THE SHAPI. ̲ ̲ LONDON:

A political and economic perspective 1066-1870

Paul N Balchin

Published by New Generation Publishing in 2014

Copyright © Paul N Balchin 2014

First Edition

www.newgeneration-publishing.com

New Generation Publishing

CONTENTS

LIST OF MAPS

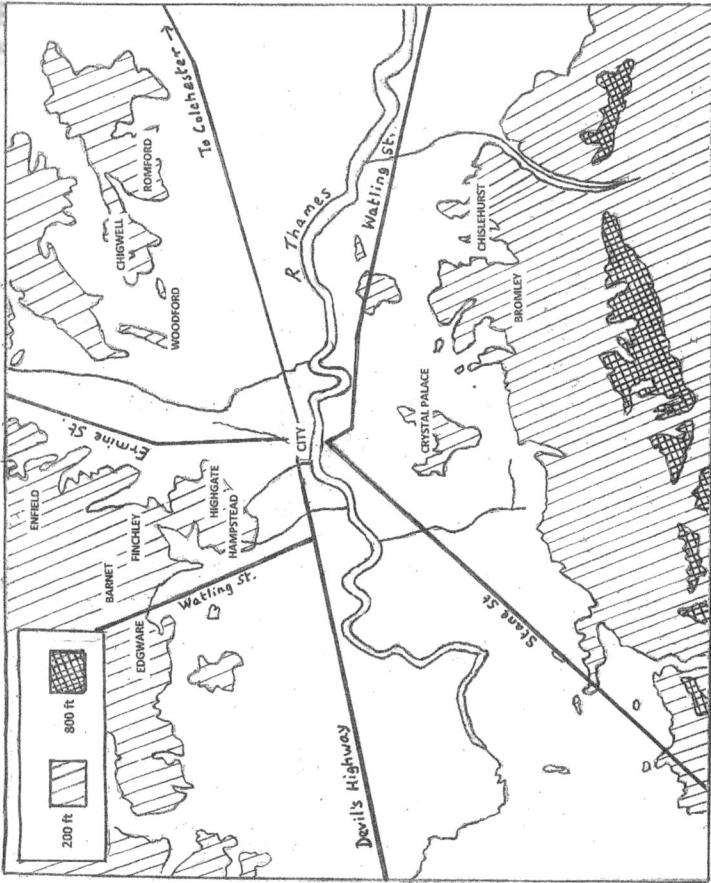

1.1 The topography of London

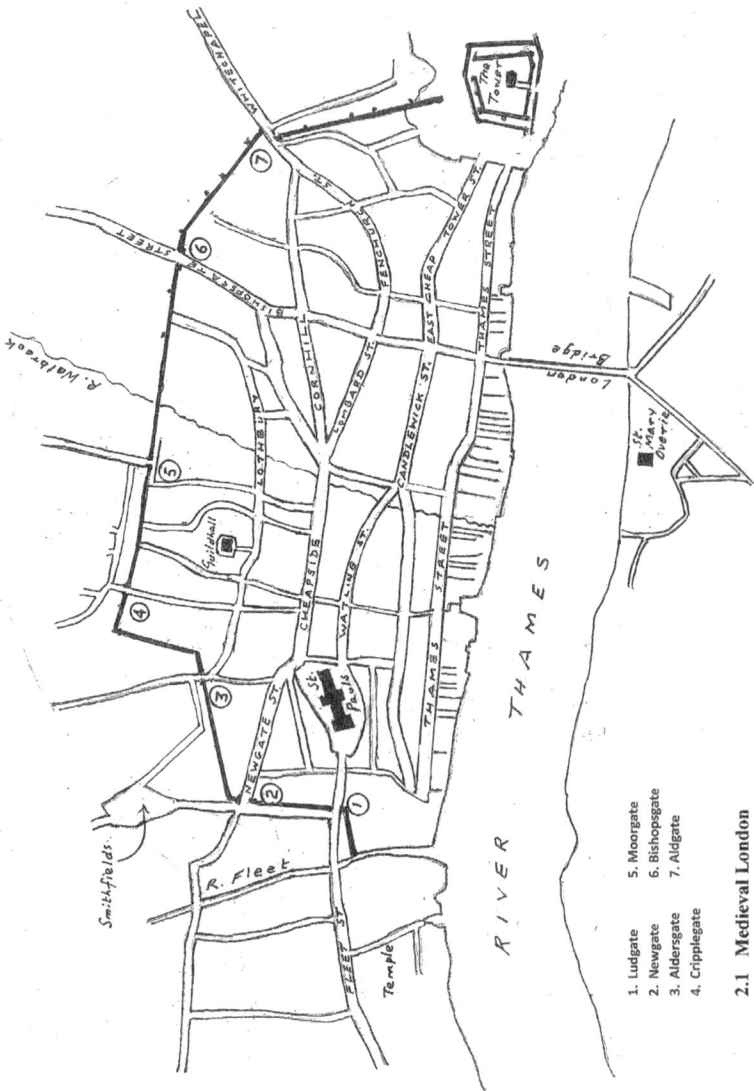

2.1 Medieval London

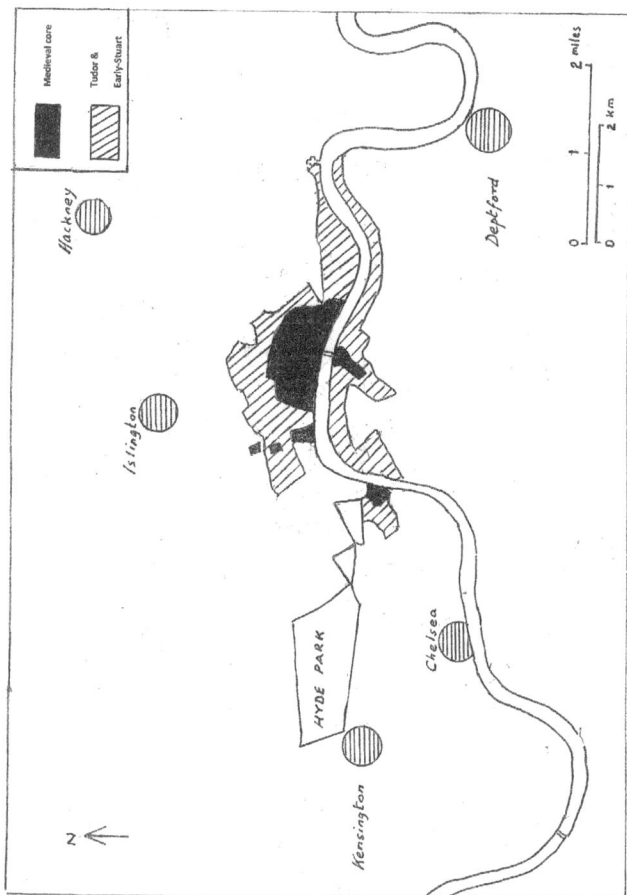

3.1 Tudor and Early-Stuart London

Map legend:
- Medieval core
- Tudor & Early-Stuart

Locations shown: Hackney, Islington, Kensington, HYDE PARK, Chelsea, Deptford

Scale: 0 1 2 km / 0 1 2 miles

N

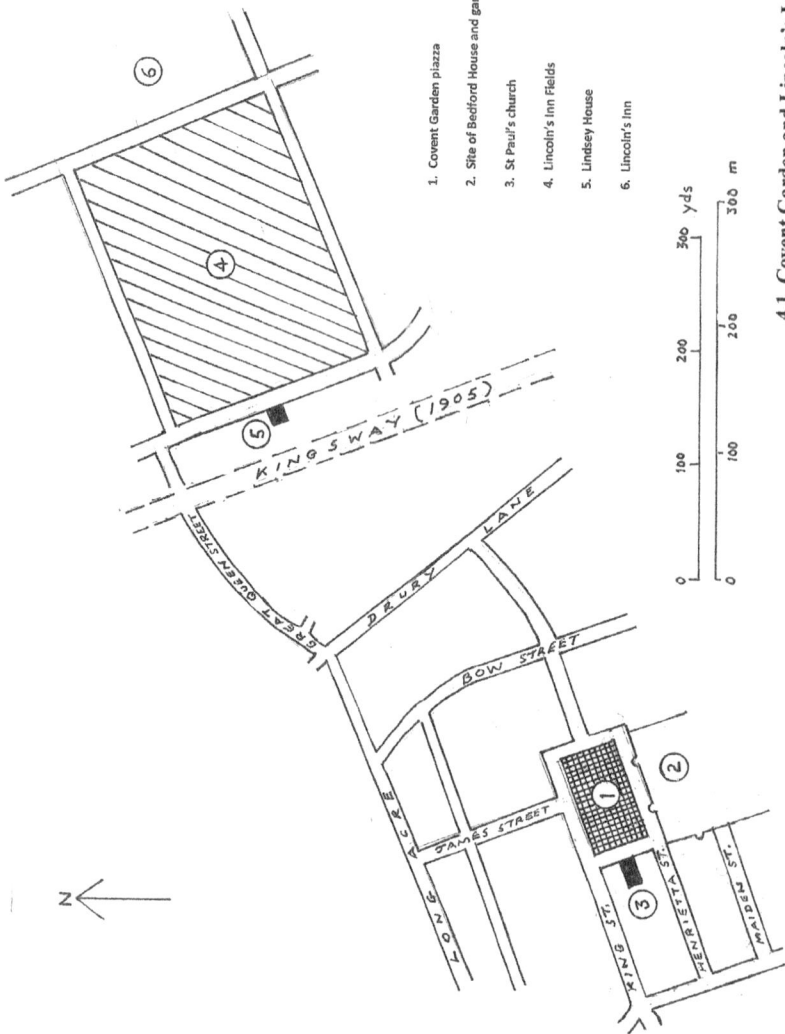

1. Covent Garden piazza
2. Site of Bedford House and garden
3. St Paul's church
4. Lincoln's Inn Fields
5. Lindsey House
6. Lincoln's Inn

4.1 Covent Garden and Lincoln's Inn Fields

8

5.1 Wren's plan for a rebuilt London

L	Ludgate	B	Bank
NG	Newgate	CH	Customs' House
AG	Aldersgate	EO	Excise Office
CG	Cripplegate	EO	Excise Office
MG	Moorgate	GS	Goldsmiths
BG	Bishopsgate	M	Mint
AG	Aldgate	PO	Post Office
		PZ	Plaza
		T	Tower

0   ½   1
mile

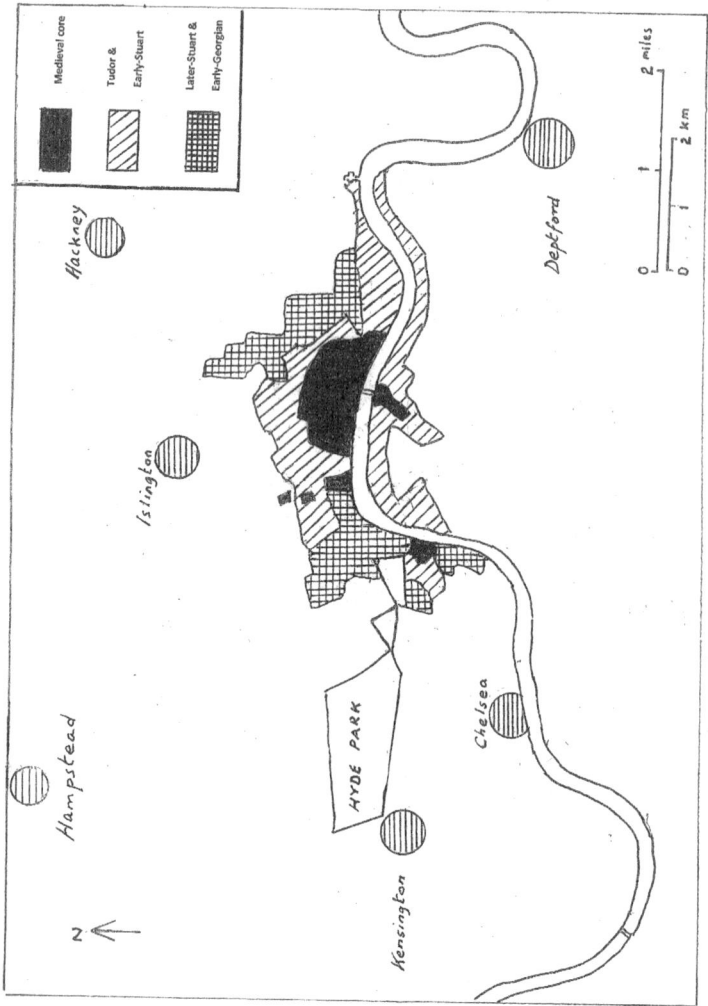

5.2 London up to 1714

Medieval core

Tudor & Early-Stuart

Later-Stuart & Early-Georgian

Hampstead

Hackney

Islington

Kensington

HYDE PARK

Chelsea

Deptford

N

0 1 2 miles

0 1 2 km

Southampton House

OXFORD ROAD

Leicester House

ST. MARTIN LANE

PICCADILLY

St.James's Piccadilly

PALL MALL

1. St.James's Square   4. Golden Square
2. Bloomsbury Square   5. Leicester Square
3. Soho Square   6. Seven Dials

0   100   200   300 yds
0   100   200   300 m

5.3 Late-seventeenth century squares

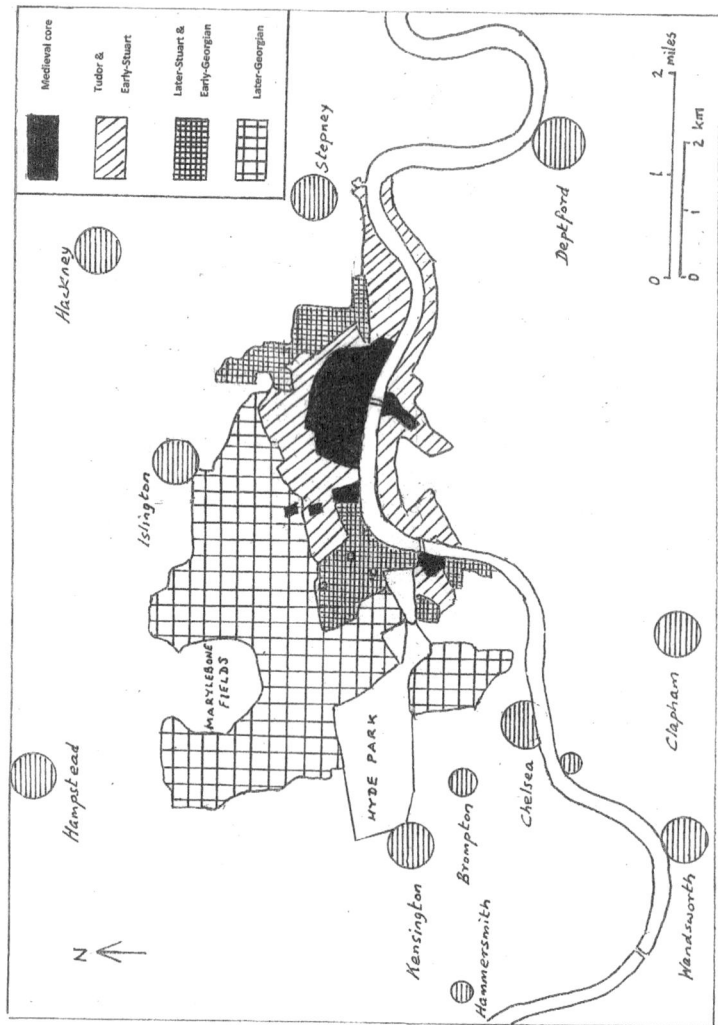

6.1 Georgian London

Legend:
- Mediaeval core
- Tudor & Early-Stuart
- Later-Stuart & Early-Georgian
- Later-Georgian

Hampstead

Hackney

Stepney

Islington

MARYLEBONE FIELDS

Deptford

HYDE PARK

Kensington

Brompton

Chelsea

Clapham

Hammersmith

Wandsworth

N

0   1   2   miles
0   1   2   km

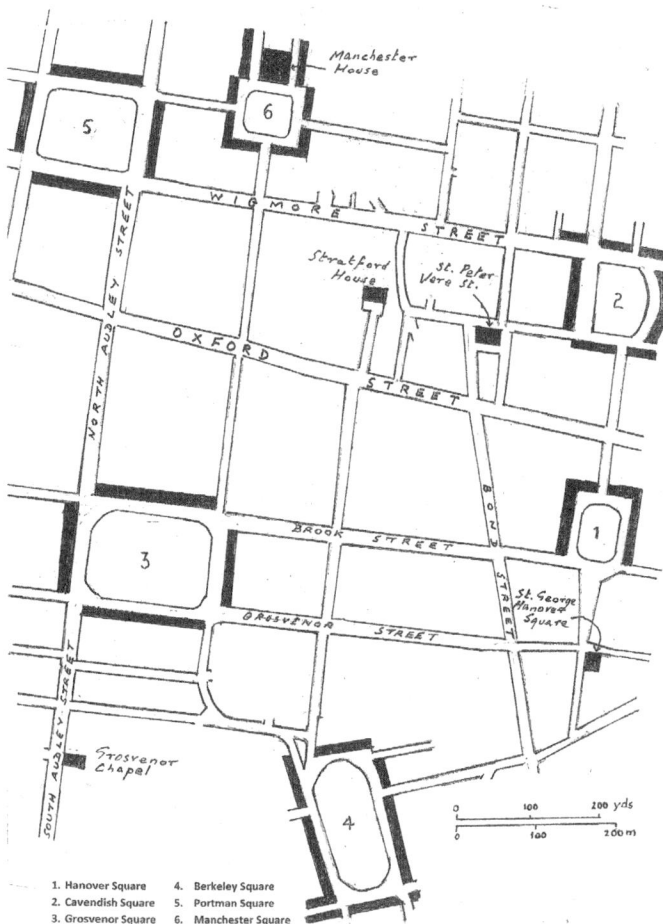

1. Hanover Square   4. Berkeley Square
2. Cavendish Square   5. Portman Square
3. Grosvenor Square   6. Manchester Square

7.1 West End Squares

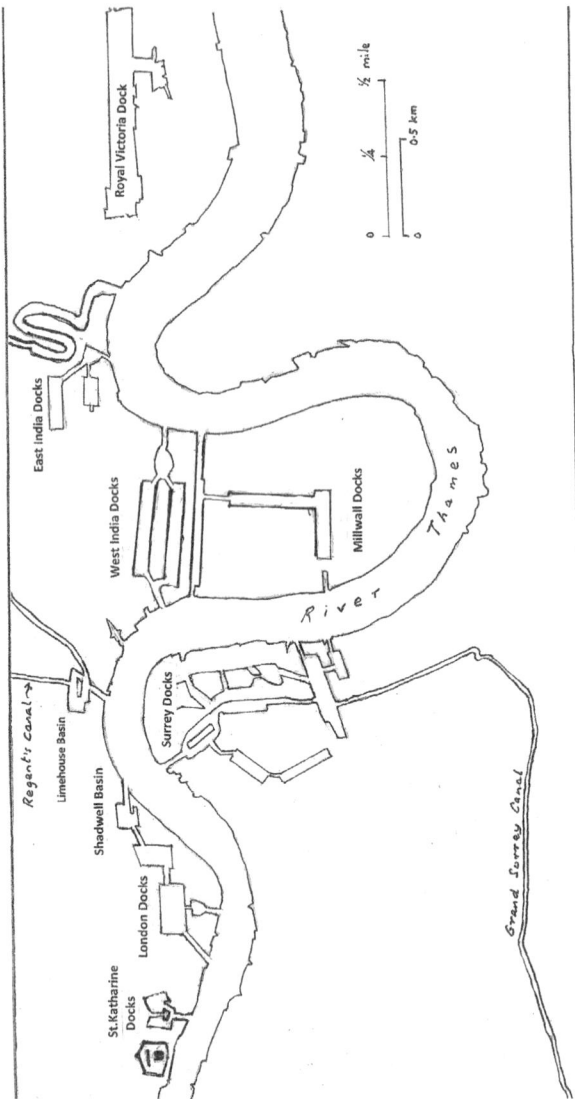

8.1 Georgian docks

Royal Victoria Dock

East India Docks

West India Docks

Millwall Docks

River Thames

Regent's Canal →

Limehouse Basin

Shadwell Basin

Surrey Docks

London Docks

St. Katharine Docks

Grand Surrey Canal

0   ¼   ½ mile

0   0·5 km

14

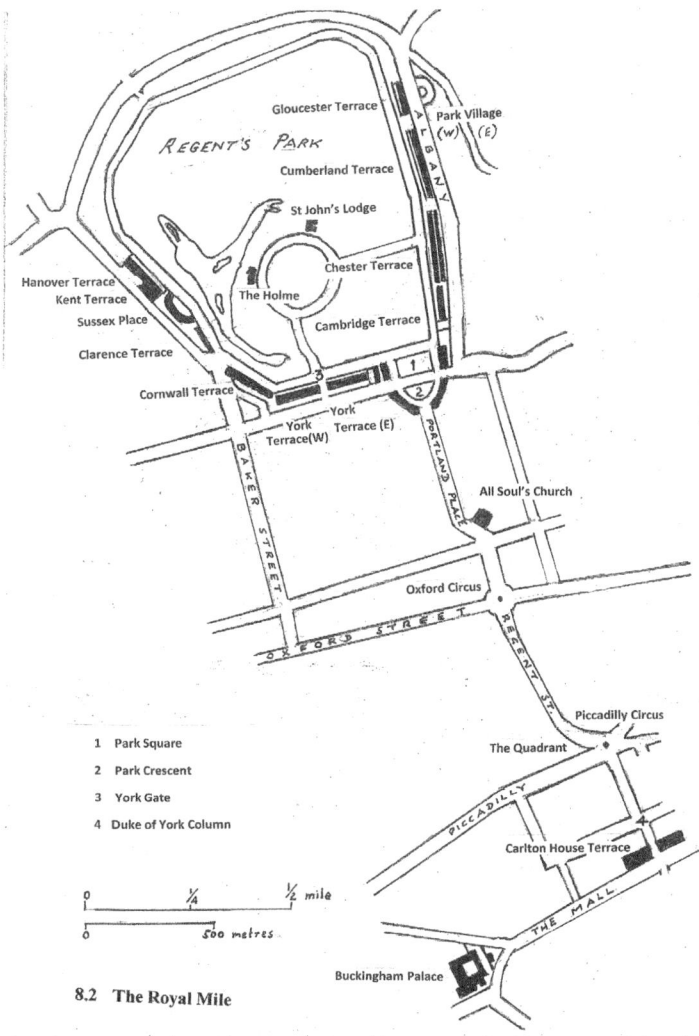

REGENT'S PARK

Gloucester Terrace

Park Village (W) (E)

Cumberland Terrace

St John's Lodge

Chester Terrace

Hanover Terrace
Kent Terrace

The Holme

Sussex Place

Cambridge Terrace

Clarence Terrace

Cornwall Terrace

York Terrace (E)

York Terrace (W)

BAKER STREET

PORTLAND PLACE

All Soul's Church

Oxford Circus

OXFORD STREET

REGENT ST.

Piccadilly Circus

The Quadrant

PICCADILLY

Carlton House Terrace

THE MALL

Buckingham Palace

1 Park Square
2 Park Crescent
3 York Gate
4 Duke of York Column

0   ¼   ½ mile

0   500 metres

8.2 The Royal Mile

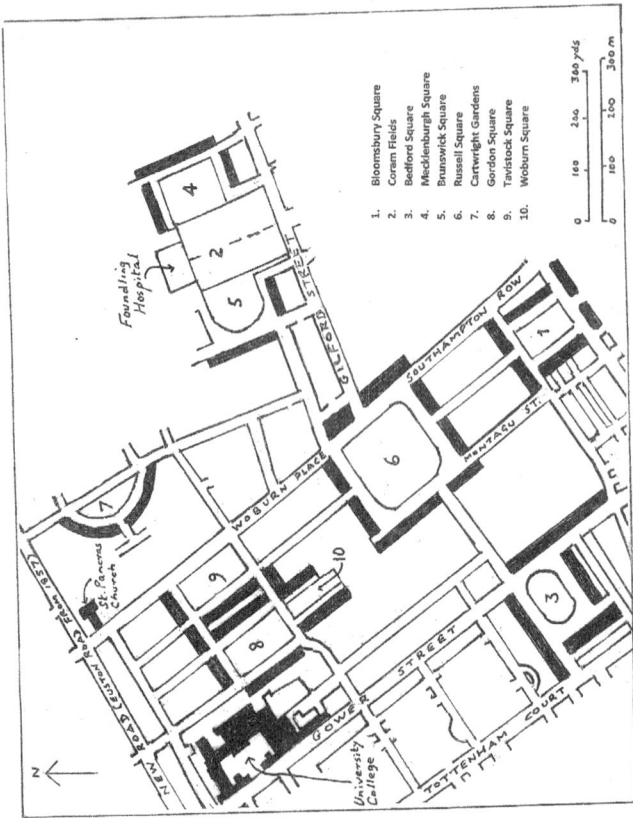

8.3 Town planning in Bloomsbury

1. Bloomsbury Square
2. Coram Fields
3. Bedford Square
4. Mecklenburgh Square
5. Brunswick Square
6. Russell Square
7. Cartwright Gardens
8. Gordon Square
9. Tavistock Square
10. Woburn Square

0   100   200   300 yds
0   100   200   300 m

Founding Hospital

GILFORD STREET

SOUTHAMPTON ROW

MONTAGU ST.

WOBURN PLACE

St. Pancras Church

EUSTON ROAD (1757)

NEW ROAD (1757)

GOWER STREET

University College

TOTTENHAM COURT

N

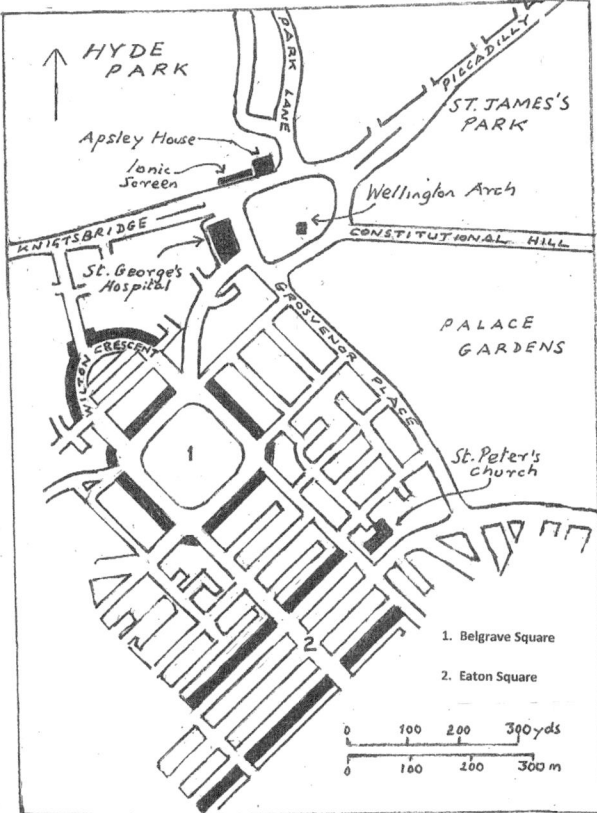

8.4 Town Planning in Belgravia

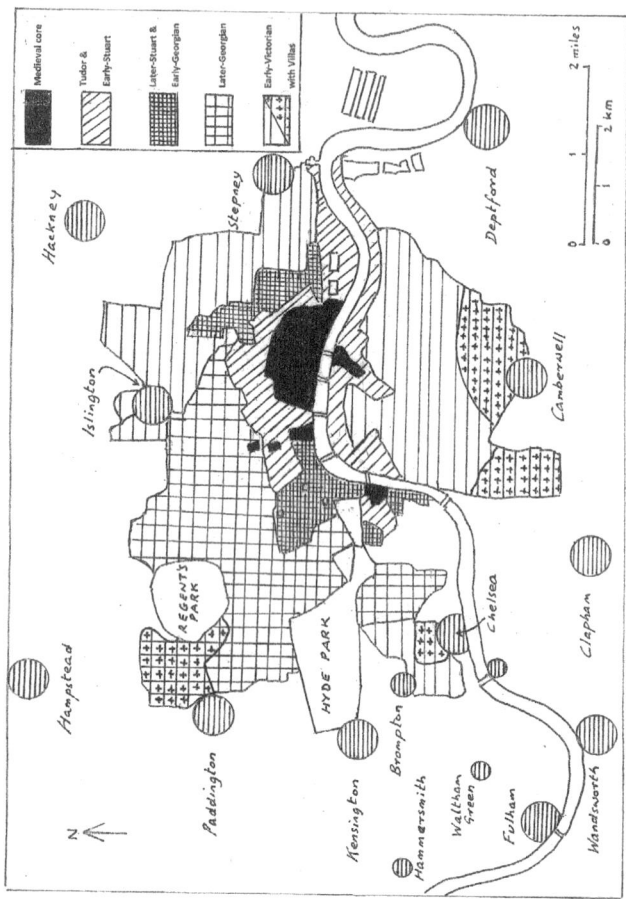

9.1 London by 1830

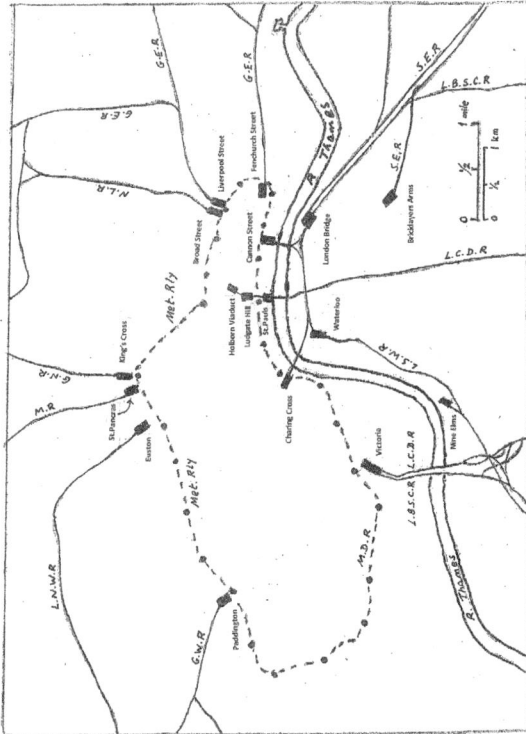

9.2 Victorian railway development

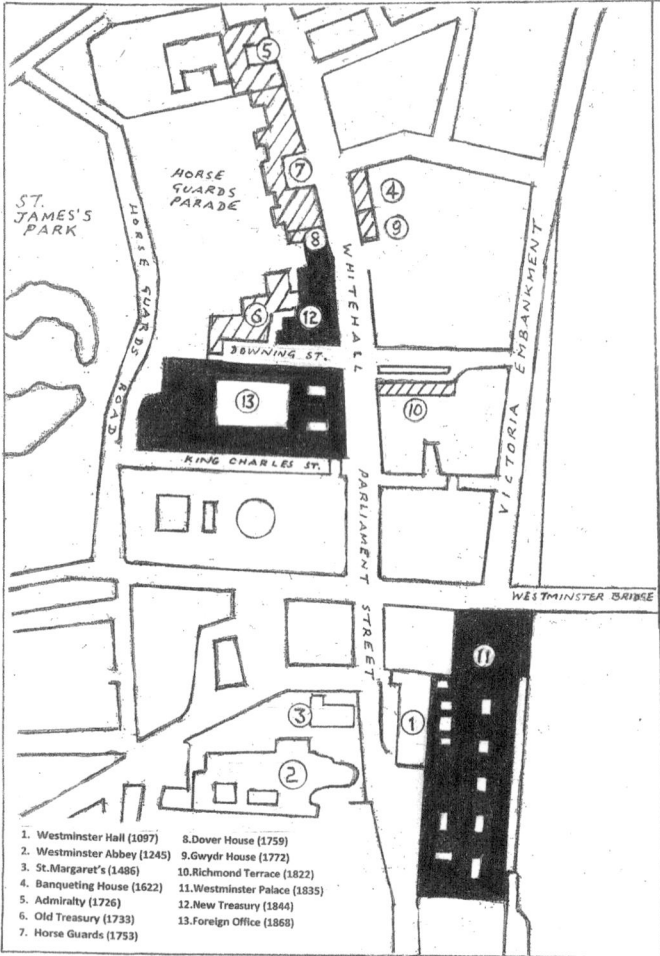

HORSE
GUARDS
PARADE

ST.
JAMES'S
PARK

HORSE GUARDS ROAD

WHITEHALL

VICTORIA EMBANKMENT

DOWNING ST.

KING CHARLES ST.

PARLIAMENT STREET

WESTMINSTER BRIDGE

1. Westminster Hall (1097)
2. Westminster Abbey (1245)
3. St.Margaret's (1486)
4. Banqueting House (1622)
5. Admiralty (1726)
6. Old Treasury (1733)
7. Horse Guards (1753)

8.Dover House (1759)
9.Gwydr House (1772)
10.Richmond Terrace (1822)
11.Westminster Palace (1835)
12.New Treasury (1844)
13.Foreign Office (1868)

9.3 Westminster by 1870

PREFACE

With a population of 8.3 million in 2012 (1), London is one of the largest cities in the world, and by far the largest city in the United Kingdom. But because of phenomenal growth in the late-twentieth and early-twenty first century the architectural heritage of this great city is being rapidly subsumed. It is particularly in central London and the boroughs of the East End that this is most apparent, though the inner-western boroughs are also under threat though on a lesser scale. How is this manifested? Quite simply, by the accelerating increase in the number of tall buildings. For three hundred years the dome of St Paul's Cathedral, and the spires of the city churches dominated the skyline of much of London, but from 1980 to 2010, Canary Wharf, Tower 42 (formerly the Nat.West Tower), the Gherkin, the Shard and the Walkie-Talkie were among other tall buildings that began to change the London skyline. However, in the spring of 2014, a survey by New London Architecture (2) showed that 236 edifices of more than 20 storeys were being either proposed, considered for approval or being constructed, of which 33 are between 40 and 49 storeys high , and 22 will have 52 or more storeys . If all the towers are built, it has been estimated that 8 will be hotels, 13 will be for mixed use, 18 will be offices, and 189 will be expensive apartments mainly or exclusively for high income owner-occupation or as investment properties. There will also be a small number of other uses. Why is all this being proposed or beginning to take place? The answer is that London has become a major centre of global finance, is considered throughout much of the world an attractive location for investment and residency, and that the current plans for its development are not being thwarted by government.

But why London? Why isn't substantial population and economic growth taking place in the other major cities of Britain during the early twenty-first century , for example in Birmingham with a 2011 population of 1,016,000 (one-eighth that of London) , in Leeds with a population of 770,800 in the same year, or in Manchester with a population of 503,000 in 2011? The answer is that London has been paramount in Britain as a global industrial and financial centre since at least 1870, and had a legacy of disproportional growth throughout most of the preceding eight hundred years. It could almost be said that in London, the twentieth century began in 1870 with its population soaring ahead from that year. It was by then that the capital had witnessed the substantial development of the railways and underground rail system, was being rapidly built-up both in the public and private sectors and often through the use of new building materials such as iron and glass, and had by far the most extensive ocean docks in Britain enabling it to fully exploit the opportunities of maritime trade with the rest of the world , opportunities that had grown throughout much of the nineteenth century because of the growth of the British Empire and the absence of any major European war since 1815.

Therefore to understand why London has achieved pre-eminence in Britain in terms of its population and as a global economic player in the early twenty-first century, it is not only necessary to look back to the end of the nineteenth century, but also to the whole period from the Norman Conquest to the first half of Victoria's reign. Thus, in reviewing the dramatic political history of England since 1066 and – to an extent – its concurrent economic history, this book suggests why and how London grew from a minor offshore settlement on the edge of Europe with around 10,000 inhabitants in 1100 to a world city with a population of 3.8 million by 1870 - a prelude to its global importance today.

It focuses on monarchical government under successive dynasties during the Late-Middle Ages and beginning of the Early-Modern period, considers the impact of Absolutism and the development of Constitutional Monarchy under the Stuart years, looks at the ascendancy of Parliamentary government under the Hanoverians, and examines the effects of public policy at the beginning of the Modern age.

Throughout much of history, and promulgated by monarchy, the nobility, the merchant class and religious faiths, a significant proportion of property has been developed in order to generate awe, respect and subservience among the population at large. Sometimes property development is the result of an arbitrary decision, but at other times it might be an outcome of market forces or a planning scheme. In examining the history of London or any other major city, it might be illuminating to consider Deyan Dudjic's observation that "architecture is [and has been] used by political leaders to seduce, impress and intimidate" (3).

Whether, for example, one looks at the reigns of William I, Edward III, Henry VIII, Charles II or George IV "political leaders [have used] architecture for political purposes. It [was] a relationship that occurred in almost every kind of regime and [appealed] to egotists of every description" (4). This view reflects the wisdom of Sir Christopher Wren who posited more than three hundred years ago that "*Architecture has its political Use; public Buildings being an ornament of a Country, it establishes a Nation, draws People and Commerce: [and] makes the people love their native Country*" (5), a sentiment almost certainly shared by many a London inhabitant, both past and present. But cities are not just inert products of decision-making by wealthy and powerful patrons, and town planners. As Sir Winston Churchill perceptively said "We shape our buildings, [but] thereafter they shape us" (6).

In acknowledging these relationships, each chapter of the book after the Introduction covers specific periods of history – Medieval, Early-Tudor, Elizab-ethan, Early-Stuart, Later-Stuart, Early-Hanoverian, Late-Georgian and Early-and Mid-Victorian, although it should not be assumed that spatial changes in the development of London or the architectural style of its buildings fit discretely into each period, nor should it be assumed that in any one specific period of history one style of architecture immediately drives out the preceding style, often the two co-exist.

For reasons of consistency, most chapters start with a look at the population growth of London and the city's spatial extent. This provides the backdrop for a detailed examination of political events both nationally and internationally and how – together with economic forces – they influenced the shaping of London particular in respect of selected buildings and public spaces.

References

1. *Annual Mid-Year Population estimates for England and Wales*, ONS, 2012.
2. *Independent building survey* , New London Architecture, 12 March 2014
3. D. Sudjic, *The Edifice Complex. How the Rich and Powerful Shaped the World,* Allen Lane, 2005, p 2.
4. Ibid, p 8.

5. L.M.Soo, *Wren's Tracts on Architecture and Other Writings*, Cambridge University Press, 1998, p 153.
6. Sir Winston Churchill, reported in *Time*, September 12, 1960

Paul N Balchin

London

Chapter 1

Introduction

Setting the Scene: The Topography of London

In many respects, the attributes of the River Thames have not been conducive to the development of London as a major city. Throughout most of the history of London the Thames was wider, shallower and slower-flowing than at present, had a greater tendency to flood and was flanked by marshland in its lower reaches, for example at Battersea, Thorney Island and Bermondsey. Despite these constraints, London owes much of its historic importance to its location astride the Thames which from the Tower is no more than forty miles from the open sea and the world-wide maritime routes that it affords. To be sure, by international standards, the Thames is a short river and with minor tributaries proves only one natural route way inland, that is from London upstream to Oxford, but between AD43-410 the Romans built a number of important roads across upland areas or river-less plains: Watling Street was constructed from Dover to London where, via a wooden bridge across the Thames, it continued north to Verulamium (St Albans), Wroxeter, Chester and Carlisle. Another north-south route, Ermine Street, connected London to Lincoln, York and Hadrian's Wall, while other roads were built south-westward to Chichester (Stane Street), westward to Silchester (the Devil's Highway) and eastward to Colchester and Norwich. However, until recently, London's wealth as a trading centre owed more to its importance as a riverside port than to its radiating road system, even though the ancient Roman roads often dictated the direction of inland trade routes in later centuries.

Since the Middle Ages, the spatial growth of London has been much influenced by its geomorphology. The city lies on predominantly flat land covered with alluvial deposits while areas of relatively high ground mark the northern and southern topographical borders of the city. Land rises to over 180 ft (55 m) in Edgware, Barnet, Finchley, Enfield, Hampstead, Highgate, Woodford and Romford north of the river, and to similar heights in Crystal Palace, Bromley and Chiselhurst to the south. Until the development of modern transport the spatial and economic growth of London has therefore been concentrated into a west-east belt flanking the Thames, and has been restrained by higher ground from expanding northwards or southwards.

The Ancient and Early-Medieval History of London

An examination of the political history of London from Roman times to the end of the first millennium will show that its demographic and economic growth was for a long time uncertain and depended very largely on the emergence of a strong ruler and a resilient community, capable together of steering the fledging settlements towards political and economic dominance in their respective spatial areas of influence. The area covering present-day London and its wider region was inhabited by Celtic tribes during the Bronze and Iron Ages, but there is no evidence to suggest that settlements were other than rudimentary, scattered and sparsely populated. It is unlikely that a pre-Roman city emerged in London or anywhere in its immediate vicinity. However, because of its rich rural hinterland

27

and its strategic position in relation to land and river transport, it came under Roman control as an outcome of Rome's attempt to expand its empire to incorporate as much of Britain *(Britannia)* as possible.

Seven years after the invasion of Britain by the Emperor Claudius in AD43, the settlement of *Londinium* was founded, though its area and population fortuitously remained relatively small since it was sacked and completely burnt to the ground by the Iceni and their queen, Boudica in c. AD60. The city was quickly rebuilt as a planned Roman settlement with a large fort, an amphitheatre, bath houses, temples, a governor's palace and the largest basilica north of the Alps. Subsequently *Londinium* continued to grow and accommodated a population of around 60,000 in the second century, in consequence replacing Colchester as the capital of Roman Britain. However, from the third century until the end of Roman rule in the fifth, political instability led to the city's slow decline, notwithstanding the construction of a substantial defensive wall around the landward side of the city between AD 190 and AD 225, and an additional riverside wall in the late third century designed to obstruct Saxon incursion. With the decline of the Roman Empire gathering pace at the beginning of the fifth century, the Roman occupation of Britain came to an end in AD 410, and for at least a century London was abandoned.

Throughout the Early-Middle Ages that followed, the growth of London was associated with the subjugation or disappearance of its indigenous population, the Romano-Celts. The London area was now on the shifting boundary between the Anglo-Saxon invaders to the east and the British defenders to the west, and by the mid-sixth century London became incorporated into the kingdom of the East Saxons. It was during this time that the East Saxons converted to Christianity, and that Melitus, the first post-Roman bishop, founded the original St. Paul's Cathedral, a modest church that was soon destroyed by pagans. By the seventh century, London within its Roman walls was very much a 'ghost town' but one mile to the west the East Saxons established a 'new town' –*Ludenvic*– in the vicinity of the present day Strand and Covent Garden. However, it is probable that when the Mercians replaced the East Saxons as overlords in the London region, around 730, the new settlement went into decline in size and status. During the reign of Alfred the Great (871-90), London within its Roman walls was resettled and the beginnings of a grid-iron street pattern emerged, a pattern that influenced the future development of the City. However, from the mid-ninth to the mid-eleventh century, London continued to be ravaged by Viking invaders to the detriment of population and economic growth.

Chapter 2

The Foundations of Medieval London: From Norman to Plantagenet and beyond; from Romanesque to Gothic

From the early-ninth century to the mid-eleventh, the history of London – like that of much of England – was marked by a continuous struggle of power between the Anglo-Saxons and Vikings. There were Viking attacks on London in 842, 851 and 871, but in 878 the invaders were defeated at the Battle of Edington by English forces under the command of Alfred the Great, and following a peace settlement between Alfred and the Viking lead Guthrum, peace ensued and Saxon rule in London was restored, notwithstanding Alfred's choice of Winchester as his capital. By about 890, settlement within the old but renovated Roman walls of London*(Londinium)* was re-established, and the city became known as *Lundenwic.* What remained of the old settlement west of the walls was renamed *Ealdwic* (the name first appearing as Aldwych in 1398). The restored city soon began to thrive. Though Alfred exercised arms-length control of London by appointing his son-in-law Ethelred as its Governor, after Ethelred's death London came under the direct control of the English kings and, because of its increasing political and commercial importance, the thriving city began to rival Winchester as the Anglo-Saxon capital of England. However, during the reign of Ethelred the Unready (r.979-1016), there was a resumption of Viking raids on London in 1013, after which Ethelred fled the city. The

Danish king Cnut and his forces eventually overran London before retreating across the North Sea, but they later returned and although Ethelred's son, Edmund Ironside, attempted to repel the invaders, he was eventually obliged to share the English throne with Cnut. After Edmund's death, Cnut became the sole King of England (r.1016-35) but following the reign of two of his Danish successors (Harold and Hardicanute), the Anglo-Saxon monarchy was restored when Cnut's stepson Edward the Confessor became king in 1042.

Old St Pancras Church (10th century, restored 1848)

It is probable that the oldest church in London to survive, albeit greatly restored in the nineteenth century, is Old St Pancras which dates back to the tenth century or earlier. Other evidence of the development of Saxon London is scarce and is confined to a small number of sites, for example the church of All Hallows Barking (often called All Hallows by the Tower) dates back to 1000-1060 and was built on land that had been endowed by the Eorconweath, Bishop of London in the late seventh century.

Dating from Roman times, London had only one bridge (a wooden structure) over its river during the Early Middle Ages, though it was repaired and rebuilt on several occasions. In 1014 King Ethelred and his Norwegian ally King Olaf ordered the destruction of the bridge to divide the invading Danish forces.

Recognising that London was more favourably located than Winchester to repel potential invaders, Edward the Confessor (r. 1042-January 4th 1066) declared London his new capital. However, in presiding over the construction of the very first Westminster Abbey (1042-1066) and the original Westminster Palace (1045-1050), he chose Thorney Island - at the confluence of the Tyburn and the Thames - as his governmental location, some two miles west of the City of London, partly in the belief that site conditions would repel possible invaders and partly because of his desire spatially to separate the Crown from the commerce and local politics of the City – the capital to this day having two centres.

The Collegiate and Church of St. Peter, more commonly known as Westminster Abbey, is depicted in the Bayeaux Tapestry woven around 1077. Inspired by the Edward's long exile in the Duchy of Normandy (1013-42), the building was almost certainly modelled on the Abbey at Jumieges, and its foundations on the northern edge of the present Abbey have recently been excavated indicating a significantly smaller structure than its successor.

But Edward was heirless, and the English throne was immediately claimed on his death in 1066 by his cousin, William Duke of Normandy. However, the Royal Council elected Harold Godwinson, Edward's brother-in-law, as king instead of William. To claim what he considered his rightful inheritance, William and his army crossed the English Channel, and after his rout of Harold's forces at the Battle of Hastings on 14 October 1066, established Norman rule in England.

London in the High and Late Middle Ages

During the High and Late Middle Ages, London was still a relatively small city. Its population of 10,000-20,000 had grown to only 80,000 by the mid-fourteenth century, but as a consequence of the Black Death and further plagues in 1361, 1369 and 1375 fell to between 35,000 and 40,000 by 1377 and probably did not exceed that number until well into the sixteenth century. By contrast, the population of Westminster had risen from around 2,000 in 1400 to a little under 3,000 by the end of the century (1). Dwarfing England's second largest city Norwich which had a population of about 13,000 inhabitants by 1400, and the even smaller cities of Bristol and Newcastle with around 10,000 inhabitants, London as a whole owed its "exceptional size and wealth in the Middle Ages to a number of factors: its convenient location at the centre of land and water routes, with easy access to the Continent; the city's long established role as a port; the growth of Westminster as a focus of government, and the growth of government itself (2).

Though the largest city in England, Medieval London was spatially small by any standards. It was largely concentrated within a relatively restricted area on the north bank of the Thames – roughly a square mile – surrounded by a single Roman wall of three miles in length (five kilometres) that dated from around 200 AD. It was initially 14.3ft (4.4 m) in height but was increased in height to about 33ft (10 m) through the addition of additional brick and stonework in Medieval times, and was pierced by eight gates which, in an anticlockwise sequence comprised Aldgate,

Bishopgate, Moorgate, Cripplegate, Aldersgate, Newgate, Ludgate and Temple Bar. All were Roman except for Temple Bar and Moorgate that date respectively from 1321 and 1472. However, the Roman wall along the banks of the Thames was allowed to decay in the Middle Ages to allow alleys to descend from Thames Street down to the water's edge. Along the Thames a strip of land of up to 350 feet had been reclaimed piecemeal, while inlets at Billingsgate and Queenhithe as well as the small haven at Dowgate were developed as landing places (3).

Whereas the main Roman wall remained extant until the middle of the eighteenth century, the grid-iron street pattern that was developed during the Roman occupation disappeared under the Saxons and Early Normans, only to be replaced by a haphazard street layout as the Middle Ages progressed, while the City, with its many church steeples was reminiscent of the great cities of the Low Countries and Lombardy (4). Most of the population of London was accommodated in timber-framed dwellings built on stone foundations, and often rising to three storeys with the upper floors jettying out. However, though buildings had been constructed at a high density, there was a proliferation of private alleys, yards, gardens and orchards – as well as lower occupancy rates and vacant houses – as the population of the city plummeted dramatically between the mid-fourteenth century and 1500. By the end of the late Middle Ages, far from expanding, the built-up area had not spread far beyond the City wall, except in the two settlements of Westminster to the west and Southwark, south of the Thames.

Through the Late Medieval period economic development was every bit as important to the well-being of Londoners as a relatively settled political and ecclesiastical environment. London was generally free from insurrection, save for the Peasants' Revolt led by Wat Tyler in 1381 and Jack Cade's rebellion of 1450, while the economy of London flourished from the thirteenth – to the fifteenth centuries. The City, in fact, was for long "extraordinarily free of serious disorder – probably a token of its broad based prosperity and the social-economic cohesion created by the guilds" (5). On the western edge of the city, multifarious commercial activities took place around and even within St Paul's Cathedral. With its long nave and tall tower the enormous edifice assumed a commanding position in close proximity to the western end of Cheapside, the city's busiest produce market which indirectly led to East Cheap, just west of the Tower.

The economic growth of London was driven by the zeal of its craftsmen and merchants in a determined effort to satisfy demand, and aided by the regulatory activities of their respective guilds, but it was also conditioned quite substantially by foreign trade. From the late fourteenth century, the Port of London provided the conduit for the flow of exports and imports, as wool exporters and woollen cloth merchants took control of England's two main exports, while other merchants organized the import of a wide range of primary and secondary goods, in aggregate stimulating the development of a strong trade axis between London and Antwerp by the late fifteenth century. Downstream, from Blackfriars and Baynard's Castle to London Bridge, the Thames was lined along its northern banks with quays such as Queenhithe, Broken Wharf and Dowgate – each facilitating trade with Flanders, while further downstream a three-acre plot known as the Steelyard provided a stronghold for the Hanseatic League involved in trade with northern Germany and the Baltic. Granted to German traders by Henry III, Steelyard was soon densely packed with warehouses, counting houses and lodgings, while its occupants were permitted to live under their own laws in the hope that their trading prowess would bring business to London. Beyond London Bridge, where river barge traffic gave way to sea-going vessels, the Pool of London was the real key to London's prosperity (6). It was here – at the Billingsgate and St Botolph's wharves – that ships loaded and unloaded their cargoes often with the assistance of man-powered cranes, while further downstream canon guarded the approach to the Pool from the Traitors' Gate at the Tower (7). Much of the wealth generated by both domestic and foreign trade found its way into property development in the City, not only directly through the construction of commercial buildings, but indirectly through the medium of banking and money lending directed at funding the physical development of London in general.

The pace of London's development, however, was largely determined by the rate at which England's monarchy took the lead in funding or promoting the construction of important secular and ecclesiastical buildings, a process very largely conditioned by vagaries in domestic and foreign policy, by war and peace.

The Development of London under the Normans

William I, the Conqueror (r.1066-1087)

After invading England in September 1066 and defeating and mortally wounding Harold at the Battle of Hastings on 14 October, William, Duke of

Normandy, secured Dover and Canterbury and subsequently sent a force to Winchester to secure the royal treasury. Though he subsequently torched Southwark to neutralise armed resistence south of the Thames, he deemed it too risky to cross London Bridge – still a wooden structure, and marched westward to Wallingford, devastating the countryside and settlements on the way. There he crossed the Thames and headed eastward to London. At Berhampstead at the beginning of December he met leading London citizens who offered him the crown. His forces arrived peacefully in London in mid-December and he was crowned at Westminster Abbey on Christmas Day 1066. He was immediately accepted by a large proportion of London's inhabitants. Although William was Norman rather than Saxon by birth, only a year had passed since Edward the Confessor had died – a revered monarch who had a Norman mother, Emma; had lived in Normandy for 25 years prior to coming to English throne; and who appointed as Bishop of London in 1041 and Archbishop of Canterbury in 1051 his close Norman friend, Robert, the former Abbot of Jumiège.

After being crowned King of England, William confirmed that Lomdon rather than Winchester was his new capital and granted it a formal charter in 1067 upholding its long established laws, rights and privileges. However, from the very outset, William set out to defend London from outside intrusion or dissent within by constructing a number of wooden castles along the north bank of the Thames, the most notable of which later became the Tower, a stone donjon located on the eastern boundary of the city on the bank of the Thames.

Only a year after his coronation, William returned to Normandy to exercise his ducal functions, but on returning to England in December 1067 he was immediately faced with the need to suppress a revolt in Exeter and obliged to conduct an 18 day siege of the city before it surrendered. In the following year he had to put down a further revolt against his rule by Earls Edwin and Morcar in Warwickshire, and then continued to York and Nottingham, Lincoln, Huntingdon and Cambridge where he built castles to exert his authority across his kingdom.

In 1069 William put down a revolt in York led by Edgar Ætheling and his ally King Sweyn of Denmark, and in the winter of 1069-70 William defeated a rebellion at Shrewsbury before building castles at Chester and Stafford. After this campaign, euphemistically known as 'Harrying of the North', William turned his attention in the Spring of 1070 to putting down a revolt in the Isle of Ely led by Hereward the Wake supported, in customary fashion, by Sweyn who had landed his Danish troops along the Humber and East Anglian coast. After securing their defeat, William returned to the Continent to deal with troubles in Maine, south of Normandy.

From early 1073 to the autumn of 1075 William travelled to and from Normandy to safeguard his interests on the Continent, but in 1075 Ralph de Gael (the Earl of Norfolk) and Roger de Breteuil (the Earl of Hereford) conspired, for reasons somewhat obscure, to overthrow William during his absence. As in earlier revolts, the Danish King Sweyn gave active support to the rebels, but the so-called 'Revolt of the Earls' in mid-1075 was suppressed by forces loyal to William, though it was left to William to deal with the Danish threat on his return from Normandy later in the year. In the following year William returned to Normandy where he spent most of his remaining life. But on his infrequent visits to England his main claim to fame was the compilation of the *Domesday Book*, an inventory of land holdings across all the counties of England south of the rivers Tees and Ribble as a record of feudal obligations and as means of assessing tax liability. Within one year of its completion in 1086, William died in Normandy at the untimely age of 59 after a serious riding accident incurred while on a military expedition in 1087.

The White Tower (begun 1077)

Despite William's frequent absence from London, his principal legacy to his capital was the Tower of London, a spectacular example of a Norman castle which in its long history has been, in full or in part, a fortress, a royal residence, a prison, a place of execution, an arsenal, a jewel house, a mint and a royal menagerie. The Tower of London in the Middle Ages and beyond thus not only epitomized the English monarch's quest for political dominance in London but for hegemony across the whole country. Occupying a 12 acre (4.9 ha) site on the eastern edge of the city where the Roman wall abuts on to the Thames, and replacing the earlier wooden castle, the Tower of London is dominated by an immense rectangular donjon (the White Tower), 118 ft (36 m) in length and 107 ft (32m) in width, with walls 105 ft (27 m) tall and 12 ft (3.6 m) thick. While William was in Normandy in 1077, work started on the construction of the edifice under the direction of Bishop Gundulf of Rochester in 1077 and using white Caen stone shipped from Normandy as well as Kentish ragstone, it was intended that the huge size and solid form of the donjon would provide both a stout defence against sea-borne invaders and a refuge for the monarchy at times of internal crisis. To provide spiritual comfort for its occupants, the Chapel of St. John was constructed on its second floor, the oldest surviving place of worship in London, and second only to Durham Cathedral as the finest example of Norman ecclesiastical architecture in England, with the four corners of the White Tower marked by a turret and its whole roofline defined by crenellations.

Upstream from the Tower, and situated south-east of Blackfriars Priory on a site where the old Roman wall and the Fleet River meet the Thames, Baynard's Castle was built by Ralph Baynard shortly after he arrived in London with William the Conqueror. Subsequently, despite its four fortified wings it was repeatedly damaged and repaired in the twelfth and thirteenth centuries. In 1428 the stronghold was burnt down and then rebuilt by Humphrey, Duke of Gloucester in the manner of the previous castle, and it was finally rebuilt by Henry VII in 1487 and remained intact until it was destroyed by the Great Fire in 1666 (8).

Built around the same time as Baynard's Castle, Montfichet Tower – an edifice around 230ft (70 m) in height – probably stood on the river side of Ludgate

40

Hill, though there is no record of its existence until the 1130s, but to defend London from military attack from the west, William the Conqueror built a motte and wooden castle between 1070-1086 overlooking the Thames at Windsor in Berkshire. Known as Windsor Castle, the stronghold is located about 22 miles (35 km) and a day's march from central London.

Notwithstanding the emphasis that William put on building defensive strongholds in and near his capital, the late eleventh century also saw the first of the very many ecclesiastical buildings constructed in London during the Central and Late Middle Ages. William granted a charter to the church of St. Clement in Eastcheap in 1067, and the monastery and college of St Martin-le Grand just to the south of Aldersgate was chartered by the king in 1068 who subsequently endowed it with land in Cripplegate.

William II (r. 1087-1100)

William I's eldest son, Robert, became Duke of Normandy, his second son Richard died of a hunting accident around 1075, and his third son, William became king of England as William II (known as 'Rufus', allegedly because of his red completion). During his first year as king, work began on the construction of St Paul's Cathedral (the fourth version to be built since its original foundation in 604). Situated on the highest point of the City, Ludgate Hill, at first stylistically Romanesque or Norman. `Old St. Paul's' (before it succumbed to fire in 1666) was one of the longest and tallest cathedrals in Europe, second only to St. Peter's in Rome. As if to balance Edward the Confessor's Westminster Abbey to the west, 'Old St. Paul's' was built on the highest point of the City of London, Ludgate Hill. Funded generously by William

II, and initially promoted by Maurice, the Bishop of London (1086 – 1107), the Late Medieval cathedral was cruciform in shape, measured 585 ft (178 m) in length, extended laterally by 290 ft (88 m) at its transepts, and with its wooden spire rose to a height of 489 ft (149 m). Built largely with Caen stone, its construction began with the rib-vaulted chancel and choir (completed in 1148), was continued with the twelve bays of the similarly vaulted nave (finished in 1200), and was temporarily concluded with the erection of the tower and spire (1221).

But cathedral-building and the construction of other ecclesiastical buildings at home coincided with military action against external threats (not unusual throughout the Middle Ages and beyond). In addition to funding St. Paul's, William II financially supported the establishment of the Cluniac Priory of Bermondsey in 1089, and in the same year he also funded a war with his brother Robert in Normandy. Only two years later, in 1091, William sent a large army to counter a Scottish invasion of the north of England which ended with the Scottish king Malcolm III accepting William as overlord, while the Treaty of Caen healed the rift between William and his brother Robert and both agreed that whichever of the two survived would inherit the domains of his brother. Though a harmonious understanding was established between the rulers of England and Normandy, William was not at peace closer to home since there was a further conflict between England and Scotland in 1093 in which Malcolm met his death, and a year later William was obliged to quell rebellions not only by English barons but also by their Welsh counterparts. Despite the vagaries and expense of war, during the 1090s a number of churches, Norman in style, were built across England. In London, for example, the church of St.

Mary-le-Bow is known to have existed in 1091, and St. Stephen Walbrook possibly dates from before 1096.

Though William's forces did not participate in the First Crusade to the Holy Land in 1096-1099, his brother, Robert of Normandy and his army joined the Crusade and were absent from the duchy throughout the full two years of the conflict. To fund his venture, Robert obtained a loan of 10,000 marks from William in return for pledging his Duchy to William in his will. The loan was equivalent in value to about a quarter of William's annual taxation and was funded by the reluctant taxpayers of England. To add to the expense, William as regent for Robert in Normandy, campaigned in France from 1097 to 1099, securing Maine and planning to invade Aquitaine.

Notwithstanding the limit on the amount of funds available, William was able to afford to rebuild Westminster Palace in 1097-1099, the building having first been constructed before the Conquest in 1045-1050. The palace henceforth became the principal London residence of the kings of England for over four centuries and its Great Hall was the largest of its day in Europe measuring 240 x 67 ft (73 x 20 m). It became the seat of the law courts, and accommodated the predecessor of England's parliament, the *Curia Regis* (Royal Council). But not all changes to the built environment in the late eleventh century were positive. After the reconstruction of the wooden London bridge, followings its destruction in 1014, it was again swept away, this time by a gale in 1091.

Henry I (r. 1100-1135)

William Rufus's reign came to an abrupt end when he was killed by an arrow through the lung when hunting in the New Forest on 2 August 1100. Accidently or not, his death was immediately followed by the coronation of his younger brother, Henry, in Westminster Abbey on 5 August, and on 11 November the new king was married to Edith daughter of Malcolm III of Scotland and Margaret of Wessex endearing him to both the Scots and his own Saxon subjects. He also became very popular in London since he later granted the City's inhabitants an exceptional charter of liberties.

However, at the beginning of Henry's reign, William's lawful successor, his elder brother Robert of Normandy, was currently returning from the Holy Land, and after arriving at his Duchy in 1101 Robert with a sense of grievance invaded England in an attempt to seize the crown from the new king. Although, in the subsequent Treaty of Alton, Robert agreed to recognise Henry as the legitimate ruler of England in return for an annual payment of 3,000 marks, Henry was unwilling to keep this agreement and in 1105 led an expeditionary force to Normandy to eliminate Robert's financial hold over him. At the ensuing Battle of Tinchebray on 28 September 1106 William decisively defeated the Duchy's army and captured Robert whom he then imprisoned for the rest of his life, first in the Tower of London and then in Devizes Castle and Cardiff Castle where he died in his eighties in 1134.

Following Tinchebray, Henry appropriated Normandy, made it a possession of England and ruled it as king of England, rather than as Duke. However, although Henry had eliminated Robert from the political stage, he felt it prudent to allow Robert's son, the 'Clito' ('man of royal blood'), to retain his freedom, a mistaken gesture since he became the focus of every plot and alliance against his uncle. In 1113 Henry attempted to enhance his standing in Normandy by securing the marriage of his son William Adelin to

Matilda of Anjou daughter of Count Fulk V of Anjou, who until then was a serious enemy of Normandy, but after William's death at sea in 1120 Henry more momentously arranged the union between his daughter Matilda (married to Henry V Holy Roman Emperor from 1110 until his death in 1125) and Fulk's son, Geoffrey Plantagenet, Count of Anjou in 1128, a marriage which eventually led (with the coronation of their son, Henry II) to the founding of the Plantagenet dynasty in England in 1154.

During most of Henry's thirty-five year reign, there was little political strife. To be sure the king felt it necessary to confiscate Baynard's Castle from its current incumbent William Baynard (grandson of its founder Robert) for supporting Robert Curtose's claim to the throne (Robert was Henry's brother), but thereafter England remained at peace domestically, and except for an invasion of Wales in 1114 when Henry seized Gwynedd and Powys it also remained at peace with her western neighbour as well as with Scotland. It is within this context that London experienced a fairly prolonged period of construction activity.

St Bartholomew - the Great (1123). Original part of St
Bartholomew's Priory.

Throughout Henry's reign, with royal castles in
place and with house building reflecting multifarious
individual needs, the provision of new ecclesiastical
buildings contributed substantially to the shaping of
London. In 1100 both the Romanesque-Gothic church
of the knightly Order of the Hospitallers, and the
Benedictine nunnery of St. Mary were founded in
Clerkenwell; in 1106 and 1108 respectively the
Augustinian Order established the monasteries of St.
Marie Overie *('across the river')* in Southwark and
Holy Trinity Aldgate; and in 1123 the Romanesque
church of St. Bartholomew-the Great was founded in
West Smithfield, by Prior Rahere, a member of the
court of Henry I. After the chapel in the Tower of
London, St. Bartholomew's is the oldest surviving
church in London. As part of the Augustinian

monastery and hospital of St. Bartholomew's the church measured as much as 300 ft (91.5 m) by 86 ft (27.9 m) – the size of a small cathedral, yet all that survives are its four-bay choir with its massive Romanesque piers, a bold ambulatory rising to a clerestory, and a double-apsed chapel.

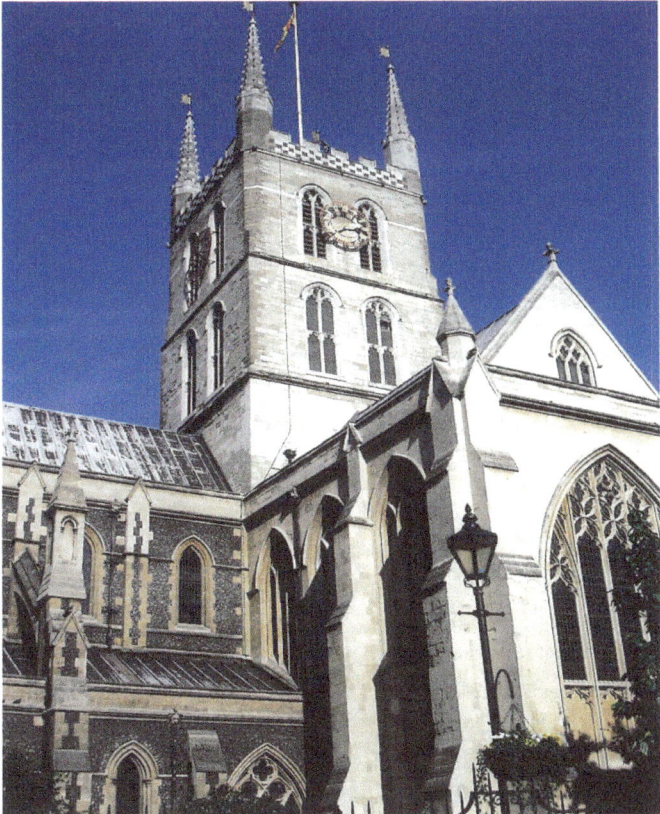

St Mary's Overie (1212), called Southwark Cathedral since the beginning of the twentieth century

But these were relatively small ecclesiastical buildings. While the very extensive Westminster

Palace was situated on the north bank of the Thames, some substantial medieval palaces were constructed on the south bank, quite possibly to provide their residents with a more pleasing physical environment than that prevailing north of the river. The first of such edifices was Winchester Palace, built by William Gifford Bishop of Winchester in 1129. Located in Southwark, close to the Augustinian prior of St. Mary Overie (literally `over the river') the palace boasted a richly decorated Great Hall leading at its west end to a buttery, a pantry and kitchen, and an extensive vaulted cellar below providing direct access to the riverside wharf. Two extensive courtyards accommodated within their walls a prison, a brewery, a tennis court, a bowling alley and a pleasure garden. The second was Lambeth Palace, the Archbishop of Canterbury's residence, but work on this building did not start until 1190 during the reign of Richard I (see below).

Stephen (r. 1135-1154)

In 1122 Stephen of England, the son of Stephen II, Count of Blois and Adele of Normandy, married Matilda of Boulogne and duly became Count of that county, and in 1135 as a grandson of William I he inherited the throne of England and reigned for nearly two decades during which time his kingdom was plunged into anarchy and civil war. From the beginning of Stephen's reign England and his possessions in Normandy were under attack from David I of Scotland, Welsh rebels and Geoffrey of Anjou, the husband of the empress Matilda who had a legitimate claim on the English throne. In 1139 the forces of Matilda and her half-brother Robert of Gloucester invaded England and a lengthy civil war ensured and continued until 1152 with neither side securing victory despite Stephen's

48

ability as a military strategist.

With most of Stephen's attention focused on military issues, and with the Treasury depleted by civil war, few if any buildings were commissioned by the king in his capital. Thus, apart from the reconstruction of the wooden London Bridge after it was burnt down in 1136, almost all building work of note in the capital during Stephen's reign occurred in the ecclesiastical sector. Although St. Anne and St. Agnes, and St. Martin Ludgate, were known to exist in respectively 1137 and 1138, and St. Andrew Cornhill was first mentioned in 1147, they probably date from earlier in the twelfth century if not before,. However in 1145 a monastic complex of a very different sort than was usual was established in Clerkenwell by a Crusading Order – the Order of St. John-in-Jerusalem (the Knights Hospitallers). With funds provided by Jordan de Brichett, a wealthy Suffolk landlord, the Hospitallers built a monastery in Clerkenwell for the care of the needy. It included a church with a round nave and an adjoining rectangular chancel and it is probable that it was based on the church of Holy Sepulchre in Jerusalem. Another new hospital, for female lepers, St. Katharines, was founded just east of the Tower by Matilda of Boulogne in 1148.

From Romanesque (or Norman) to Gothic

From the reign of William I to that of Stephen, a period of only 88 years, the predominant architectural style employed in the construction of notable new buildings – both secular and ecclesiastical – progressed from Romanesque or Norman to Gothic. After slowly emerging in the Ottonian Empire and Burgundy in the tenth century, Romanesque architecture made its appearance in Normandy and England in the early-twelfth. By then the principal features of Romanesque cathedrals, abbeys and churches were thick walls, sturdy piers, round arches and tunnel vaults though in some buildings, such as Durham Cathedral, groin or rib vaults were used as early as 1130. In the grander churches, ambulatories and radiating chapels at the east end are also common features. In Northern France and England, a variant of the Romanesque style is often referred to as 'Norman'. It is endowed with broadly the same attributes, but the west front of some Norman cathedrals are adorned with two towers and a tower over the crossing such as at St-Etienne in Caen and at Southwell in Nottinghamshire. In London both Westminster Abbey and the cathedral of 'Old St. Paul's' retained many of their Norman attributes until the fourteenth century or later.

In addition both Westminster Hall (1087-1100) and Winchester Palace (begun in 1129) were built in the Norman style shortly after the Conquest, notwithstanding the need to adapt church architecture to the requirements of secular use. Romanesque castles and their Norman equivalent are even more different architecturally. They tended to be square or oblong *donjons* or keeps, with massively thick walls, but since they were built *poste-haste* soon after the Conquest they were normally without the protection of one or more curtain walls or even a moat , as at the White Tower and of similar age at Baynards Castle and the Montfichet Tower.

Derived from the French Early Gothic paradigm, the Early English Style, was first employed in a rudimentary manner the east end of Canterbury Cathedral by William of Sens and William the Englishman in 1174-1185, but in a more enhanced way at Wells, (1175-1229) and Lincoln (c. 1190-1239) . Throughout the many ecclesiastically buildings, Early English in style, there is an ubiquitous use of rib vaults, pointed arches, and much architectural ornament, particularly shaft work (9). Then followed the decorated style of Gothic architecture, exhibited in ecclesiastical architecture between c. 1250 and c. 1350 and epitomised by the use of tracery, sculptured ornament and – towards the end of its popularity – the ogee arch. While found in a plethora of English cathedrals, for example in the east end of Bristol Cathedral (begun in 1298) and Wells Cathedral (c.1290 – c.1340), "no other country has anything as novel, as resourceful and as lavish as the English Decorated style" (10). The final form of English church Gothic is the Perpendicular, a style in vogue from the mid-fourteenth century to the sixteenth, and employing "rectilinear surface panelling, flattish four-centred arches and multi-ribbed or fan vaulting" (11). Reaching its apogee in the chancel of Gloucester Cathedral in 1337 – 57, and in the naves of Canterbury (1379 – 1404) and Winchester (c.1360), it was later used at King's College Chapel at Cambridge (1446-1515) and at St. George's Chapel, Windsor (begun 1474) before making its appearance in London in the early-sixteenth century (see below). Like the English Decorated style, there is an absent of Perpendicular Gothic on the Continent.

Though Gothic architecture emanated in France rather than England, in ecclesiastical buildings its development occurred broadly simultaneously in Paris and London. The initial stage in the construction of St. Paul's was completed by 1148, whereas Notre Dame was started in 1163. However, St. Mary Overie and Westminster Abbey were begun respectively in 1215 and 1220. Similarly, smaller churches in Paris and

51

London were constructed at broadly the same time. In Paris, Gothic elements were added to the Romanesque church of St-Germain-de-Pres in 1150 and St-Germain-l'Auxerre in 1220. while in London the largely Romanesque St. Bartholomew the Great (1144) and the Temple Church (1185) exhibit some Gothic attributes in contrast to St. Helen's Bishopsgate (1200-1215), St Etheldreda's Ely Place (late-thirteenth century), All Hallows by the Tower (fifteenth century), and St Margaret Westminster (1485-1523) that are all Gothic.

In contrast to church architecture, the construction of secular buildings of Gothic design was relatively insensitive to evolving changes in style, and like Romanesque or Norman secular buildings only accommodated those attributes that were considered appropriate to the needs of the user. In London, for example, palaces were constructed at Eltham and Lambeth in the thirteenth century and Greenwich from 1447, and the Guildhall was started in 1411 (though an earlier Romanesque hall might have been built on the same site in the early twelfth century). Uniquely, castle building in Gothic England was influences by the design of Crusader castles built in the Levant. New or existing *donjons* were now completely or partly surrounded by one or more defensive walls, sometimes regularised by the provision of four ranges with angle towers round a new or earlier square or oblong *donjon*, as, for example, at the Tower of London or Windsor Castle.

The Plantagenets and the Growth of London

Henry II (r.1154-1189)

Following Stephen's death in October 1154, Henry Plantagenet, son of Geoffrey of Anjou and Matilda, inherited the English throne and as Henry II reigned England for thirty-five years. Also having married Eleanor of Aquitaine in 1154 after the recent annulment of her marriage to the French king Louis VII, Henry not only ruled over England and re-established hegemony over Wales but also gained full control of what was later known as the Angevin empire incorporating the lands of Anjou, Maine and Touraine. Not content with his enormous territorial dowry, and often at Louis VII's expense, he subsequently extended his imperial possessions to include Brittany and set his sights on Central France and Toulouse.

In the 1160s, the Becket controversy overshadowed many other aspects of Henry's reign. Appointing Thomas Becket, the English Chancellor, as Archbishop of Canterbury in 1162 after the death of the former incumbent Theobald of Bec, Henry wrongly anticipated that Thomas, an old friend, would defer to the king on controversial matters that concerned both the monarchy and the church. However, the king and archbishop disagreed on a number of issues, for example concerning Becket's attempt to recover land lost to the archbishopric, disputes over Henry's taxation policies, and disagreements over who should try clergy allegedly guilty of secular crimes - the Crown or the Church? Differences of opinion became increasingly personal and international, and matters were made worse when

Becket fled to France in 1164 to seek the support of Henry's enemy, Louis VII, and subsequently excommunicated religious and secular allies of Henry. However, eventually Henry and Becket came to terms in July 1170 and the prelate returned to England in December, but Becket continued to excommunicate supporters of Henry, but to his cost. After refusing to be arrested in Canterbury Cathedral by four knights for allegedly breaking his agreement with Henry, he was hacked to death by his knightly assailants on 29 December 1170 horrifying Christian Europe and demonising Henry.

In 1173 Henry II's sons 'Young Henry', Richard and Geoffrey and their mother Eleanor rebelled against the king, but the 'Great Revolt' as it was called was put down magnanimously by the king but Young Henry and Geoffrey revolved again in 1183 resulting in the former's death. A final rebellion broke out in 1189 when Richard and Godfrey feared that Henry would make John, his youngest son, the next king of England, and defeated by Richard and Godfrey and in poor health Henry retreated to Chinon in Anjou where he died on 6th July 1189. Though Henry's empire rapidly collapsed after his death, many of the changes he introduced were of long-term importance, for example his legal innovations form the basis of English Common Law, his intervention in Wales, Scotland and Brittany influenced the development of their systems of government, and to an extent during his long reign he commissioned, or encouraged, the construction of a number of important buildings across London or on the edge of his capital.

Windsor Castle – Round Tower (1170)

Perhaps the most spectacular project was the reconstruction of Windsor Castle. Throughout a large part of Henry II's reign, the original wooden castle at Windsor was rebuilt in stone by the king and it was soon surrounded by an outer wall, also made of stone. The awesome Round Tower, that symbolises the strength of the castle, finally reached a height of about 50 ft (15 m) in the nineteenth century, and is far from cylindrical since the motte on which it stands is more oval than circular. Henry recognised that the castle represented the capital's first line of defence should it be attacked from the west.

But the local economy was just as important to Londoners as defence, not least to those employed in the weaving industry, perhaps the most important manufacturers in the City. In an attempt to enhance their role in the economy, weavers were granted a charter by Henry II in 1155, and from their hall built in Basinghall Street operated as the first craft guild in London. Under their direction, woollen cloth soon became the stock-in-trade of several leading City guilds, the mercers, drapers, tailors and haberdashers and was soon the most important commodity in London's later medieval overseas trade" (12).

Temple Church (1185)

However, it was in the ecclesiastical rather than the trading sector that most new notable buildings were constructed in the second-half of the twelfth century. For women, the Augustinian Priory of St. John the Baptist in Shoreditch was built in 1158, but perhaps the most important edifice to be constructed was the monastic complex of the Knights Templars. Situated on land that they had recently acquired south of the Strand, and funded from the charitable donations and wealth derived from their campaigns in the Levant, the Temple Church – reminiscent of the Holy Sepulchre in Jerusalem – was built by the Knights Templar in 1185. With a round nave and a larger rectangular chancel, the church "represents a most unusual and interesting point in the history of medieval architecture at the transitional stage between Norman and Gothic" (13). At its west end, its portal is distinctly Norman, while the entire interior is Gothic, its chancel (1240) being "built as a hall with aisles of the same height" (14).

Unlike the Knights Hospitallers in Clerkenwell (see above), the Knights Templars – an international order – were engaged in a wide range of activities, religious, economic, political and military, but probably because of their wealth they provoked jealously among their temporal rulers, not least in France where Philip IV brought questionable charges of blasphemy, heresy and sodomy against them in 1307. In consequence the Order was disbanded by Pope Clement in 1312. Subsequently, the London knights were arrested, imprisoned in the Tower and their property was confiscated and passed to the Hospitallers.

Meanwhile, further parish churches were built in London to cater for local needs. Though both St. Vedast and All Hallows Staining date from 1170-77 (or even earlier in the century), in the middle years of the twelfth century Benedictine monks built the church of St Margarets very close to the north façade of Westminster Abbey to provide a parish church for local residents who – in their desire for simpler worship – did not wish to use the Abbey.

St Margaret Westminster (Founded in the twelfth century, but the present church dates from 1485)

During the reigns of Henry II, Richard I and John one of the most famous of all medieval buildings, London Bridge, was built between 1176 and 1216. It remained the only bridge across the Thames for as long as 600 years, but unlike its three predecessors that were of wood, the new London Bridge had 19 small stone arches, a drawbridge at its southern (Southwark) end to allow ships to pass through, and in its centre a chapel built by Peter of Colechurch and dedicated to St. Thomas Becket. It also accommodated a severely congested roadway flanked either side by houses and ground floor shops at high density which in total rose three to seven stories in height. It nevertheless enhanced the local economies of the north and south banks of the Thames, and probably improved the effectiveness of London's government.

London Bridge (1176-1216)

Richard I (r. 1189-1199)

As the eldest son of Henry II, Richard I was crowned king in Westminster Abbey on 20 July 1189, and was also Duke of Normandy, Duke of Aquitaine, Duke of Gascony as well as being at various times Lord of Cyprus, Count of Anjou, Count of Maine, Count of Nantes and Overlord of Brittany. Understandably, he spent very little time in England nor spoke English, and resided mainly in Aquitaine in south west France. As Richard Coeur de Lion (the Lionheart) he is perhaps best known for being the central Christian Commander during the Third Crusade and for defeating the Saracen leader, Saladin, in the field, though he was unable to reconquer Jerusalem. However, in England, he became notorious for raising taxes and depleting the Treasury of funds to facilitate his involvement in the crusade, and eager to increase his resources further he was even said to declare "I would have sold London if I could find a buyer". Though a somewhat flippant remark, together with the king's high propensity to tax it was sufficient to encourage the citizens of London in 1193 "to form themselves into a 'commune' and elect their first mayor, Henry Fitz-Ailwyn" (15). The mayor's authority, supported by his aldermen and scrutinised by councillors, formed the essential foundation for strong local government in the capital, a template soon emulated by around 30 medieval towns across England.

All Hallows by the Tower (15th century, restoration completed 1957)

With taxation rising an unprecedented level and with Treasury funds being fully stretched because of Richard's participation in the Third Crusade and his heavy expenditure on castle-building in Normandy, only minimal financial resources were available for the construction of major buildings anywhere in England and Wales. In London, for example, the only notable buildings constructed during the reign of Richard I were three small edifices: St. Mary Spital on the east side of Bishopgate founded in 1197, the Lady Chapel of All Hallows Barking (by the Tower) built in 1189-1199 and allegedly where Richard's heart is buried, and St. Margaret Lothbury which dates from 1197. However, at the time this may have been no bad thing. London was now so cramped that it was frequently devastated by fire. Thus the mayor, Henry Fitz-Ailwyn, introduced the city's first Building Act that prohibited thatched roofs and stipulated that stone was to be used for partition walls. But, of course, it was many years before these statutory provisions were implemented, and then only partly.

John (r. 1199-1216)

John, the youngest of the five sons of Henry II and Eleanor of Aquitaine, was crowned King of England on 27 May 1199 when he was twenty-nine years old. In 1200 John married Isabella of Angouléme and in the same year, and in return for giving up the Vexin region in Normandy and a payment of 20,000 marks, he secured the Angevin lands in France at the peace treaty of Le Goulet, but the termination of hostilities was short-lived. The war resumed in 1202 and within two years John lost the whole of his empire in northern France and spent most of the next decade attempting to win it back which necessitated a huge increase in tax revenue and military expenditure as well as establishing new continental alliances.

At home, John's judicial reforms enhanced English common law and provided an extra source of revenue, but a disagreement between the English king and Pope Innocent III in 1209 over the pontiff's choice of Stephen Langton becoming the next archbishop of Canterbury heralded John's excommunication in 1209, but under continual pressure from the pope John eventually accepted Langdon as his principal primate in 1213. He feared that if he did not, Innocent would encourage the French to invade England.

But when England was at war with France in 1214, John suffered a severe setback when the French army of Philip II defeated John's German allies at the battle of Bouvines in 1214. To make matters worse, on returning to England John was faced with the First Baron's War, a rebellion by many of his barons who were opposed to his fiscal policy and unhappy about the way he treated many of his nobles. Fearing for his life John retreated to the Tower while armed bands roamed outside, and siding with the barons Archbishop Langdon proposed that they should "set out a demand for specific liberties in the name of 'the community as a whole land' (16). Cognizant of the archbishop's advice to his opponents, John travelled up the Thames to Windsor in June 1215 where he compiled the Magna Carta, a document of sixty-one clauses aimed at placating the barons. He then met them in a meadow by the Thames at Runnymead, applied his seal, secured their signatures and returned grudgingly to Windsor. The document became the "first charter of rights in Europe specifically to underpin civil liberties in a rule of law ….[and]….ranks among the foremost documents of the rule of law against raw power" (17) It was neither to the king's nor the barons' credit that neither side complied with its conditions, while Pope Innocent wrote that the charter was "'not only shameful and base, but illegal and unjust"(18).

In consequence, a civil war broke out that was compounded by the barons inviting Philip II's heir, Louis, to invade England to seize the crown. In 1216, Louis consequently captured all the Cinque Ports on the Channel coast except for Dover, marched his troops to London and installed himself in the Tower where he received declarations of loyalty from the English barons (19). Meanwhile, Llywelyn the Great of Wales and Alexander II of Scotland took advantage of the opportunity to also invade England, the Scots king even reaching Dover with the intention of paying homage to Louis. John was now a fugitive, moving haphazardly across his kingdom devastating rebel territory and destroying towns and villages unable or unwilling to help him. In early October 1216, John contracted dysentery and lost the Crown Jewels and other treasure while crossing the Wash, and died in Newark Castle on 18 October, allegedly of poison or a surfeit of peaches.

St Helen's, Bishopsgate (1216)

During a reign of questionable merit, and at a time of high taxation, a miscellany of notable buildings were constructed across London. Upstream from West-minster, Hubert Walker, archbishop of Canterbury, redeveloped his London residence, Lambeth Palace in 1207; Robert Fitzwilliam rebuilt Baynard's Castle in

1215 after being forgiven by John for being the leader of the barons' rebellion; and William Fitzwilliam (the son of a goldsmith) founded, in parallel to an existing Benedictine nunnery, the parish church of St. Helens Bishopgate c. 1200-1215. Since the church is very similar in size and style to the nunnery, the integrated building boasts a twin gabled façade and two main entrances: one for the nuns and the other for laity, although the two naves became one when the whole building became a parish church in 1538 with dissolution of the monasteries. However, the development of the built environment, the growth in the economy of London, and public safety each suffered a major setback in 1212-1213 when London Bridge was devastated by a fire with the alleged loss of 3,000 lives.

Henry III (r. 1216-1272)

With the death of King John, the barons and bishops of England no longer wished to see their country ruled by a French prince. They decided that the deceased king's son, nine-year old Henry, should succeed to the throne and arranged for him to be taken to Gloucester where, on 28 October 1216, his coronation took place. Soon after being crowned with his French mother's tiara – the authentic crown being lost in the Wash – Louis immediately gave up his claim to the English throne after a chaotic battle at Lincoln and maritime skirmish at Dover, retreated to France in 1217 and recognised the young Plantagenet as Henry III, the legitimate king of England. Throughout his minority, "the spirit of the Magna Carta was retained. Demands for tax were accompanied by reconfirmations of the charter to reassure the barons that there would be no return to arbitrary government" (20).

Until he was twenty-five in 1232, Henry's 'justiciar'

or chief minister, Hubert de Burgh acted as the *de facto* ruler of England, but because of his incompetence and doubts about his loyalty, Henry acrimoniously dismissed him from office. This experience possibly accounts for Henry becoming enamoured with the French system of monarchy where courtiers rather than council officials were more likely to support their king 'come rain or come shine'. As an obvious Francophile, Henry's admiration of all things French did not stop there. In commissioning the reconstruction of Westminster Abbey, not only was his master mason French but the architecture of the new Abbey was overtly French High Gothic. In retaining his French connection, Henry appointed a new justiciar, Peter des Roche, the Bishop of Winchester, possibly an unwise choice since Des Roche had been a close associate of King John. As an authoritarian and a keen tax-collector, he soon became unpopular with the nobility, and like de Burgh before him became, in-effect, the ruler of England. Henry therefore had little choice but to dismiss him only two years after his appointment.

From 1234 to the late 1240s peace ensued, in large part due to the poverty of the crown, a legacy of Magna Carta that put a constraint on the ability of the monarch to impose high levels of taxation. This, together with his committed expenditure on the Tower of London and Westminster Abbey, prevented him from recovering the French possessions of his grandfather Henry II, but lost by his father. During these years, relations between Henry III and the nobility were favourable since they were not asked to contribute unacceptable sums to further the king's ambitions. However, because of a shortage of tax revenue, Henry was increasingly in debt to the papacy and to a number of great families across Europe, but to Henry's chagrin the English nobility refused to bail him out. Criticism of the king intensified after he married Eleanor of Province in 1236. Over the following decades, he showered her Savoyard family with land and titles and even made her uncle, Boniface, archbishop of Canterbury in 1270 while other members of her family became councillors. Another influx of French relatives came to England from 1247. These were the Lusignans, Henry's half siblings from his mother, Isabella of Augouléme's second marriage, and again they were received by Henry generously.

Since both the Savoyards and the Lusignans increasingly gained political and economic power they provoked much resentment among the English nobility, and it was surmised that both families were encouraging Henry to become more and more tyrannical. In their opposition, the barons turned to Simon de Montfort, the Earl of Leicester, who, although of French origin, abhorred Henry's autocratic style of monarchy and was particularly antagonist to the Lusignans.

Though Henry, in an attempt to reduce opposition from his political critics, ordered the compilation of the Hundred Rolls in 1255 to provide information on royal privileges, he was very reluctantly obliged to agree to the 'Oxford Provisions' of 1258, the outcome of a meeting of Parliament (formerly 'council') that was convened at Oxford instead of at Westminster. The provisions drew up revolutionary plans to turn England into a crowned republic, an unprecedented constitutional arrangement unknown anywhere else in Europe, though it contained some constitutional elements found in the city-states and communes of Italy or Germany. Fearful of recriminations against their role in domestic politics the Lusignans fled the country, leaving Henry politically very much on his own. In a show of bravado he attempted to avenge himself by resorting to armed conflict against De Montfort and the barons, but Henry and his army were duly defeated by de Montfort's forces at the Battle of Lewis in 1264, and soon after was compelled to agree to the terms of the Oxford Provisions.

Though De Montfort's parliament was the first directly elected parliament in Europe, it benefited from having its membership broadened to include not only knights from each county but also burgesses and others from the larger towns, but in the view of many of his critics its members "proved to be as selfish and grasping as the king's fallen favourites" (21). Recognising that he must support Henry, with the help of his son Edward (later Edward I), he raised an army in 1265 to confront de Montfort's forces, and at the ensuing battle of Evesham, De Montfort met his death and was duly dismembered. In the following year the Dictum of Kenilworth restored Henry's full authority, but during the final years of his fifty-six year reign little happened and Henry expired on 16 November 1272 aged sixty-five. He was subsequently entombed in splendour at his beloved Westminster Abbey, the building arguably being his greatest legacy.

Despite the shortages of funds available to the king and his subjects, many construction projects were undertaken throughout most of Henry's reign in both the secular and ecclesiastical sectors. Of some urgency, the damage done to Windsor Castle when it was under siege by baronial and French troops in 1216 was repaired by 1221 by the citadel's constable, Engelard de Cigogné, who at the same time was instrumental in strengthening the castle's defensive ramparts. The walls of the Lower Ward were rebuilt of stone and incorporated a gatehouse in 1224 – 1230 (on the site late occupied by Henry VIII's sixteenth century gate). The Middle Ward was likewise reinforced with a stone wall, and protected by the new Curfew, Garter and

Salisbury towers. Windsor Castle was undoubtedly one of Henry III's favourite residences and he spent more money on the castle than on any of his other properties. After his marriage to Eleanor of Province in 1236 he built a magnificent palace in 1240-63 adjacent to the north side of the Upper Ward, while along the north side of the ward the Great Hall was repaired and enlarged at a cost of around £10,000, though it was later destroyed by fire (in 1296) and not rebuilt.

In the City of London, however, the first buildings of any note to be constructed soon after Henry's accession were relatively small parish churches. Though the church of St. Andrew Castle Baynard was known to exist in 1244, it was probably founded very early in Henry's reign or even before Henry came to the throne. However, there is evidence that the church of St. Michael Paternoster Royal was built in 1219, only three years after his accession, and some way through Henry's reign, the eleventh century wooden church of St. Olave was replaced by a stone structure. However, throughout most of the century, hospitals became the most prolific of the ecclesiastical edifices constructed in London. Rather than supplying medical treatment, they were essential providers of protective care, and they were managed by religious communities and generally funded by the Crown, rich landowners and courtiers (22).

With the arrival of the mendicant orders in London, there was a proliferation of new monasteries as bases for local preaching. The Dominicans (or Blackfriars) were the first to build such a monastery, initially in Holborn (c.1221), the Franciscans (Greyfriars) became located on a large estate granted by a rich sheriff, north of Newgate (1225); the Cartmelites (Whitefriars) were given a large plot of land to the west of the wall (1241); the Augustinians added to their property portfolio by being granted a large area of land in the north of the City (1253); and the Crutched or Cross friars were given two acres north west of the Tower on which to build its monastery (23). However, these were comparatively small ventures.

In the middle part of his reign, Henry commissioned two major and lengthy building projects: first, the further development of the Tower and second, the reconstruction and expansion of Westminster Abbey, both buildings in their current forms having been founded by William the Conqueror. On Henry III's orders, the Tower's keep was whitewashed in 1240 to make its bulk visible from afar, hence the origin of its name, the 'White Tower'. Inspired by Crusader castles, inner and outer defensive walls were erected around the keep throughout Henry's lifetime (they were started in the late-twelfth century and completed in the early-fourteenth), and Henry himself commissioned a new defensive wall that linked the Bell Tower (built during the reign of Richard I) with the Devereux, Martin and Salt towers.

Westminster Abbey – north transept (1246-72), by Henry de Reynes

At Westminster Abbey building work in 1220, funded and directed largely by the Benedictine Order, transformed the rounded east end of the Abbey into a squared-off structure containing a Lady Chapel. However, on its completion, further development was put on hold, probably because of a depletion of resources. However, it was largely Henry III who ordered the demolition of the Romanesque edifice built for Edward the Confessor between 1042 and 1066, and its replacement by a new abbey built mainly between 1246 and 1272, though it was subsequently enlarged over the following three centuries using, in various combinations, the use of Caen and Portland stone, tuffean from the Loire valley and Purbeck marble.

In 1245, the year before rebuilding work began , Henry III – in his desire to build a shrine for his favourite saint Edward the Confessor – assumed the whole financial responsibility of reconstructing the building, and employed a master mason, Henry de Reynes (possibly from the cathedral city of Reims) to extend the new abbey further to the west. Encouraged by the king, who was familiar with such buildings as the Abbey Church of St-Denis and the Sainte-Chapelle, Henry de Reynes eschewed the Early English style of Gothic architecture and opted instead for French High Gothic currently in vogue in the Ile-de-~France and Paris. Based on the Abbey of Royaumont (1228-36) or Reims Cathedral (finished 1242), De Reynes added a French chevet (incorporating an apse, an ambulatory and small radiating chapels) to the existing Lady Chapel at the east end and, building progressively westward, constructed a tall and narrow rib-vaulted choir rising to 103 ft (31.3 m), north and south transepts projecting from the crossing, and the first two bays of the rib-vaulted nave with its narrow aisles. Other French features adopted mid-century include the use of pointed arches, flying buttresses (on the south side of the nave), the absence of a wall passage in the clerestory, and naturalistic foliage capitals. In the 1260s, rose windows in the Flamboyant style were being incorporated into the north and south walls of the transepts, virtually replicating those being currently installed in the Notre Dame (24).

In 1250-53, work was completed on the abbey's octagonal chapter house. Stemming from the south transept, the 60 ft (18 m) wide building is noted for its bar-tracery developed at the Sainte-Chapelle in Paris from the 1220s to 1240s, while its "windows are far more expansive than those in the church, being grouped in four lights surmounted by two quatrefoils and then by a large six-foiled circle" (25). Even richer tracery, reminiscent of that found in the Sainte-Chapelle, graces the vestibule of the chapter house and around part of the cloister. The chapter house accommodated Henry III's Great Council on 26 March 1257, and from the middle of the fourteenth century to the middle of the sixteenth it was used for the meeting of the House of Commons. During the last decade of Henry's reign, work on the Abbey slowed down till his death in 1272, by which time a total of £45,000 had been spent on the construction of the rebuilt Abbey (26),

Old St Paul's (1258-1314). Its steeple was struck by lightning in 1561 and not replaced.

At the City of London's expense, the rib-vaulted chancel and choir (with new traceried windows) of St Paul's were rebuilt in the Early English Gothic style between 1258 and 1314, and the octagonal Chapter House designed by William de Ramsey in the novel Perpendicular Gothic style was added to the main structure in 1332. The cathedral also boasted a magnificent rose window with a series of lancets at its eastern extremity whose design was "taken directly from Westminster transepts which were themselves based on Pierre de Montreuil's south transept at Notre Dame" (27). However, all was lost in the Great Fire of London in 1666.

Edward I (r. 1272 – 1307)

The coronation of Edward I occurred on the 19 August 1274, nearly two years after the death of his father Henry III. During this gap, Henry had participated in the ninth and last Crusade, and on his long way home engaged in tournaments and put down a rebellion in Gascony. From the beginning of his reign he undoubtedly reminded himself of how Simon de Montfort humiliated his father, and the cost of being a weak king. Not only was he six foot two inches (1.88 m) in height and acquired the nickname 'Longshanks', he had a strong physique and was determined to rule without any mercy shown to his foes. To reinforce the rights of the crown he eliminated the causes of discontent in England and waged a three-pronged attack on Wales, Scotland and France.

At home he put an end to the smouldering baron's revolt by encouraging them to buy back their property that had been appropriated by his father, a ploy that was not only popular among his former enemies but also raised a substantial amount of revenue for the Treasury. He also attempted to put an end to official corruption by extending the content of the Hundred Rolls of 1255 by adding, in 1274-78 and 1279-80, a census of liberties and land-ownership that could be used for judicial and taxation purposes. Because of its accumulation of a vast amount of unwieldy information, few prosecutions took place but the rolls were important in demonstrating that, when law was in action or tax demands were made, there were, at least nominally, equal rights for all.

From the beginning of his reign Edward was aware that, with Llwelwyn ap Gryffydd exerting his power over most of Wales from his base in Snowdonia, his kingdom's authority over the province was being severely diminished. Edward, however, was completely opposed to giving the Welsh independence, and because he could not secure homage from Llwelwyn on four repeated occasions, declared a costly war on England's western neighbour in 1277. Opposed by Edward's army of 15,500 men, Llwelwyn surrendered to the English king and his countrymen were compelled to accept alien English laws. This they found unacceptable and rebelled again in 1282 and thereby provoked Edward with his vast army to lay siege to Llwelwyn in Snowdonia and to starve him out. A brutal and expensive military occupation ensued, strengthened by the construction of English castles, particularly at Conwy, Harlech, Caernarfon and Beaumarais. But English suppression did not stop there. Edward proclaimed that to wage war against him was an act of treason, a crime that would receive the most severe punishment. The first person to be accused of this 'new' offence was Llwelwyn's brother, Daffyd ap Gryffydd who, among other forms of mutilation, was hanged, disembowelled, beheaded and quartered.

In contrast to Wales, Scotland for generations had been partly integrated with England through the intermarriage of royal houses, Scotland owning vast landholdings in England, and the Scots having the right to participate in English councils and parliaments. With the early death of Margaret, the Maid of Norway in 1290, the throne of Scotland became vacant, and Edward considered that, as a feudal suzerain, he had the right to select the next ruler. In choosing John Balliol, a major landowner in England, as the next king of Scotland Edward preserved the right to remain the country's overlord and responsible for its justice and government, and when necessary he would overrule Balliol's judgements. To Balliol's embarrassment, and to the wrath of the Scots, Edward summoned Balliol to Westminster to remind him of their respective responsibilities, and in provocation the Scots rebelled and Edward responded by sending an invading army north of the border. Taking Berwick, Dunbar, Edinburgh and Stirling, the English army conquered Scotland in only five months, and Edward achieved his much wanted prize, the direct rule of Scotland. Balliol was stripped of the Scottish crown, and the Stone of Scone, which for 400 years had been placed under the Scottish coronation throne, was removed and relocated by Edward at Westminster Abbey where it remained for a further 700 years. Clearly, in the view of Richard Starkey, "Scotland had ceased altogether to be a kingdom and became a mere province of England" (28).

As a result of an alliance between Philip IV of France and John Balliol, the French king confiscated the remaining English territories in France as a reprisal for Edward's stance on Scotland. Therefore, to raise taxes to fund a war against France in an attempt to recover his lost possessions, Edward summoned what became known as the Model Parliament in 1295, an assembly of prominent townsfolk, country gentlemen and knights, and ironically shared with Simon de Montfort the epithet of being the father of Parliament. Edward was soon at war with the French and Scots on two fronts, and to address the concerns of his subjects about the escalating costs of war, found it expedient to reissue the Magna Carta and pledged that there would be no increase in taxation without full consultation. The Scots fiercely defended their homeland, but their resistance leader William Wallace was betrayed and taken to London where he was put on trial in Westminster Hall. Found guilty of a plethora of traitorous and other offences, and taken to Smithfield for his execution, he shared virtually the same horrific fate that fell on Daffyd ap Gryffydd, twenty-five years earlier. But this did not stop Scottish resistance to English rule. Notwithstanding the absence of a Scottish crown and the Stone of Scone, Robert the Bruce was crowned king of the Scots in 1306 and continued to antagonise the English. The effect was to encourage Edward to wage punitive campaigns across the border and conduct brutal reprisals on his enemy, but on a campaign in 1307 Edward died at the age of sixty-eight and like his father was buried in Westminster Abbey.

The reign of Edward I was particularly notable for its almost continuous and costly wars, necessitating frequent increases in taxation and stretching funds to their limit. It is therefore surprising that quite a few notable buildings were constructed in London during the late-thirteenth and very early-fourteenth centuries, both ecclesiastical and secular.

Perhaps at a time of warfare it was to be expected that Edward I prioritised expenditure on improving his own defences, albeit at some distance where military action was being taken. Thus throughout his reign, the Tower of London was greatly extended. An outer wall was erected that – on the riverside – linked together a succession of new stone edifices: Cradle Tower, Wakefield Tower, St. Thomas's Tower, the Traitors' Gate and the Byward Tower (a gatehouse) before continuing on its rectangular course around the White Tower. In addition Edward ordered the construction of a new moat on the western, northern and eastern sides of the outer wall, the isolated Middle Tower on the far side of the moat, the Beauchamp Tower on the western edge of the inner defensive wall, and the church of St. Peter ad Vincula in the inner ward.

While most of the mendicant orders established in London early in the thirteenth century stayed put, the Dominicans (or Blackfriars) relocated their monastery in 1274 from Holborn to a site of the former Montfichet Tower between Ludgate and the Thames, and in the following year the same order acquired Baynards Castle, the building by 1279 providing a precinct for the enlarged monastery, while to the east of London wall in 1293, the Minoresses of St. Clare began to provide a refuge for women in need of care and protection.

Expenditure by the state on public buildings in the capital was also maintained. From the reign of William II, Westminster Palace had accommodated the predecessor of England's parliament the *Curia Regis* (the Royal Council), but from 1295 it housed the country's first official parliament (the Model Parliament) and the seat of the Royal Courts of Justice.

Edward II (r.1307-1327)

During Edward II's twenty year reign England was at war with Scotland for much of the time (the highlight of the conflict being her defeat at Bannockburn in 1314, while famine spread across the kingdom in 1314-15). Comparatively little building work of note was therefore undertaken in London during this period. Most of the Tower of London had been built in the thirteenth century though it was not until the reign of Edward II that construction was virtually complete, while building work in the ecclesiastical sector was minimal. There were already 110 churches in London in the early-fourteenth century, and these were very evenly spread across the City to ensure "that most people could belong to a relatively small and intimate group for religious worship" (29). However, the church in the English capital was a major landowner, and thus "played an important role in shaping the appearance and character of medieval London" (30). Though bequests and investments dramatically expanded its holdings of commercial and residential property, the church was exempt from taxation, and thus in 1312 London's "mayor and the aldermen complained that monasteries and other religious landlords, owning a third of the city's rental income, paid nothing towards its walls and defence" (31). To an extent Edward II involved himself in ecclesiastical matters, for example when the Knights Templars ceased to gain royal support, the king took control of their monastery in 1307 and presented it to his cousin the Earl of Lancaster before passing it to the Knights Hospitallers.

Edward III (r. 1327-1377)

Temperamentally more like his grandfather, than his father, Edward III lacked Edward I's aggressive authoritarianism while in his endeavours to rule England with the full co-operation of the barons he brought about a quiet revolution by attempting to rule with the full co-operation of Parliament and only going to war if it were in the national interest. However at the very beginning of his reign he found himself marginalised by his mother Isabella's lover, Roger Mortimer, the 1st Earl of March. Mortimer accumulated both power and land for himself, and in overshadowing the influence of the young king and the nobility created a new tyranny. Though only eighteen years of age in 1330, Edward with his close followers overpowered and arrested Mortimer at Nottingham Castle, and he was subsequently taken to London and hanged as a common criminal at Tyburn whilst, for her part in aiding and abetting Mortimer, Edward's mother was imprisoned for life.

In 1332, and being aware of how Scotland eluded his grandfather and humiliated his father, Edward turned his attention to regaining England's influence and authority north of the border. Using the longbow for the very first time, Edward's army won a resounding victory over the Scots at Haldon Hill on the outskirts of Berwick, avenging his father's defeat at Bannockburn eighteen years earlier, and for the first time in thirty years safeguarded the north of England from a Scot's invasion.

Deteriorating relations between France and England gathered pace in 1337 when Philip VI ceased to recognise the legitimacy of English lands in France and began invading Aquitaine. In response Edward declared that since he was the only male descendent of Philip IV he, rather than the current incumbent Philip VI, was the only true king of France. Hostilities between the two countries commenced in 1340 with a naval battle at Sluys, which when won by Edward's fleet gave England control of the Channel and enabled her to transport an army to France without hindrance, and so the Hundred Years War began. But if Edward wanted a war with France it not only required Parliament to scrutinise the King's demand for money but Parliament was also expected to provide the king with advice and consent. In so doing, Edward could be assured that his war with France (or any other country) "was a joint enterprise between the King and the English nation" (32).

Because of the length and scale of fourteenth century wars, Parliament deemed it necessary to expand the system of taxation. Therefore in addition to retaining direct taxation on income and property, indirect taxation on trade was introduced which not only helped to fill royal coffers but, through the levying of heavy export duties on for example wool, resulted in the incidence of taxation shifting from English taxpayers to foreign purchasers who, of course, were not represented in Parliament. Eventually, in 1346, Edward III invaded France with an army of 10,000 men, and after failing to take Paris withdrew to the Somme where at the Battle of Crécy on 26 August it defeated an even larger army of Philip VI through the skill of Welsh longbowmen and the previously unknown force of the cannon, notwithstanding the heroism of the French cavalry. Soon after this, on 17 October, an English army defeated Scottish forces at the Battle of Neville's Cross in Durham, freeing Edward to focus his attention on France, where, from 4 September 1346 to 3 August 1347, his enormous force that now exceeded 35,000 men laid siege to Calais, an *enpasse* that only ended with the surrender of six of the town's burghers.

Soon after, 1348, Europe was ravaged by the Black Death or bubonic plague which reduced the Continent's population by a third or more. With further outbreaks of the plague later in the century the population of London fell by as much as a third. However, because of the resulting shortage of labour across England, Parliament deemed it necessary to peg wages at pre-plague levels through the Statute of Labourers of 1351, and for the first time appointed justices of the peace to ensure that the statute was enforced. But despite the Black Death the war with France intensified, and battles were not only fought in Normandy but in Scotland, an old ally of the French. But it was in France that the English army was most engaged. In 1355

Edward III allowed his sons, Edward the Black Prince and John of Gaunt to rampage across Brittany, Gascony, Armagnac and Languedoc, and in the following year the Black Prince fought a victorious battle against the French at the battle of Poitiers in 1356 where English forces vanquished a much larger French army. However, despite resounding English victories in France, Edward III was unable to achieve his goal of sitting on the French throne. At the Treaty of Bretigny in 1360, with the consent of Parliament and in the perceived interests of England, he traded his claim to the French throne and the lands of Anjou, Normandy and Brittany for the consolidation of substantial swathes of land across France.

It might be argued that after 1360 Edward "was more closely identified with the interest of his people and ... would never again rule effectively without the consent and cooperation of Parliament" (33). This of course did not stop Edward from resuming his costly campaign in France in 1369, initially in an attempt to retake Aquitaine and then in 1370 authorising the Black Prince to sack Limoges with a loss of 3,000 lives. However, in 1372 French troops recaptured Poutou and Brittany, and at the Battle of La Rochelle the French regained control of the Channel in 1373. In response, England yet again invaded France, and although John of Gaunt took his army as far as Burgundy, his efforts were wasted since, at the Treaty of Bruges in 1375, England lost all her French possessions except for the coastal towns of Calais, Bordeaux and Bayonne. In 1374, John of Gaunt had already taken the opportunity to return to England to grab the levers of power during Edward's dotage and the Black Prince's illness and premature death in 1376, but his moment of glory was short-lived since in 1377 and after an exhausting reign of fifty years, Edward III died at Sheen Palace in

Surrey, and was buried like his grandfather in Westminster Abbey.

Despite the enormous expense of contemporary warfare, a relatively low tax base (notwithstanding the introduction of indirect taxation) and the increased power of Parliament to control expenditure, a wide range of secular and ecclesiastical buildings were commissioned in and near London in the thirteenth century. Although only a small number of modest buildings of note were constructed during the first year of Edward III's reign such as the livery halls of the Merchant Taylor's in Threadneedle Street in 1327 and that of the Skinners in Dowgate Hill founded in the same year, throughout the rest of his reign, the scale of building projects increased substantially, so much so that it could be claimed that Edward "eclipsed his great predecessor Henry II and became the greatest patron of English architecture in the Middle Ages" (35).

In 1336, the Great Hall of Winchester Palace was adorned by the insertion of a rose window at its west end, while St Stephen's Chapel in Westminster , like its Parisian counterpart, the Sainte Chapelle of 1248, and to an extent like the choir of St. Denis (begun 1231) "made ample use of tracery patterns inspired by the French court style, and thereby anticipated the Perpendicular style of the following century. Internally, the spandrels of the chapel's arched windows were adorned with vertical tracery patterns, and their descending mullions passed through a dado arcade, while externally, "the mullions of the main windows descended in a kind of curtain in front of the crypt windows and so to the ground" (34). Though tracery of the sort employed in St Stephen's is of French origin, it was also employed by the designer of the chapter house of Old St Paul's, William de Ramsey, who simultaneously worked as a mason at St Stephen's before being put in charge of work there from 1337 . Though St Stephen's was used as a place of worship for the monarchy until the reign of Henry VIII, thereafter it became a debating chamber of the Commons and was eventually destroyed – with the rest of the Palace of Westminster – by fire in 1834.

St Stephen's Chapel (1327)

Construction work in the ecclesiastical sector also included the establishment of a hospital and two monasteries. Situated in Cripplegate, The Elsing Spital was founded by a mercer, William Elsing in 1329, and from the beginning the hospital was administered by a rector and four secular priests but they were replaced in 1342 by four Augustinian canons. East of Smithfield, the Cistercian abbey of St. Mary Graces was founded by the king in 1349 and, on a site used as a burial ground for victims of the Black Death, Charterhouse was founded by Sir Walter Many in 1370 and built by the master mason Henry Yevelve on a 13 acre [5.3 ha] site north of Smithfield (35).

From 1350 to 1377, Edward renovated Windsor Castle at a cost of £51,000, the largest amount spent by any English monarch on a single building project, and over one and a half times his annual income. Some of the money came from ransoms derived from English victories at Crécy, Calais and Poitiers, but the rest came mainly from domestic taxation. Windsor Castle rebuilt became "the most expensive secular building project of the entire Middle Ages in England" (36). Construction was concentrated on the northern side of the Upper Ward of the castle including most notably the enormous St. George's Hall (rebuilt in the eighteenth century). The main body of the building accommodated a new hall and a new chapel, was pierced by sixteen large windows looking out across the ward, and was framed at either end by two symmetrical gatehouses. Overall, the extensive hall is architecturally uniform in respect of its roof and cornice lines, and its window, floor and ceiling heights.

Around the same time of this renovation, the Jewel House was constructed on the south-west edge of the Palace of Westminster. Designed as a mini-keep to protect the royal valuables, the building was designed in a somewhat archaic style – more Romanesque than Gothic. Being detached from the palace itself, it therefore survived the fire of 1834 that devastated the parliamentary buildings.

Jewel House, Westminster Palace (1365-6), by Henry Yevele.

Further construction work occurred in the commercial sector. The Goldsmiths' guild hall was established in 1339 in Foster Street, and the Drapers' guild in Throgmorton Street and Vintners' guild in Upper Thames Street were both founded in 1364.

Richard II (r. 1377 – 1399)

As son of Edward the Black Prince and the surviving heir to the throne, Richard Plantagenet was only ten when he succeeded his grandfather Edward III as Richard II King of England in 1377. Though his uncle was Richard of Gaunt, Gaunt was so distrusted that the king's councillors denied him the regency and instead allowed friends such as Simon de Burley and Aubrey de Vere to exercise a great deal of control over royal affairs. However, their role was abolished by the Commons in 1380 since they imposed the heavy burden of the poll tax on the king's subjects three times between 1377 and 1381 to facilitate spending on military campaigns on the continent. The last of these taxes in 1381 and the unpopularity of the post-plague Statute of Labourers of 1351, that pegged wages at pre-plague levels, triggered the Peasants' Revolt, a misnomer since it was an uprising of yeomen and craftsmen. Though discontent was endemic throughout south-east England, the full force of the rebellion started in Kent in late-May and spread the following month to London via Blackheath under its leaders Wat Tyler, John Ball and Jack Straw. Demanding the end of the poll tax and last vestiges of serfdom, the rebels burnt to the ground John of Gaunt's Savoy Palace, and killed the Archbishop of Canterbury, Simon Sudbury, and the king's Lord High Treasurer, Robert Hales. Seeking refuge in the Tower, it was clear to the king that the Crown did not have sufficient forces to dispel the rebels and therefore he was obliged to negotiate, notwithstanding the fact that he was still only fourteen years old. On 14 June, Edward met the rebels at Mile End and agreed to their demands, but at a meeting with the king the following day at Smithfield, Wat Tyler doubted Richard's sincerity and outraged the king's supporters particularly William Walworth, the mayor of London, who dismounted Wat Tyler from his horse and killed him. Richard, aware of the escalating tension, led the rebels away from the scene, saying 'follow me. I am your captain' and granted them clemency, but since the disturbances continued Richard revoked his concessions to the rebels and accompanied a small army into Essex where at Billericay it finally put an end to the uprising.

But as Richard matured it was evident that, unlike his father and grandfather, he lacked the warrior spirit and showed more interest in architecture and art than martial pursuits. Though he married Anne of Bohemia in 1382 at the age of fifteen, Robert de Vere, Marquis of Oxford and Michael de la Pole, Earl of Suffolk, became his close companions. In 1388, with Richard of Gaunt pursuing his claim to the throne of Castile, both the Duke of Gloucester and Gaunt's son Henry Bolingbroke felt free to censure both Oxford and Suffolk through the 'lords appellant', and unable to gain support from the humiliated king both rapidly fled the country.

When Richard of Gaunt returned from Spain in 1389 Richard II was twenty-two and was determined to reign in his own rite. With the Hundred Years War in abeyance, not least because of its demands on the Treasury, it was possible to free the rich of taxes and to enable chapels and colleges to spend heavily on their buildings and other material assets. In 1397 he was particularly driven to take revenge on those nobles that eliminated his favourites from power some nine years earlier, and was duly involved in the murder of his uncle, Gloucester, in France. He also abolished the parliamentary council and replaced it with a committee of eighteen friends whose first task was to exile Bolingbroke abroad, a somewhat reckless act since Bolingbroke and his forever-loyal elderly father, Gaunt, were enraged and probably unforgiving. After Gaunt's death in February 1399 Richard, avariciously sequestrated the entire Lancastrian estates that would otherwise have passed to Bolingbroke, but rather naively Richard invaded Ireland with a small army to put down a minor revolt enabling Bolingbroke to return to England where he joined forces with the Percys, earls of Northumberland and intercepted and arrested Richard in north Wales on his return from Ireland. Taken to London as a prisoner, Richard was forced for fear of his life to abdicate, and Bolingbroke was subsequently crowned Henry IV on 13 October 1399. By the end of the year Richard was taken from the Tower to Pontefract Castle where he starved to death on or around 14 February 1400.

Westminster Hall (1390s), by Henry Yevele

Notwithstanding his many flaws, Richard II's contribution to the architecture of his capital was outstanding. First and foremost he ordered the reconstruction of Westminster Hall. Initially the hall, the largest in Europe, had timber supports for the roof, but in the 1390's Richard commissioned the mason

Henry Yevele to renovate the hall, and the carpenter Hugh Herland to replace the supports with a hammerbeam roof.

Westminster Abbey – western bays, south facade (1375-1400) , by Henry Yevele. The upper towers were built in the early-18th century.

After an interval of about a hundred and fifty years, and largely funded by a succession of kings, the remaining fabric of Westminster Abbey was finally demolished, and at long last the five western bays of the *retardetaire* nave with its rib vaults and narrow aisles were constructed between 1375 and 1400, mainly during the reign of Richard II. Built by the king's master mason throughout this period, Henry Yevele, the western part of the Abbey was successfully constructed in the same style as its long-since-completed eastern part to maintain the unity of the building. It was left to Henry VII in the early sixteenth century to finally complete the west front with its imposing perpendicular window.

Commercial activity in London continued to be regulated and arguably increased by the guilds, and during the reign of Richard II their influence was enhanced by the establishment of the Mercers' Guild in Ironmonger Lane in 1394, and the Fishmongers' guild in Knightrider Street in 1399.

The legal profession in particular attempted to increase its prestige, power and influence through the construction and establishment of a plethora of specialised inns along the Strand. By the beginning of the fifteenth century "there were ten Inns of Chancery and four great Inns of Court [Lincoln's Inn , Middle Temple, Inner Temple and Gray's Inn] with 700-800 lawyers and 200-300 students" (36).

However, the construction of ecclesiastical buildings, other than Westminster abbey, reached a low ebb. Very largely because London was very well endowed with churches dating from the thirteenth century or earlier, St. Martin Ludgate (1437) was about the only notable church initially built in the High Middle Ages to be reconstructed in the fifteenth century.

The House of Lancaster

Henry IV (r. 1399 – 1413) and Henry V (r. 1413 – 1422)

The reigns of Henry IV and Henry V were largely unproductive years in the creation of London's fabric largely because rebellions and the war with France put a substantial strain on the Treasury and diminished non-military expenditure. The only notable building to be completed was the Leadenhall market designed to contain a granary and wheat and cloth warehouses, rendering it London's principal merchandising centre (37), and although work began on the new Guildhall in 1411 the building was not completed until many years later (see below).

Guildhall (1411-30), by John Croxton. The medieval building is partly obscured by an eighteenth century frontisplease.

Henry VI (r. 1422-1461 & 1470-1471)

As Henry V's only child and heir, Henry VI was King of England twice in the fifteenth century and the disputed King of France from 1422 to 1453, yet until he came of age at 16 in 1437, his realm was governed by a regency council headed by his father's surviving brothers, John, Duke of Bedford (who died in 1435), and Humphrey the Duke of Gloucester. Throughout his regencies and for a while after, England had been at war with France, but this found little favour with the young Henry. To his credit, he helped formulate the

Treaty of Tours in 1444 that brought peace between England and France, but at great cost to his personal prestige. In the treaty, Charles VII of France agreed to the marriage in 1445 of his daughter Margaret of Anjou to Henry but, instead of Charles complying with normal procedure by providing a dowry, Henry generously granted the lands of Maine and Anjou to France much against the will of the English parliament from whom their loss was initially kept secret.

In the middle years of Henry's reign, the king became increasingly unpopular. Law and order had broken down, corruption was rife at the highest levels of government, crown finances were in a dire state and there was a steady loss of territories in France. In 1447 William de la Pole, the Duke of Suffolk, was thought by many to be responsible for promulgating the king's unpopularity and was duly exiled and *en route* murdered. In 1449, Edmund Beaufort, the Duke of Somerset, reopened hostilities in Normandy, but within a year the English army was in disarray and the French retook the whole of the province, previously won by Henry V. In 1450, Henry faced the dangers of an insurrection at home when Jack Cade, in sympathy with the House of York, led a rebellion in Kent and descended upon London, but with the help of the capital's residents rather than the king's army London was retaken after a few days, but even so the rebellion was a reflection of growing discontent among the king's subjects. To add insult to injury, in the following year Henry lost the Duchy of Guyenne held by the English since Henry II's time, and despite an effort to regain the duchy lost it again in 1453 leaving the enclave of Calais as England's only possession on the continent. Probably as a result of this disaster, Henry immediately had a serious mental breakdown though he regained his senses on Christmas Day 1454.

Meanwhile, disaffected nobles of the House of Lancaster, particularly the Earls of Warwick and Salisbury, backed claims by the rival House of York to the English throne, and after a prolonged and violent conflict between the houses of Lancaster and York, Henry was deposed and held captive by his cousin the Duke of York, who as Edward IV was declared king in 1461. Henry, however, escaped and with his Queen sought refuge in Scotland, but ironically two of Edward's principal supporters, Richard Neville, the Earl of Warwick and his brother George Neville, the Duke of Clarence, became disenchanted with the Yorkist rule, and after returning from his son's wedding in France, Warwick forced Edward IV into exile and restored Henry VI to the throne on 3 October 1470. However, because of Henry's poor health, Warwick and Clarence ruled in his name, but only for a short while. Edward returned to England in early 1471, split the alliance between Warwick and Clarence into two, allied himself with Clarence and fought Warwick to his death at the Battle of Barnet before gaining a decisive victory at the Battle of Tewksbury on 4 May 1471. Henry, who was imprisoned in the Tower, died soon after on 22 May 1471 and was probably murdered. Notwithstanding his tumultuous reigns, Henry both through his own initiative or the effort of others left a fine legacy of buildings in London and its outer reaches, some of which grace the capital to the present day.

First and foremost, Henry developed his principal royal residence at Greenwich, which was 5.4 miles (8.7 km) downstream from central London, though he retained Westminster Palace as the seat of government. Though there is some evidence English monarchs from Edward I to Henry V intermittently owned a manor in what later became Greenwich Park, it was not until

1447 that the royal family, notwithstanding its unpopularity, eventually found a residency in keeping with its status. In that year, a substantial property known as Bella Court built and owned by Humphrey, Duke of Gloucester, was acquired by Queen Margaret of Anjou after the duke had been arrested for treason. Build around 1422, Bella Court remained largely unchanged until Henry VII substantially extended the building c. 1500-1506 and renamed it 'Placentia'.

Throughout Henry's reign, the City of London, asserted itself as the commercial heart of the kingdom. By 1423 there were over 100 chartered guilds in the City, and later the Grocers in Old Jewry (1428), the Haberdashers in Staining Lane (1448), and the Ironmongers in Fenchurch Street (1463) were added to this number. Overarching the role of the guilds, for centuries the Guildhall has been the centre of government in the City where meetings of the Court of Common Council are held regularly, and where Lord Mayors and Sheriffs are elected. The first guildhall dated back to at least 1128, when its existence was recorded in an inventory of property owned by Old St. Paul's (38), but in the early fifteenth century the building was substantially reconstructed. Initially under the direction of the master mason, John Croxton in 1411 – 1429, the Guildhall – Gothic in style – became the largest and finest building in the City after St. Paul's, a reflection of the enormous power of the City's governors and Mayor. Its new Gothic porch was finished in 1430 and its main structure, a hall 152 ft (46 m) by 41 ft (12.5 m) was completed nine years later, making the Guildhall the largest enclosed space in London after Westminster Hall. Subsequently, a chapel adjoining the hall was dedicated in 1444, and in due course kitchens were built on the side of the hall to cater for the annual Lord Mayor's banquet (39).

Eton College Chapel (1441-61)

St George's Chapel, Windsor (1475)

Henry, as a deeply religious man, undoubtedly welcomed the reconstruction of churches in his capital, St. Stephen Walbrook, first mentioned in 1096, was rebuilt in 1429-1439 and St. Margaret Lothbury dating from sometime before 1197 was rebuilt in 1440, while at the Archbishop of Canterbury's palace at Lambeth, the Lollards Tower was erected in 1435. However, in the Late-Middle Ages, the English church was gradually losing its educational monopoly. Though grammar schools under ecclesiastical control continued to grow in number, Eton College, less than a mile north of Windsor, was founded by Henry VI in 1440 as one of the first independent boy's schools to be established in England, only Winchester was older dating from 1382. Its Cloister Court and College Hall, like its counterparts at Winchester, was virtually replicated in many an Oxford and Cambridge college over the years ahead. But Eton's most notable medieval building is its chapel intended originally to rival any cathedral in England both in its scale and magnificence. Perpendicular in style, it was intended to have 17 of 18 bays, but it contains only eight. The edifice comprises a choir and transepts, but it is devoid of a nave since building work ceased on the death of Henry VI in 1461 when funds ran out, and the Wars of the Roses with their uncertainties deterred further royal support. Eton College nevertheless inspired the construction of an even finer example of the Perpendicular, King's College at Cambridge, a masterpiece constructed over a number of years and completed in 1515.

The House of York

Edward IV (r. 1461-1483)

The only regal member of the House of York to fund major building works in the capital, or at least in its outer environs, was Edward IV (r.1461-1483). Edward provided resources for the extension of Eltham Palace where its Great Hall with its hammerbeam roof was added to the building's fabric in 1470, and five years later, Edward ordered work to begin on the construction of the lower ward of Windsor Castle together with its most notable building, St. George's Chapel, a superb edifice designed in the Perpendicular style. Over the following centuries, the castle became increasingly a monarchical residence rather than a stronghold, and an upper ward was built to accommodate the royal apartments and the more formal state rooms including St. George's Hall.

References

1. S. Inwood, *The History of London*, Macmillan, 1998. p 88.
2. H. Clout, *The Times History of London*, Times Books, 5th Edit, 2007, p 44.
3. Ibid, p 48.
4. R. Porter, *London. A Social History*, Penguin Books, 2000, p 17.
5. Ibid, p 38.
6. Ibid, pp 16-17.
7. Ibid, p 17.
8. B. Weinreb and C. Hibbert, *The London Encyclopaedia*, Macmillan, 1993, p 129.
9. N Coldstream, *Medieval Architecture*, Oxford University Press, 2002, p 40
10. J..Fleming, H.Honour & N.Pevsner, *Architecture and Landscape Architecture*, Penguin Books, 1999, p 117.
11. N.Coldstream, *Medieval Architecture*, Op. Cit., p 40.
12. S. Inwood, *The History of* London, Macmillan,

1998, p 99

13. R. Woodley, *City Guide, London*, Black Norton, 17th Edit, 2002, p 141.

14. Ibid, p 141

15. S. Jenkins, *Landlords to London. The Story of a Capital and its Growth*, Book Club Associates, 1975, p 65

16. Ibid, p 67

17. Ibid, pp 68-9.

18. Ibid, p 69.

19. Ibid, pp 69; 71.

20. D. Starkey, *Crown and Country, the Kings and Queens of England*, Harper Press, 2011, p 203.

21. Ibid, p 211.

22. S. Inwood, *The History of London*, Macmillan, 1998, p 138-9.

23. Ibid. p 144.

24. D Watkin, *English Architecture*, Thames & Hudson, 2001, p 48.

25. Ibid, p 48.

26. S. Thurley, *The Building of England. How the History of England has Shaped Our Buildings*, William Collins, 2013, p 125.

27. D. Watkin, *English Architecture*, Thames & Hudson, 2001, p 50.

28. D. Starkey, *Crown and Country, the Kings and Queens of England*, Harper Press, 2011, p 218.

29. H. Clout, *The Times History of London*, Times Books, 5th Edit, 2007, p 51.

30. Ibid, p 50.

31. S. Inwood, *The History of London*, Macmillan, 1998, p 144.

32. D. Starkey, *Crown and Country, the Kings and Queens of England*, Harper Press, 2001, p 230.

33. Ibid, p 233.

34. D Watkin, *English Architecture*, Thames &

Hudson, 2001, p 66.

35. S. Thurley, *The Building of England. How the History of England has Shaped Our Buildings*, p 164.
36. Ibid, p 188
37. R. Porter, *London. A Social History*, Penguin Books, 2000, pp 17-18.
38. B. Weinreb and C. Hibbert, *The London Encyclopaedia*, Macmillan, 1993, p 353
39. Ibid, p 354

Chapter 3

Early-Tudor London: From royal displeasure to a capital fit for a king

Diminished in size since the Black Death of 1348-1349, London, with a population of about 40,000 in 1500, was still environmentally medieval at the beginning of the sixteenth century, while the renaissance in architecture, that had rapidly changed the face of so many Italian cities in the fifteenth century, showed few signs of exerting its influence on the English capital. Without patrons such as the Medici of Florence, the Sforza of Milan or the Gonzaga of Mantua, London remained an architectural backwater. Notwithstanding the very great importance of London as England's largest city, it was often shunned as a place of residence by a succession of English monarchs.

No Place for a Monarch

Henry VII (r. 1485-1509)

In 1500 the population of London was only 50,000 compared to around 80,000 in the years immediately preceding the Black Death, and it was by no means an attractive location for a monarchical residence. For reasons of environmental appeal and privacy, Henry VII, the first of the Tudor monarchs, largely shunned London and resided at Greenwich Palace, a resplendent edifice built for the Duke of Gloucester in 1426 some five miles to the east of the capital. Henry also frequently resided at Richmond Palace (before it was destroyed by fire in 1499), ten miles to the west, and often at Windsor, a further 20 miles upstream, all of which were connected by the River Thames. Alternatively he would frequently stay at his *maisons de retraite* at Hanworth in Middlesex or Wanstead in Essex, locations that offered ample opportunities for hunting. His son, Henry VIII, had similar proclevities during the earlier part of his reign (from 1509 to say 1529), and following a childhood spent mainly at Eltham Palace not only inherited his father's residences (Richmond Palace was rebuilt in 1510) but rebuilt the medieval gatehouse at Windsor Castle (1512) and constructed sumptuous manor houses at Newhall in Essex, at Easthampstead in Berkshire and at Ampthill in Bedfordshire for is personal use. In addition, both monarchs indulged in progresses around their kingdom and resided throughout many a summer in far-flung residences of their own or as guests at their courtiers' houses. Westminster Palace, nevertheless, remained the formal royal residence even though its use was mainly confined to the winter months, while in the City the Tower and Bridewell Palace provided alternative accommodation from time to time. During the reign of Henry VII, therefore, it is thus highly probable that some of the king's major policy decisions often emanated from his residences outside of London, and most notably from Greenwich or Richmond, such as the decisions to: defend the throne against a Yorkist army led by the royal imposter Lambert Simnel in 1487; to formulate the Treaty of Etaples in 1492 in which English forces would withdraw from Boulogne after attempting to protect Brittany from invading French troops; to counter attack James IV's raid on northern England in 1496 in support of another royal imposter,

101

Perkin Warbeck; to quell a march of Cornish rebels on London in 1497; to offer a peace treaty to Scotland in 1499, and to arrange the marriages of his son Arthur, Prince of Wales, to Catharine of Aragon in 1501 and his daughter, Margaret, to James IV of Scotland in 1502.

Greenwich Palace (Placentia) (1426)

Richmond Palace (Rebuilt in 1510 after fire of 1499)

But, in defending his throne, the king did not neglect London altogether. His greatest gift to the capital was the magnificent Henry VII chapel at the east end of Westminster Abbey and immediately opposite Westminster Palace. Constructed under the supervision of Robert Janyns, Master Builder, in 1509-12, the chapel's fan-vaulting is the most outstanding example of Tudor building in the late-Perpendicular style.

Eltham Palace (1479)

Windsor Castle, Henry VIII's gatehouse (1512)

Henry VII's Chapel (1509-12), by Robert Janyns

London at the beginning of the sixteenth century

As in previous centuries, most inhabitants of the English capital lived in timber-framed houses, of two to three storeys in height, often with shops or workshops on the ground floor and with jetties over the street. However, a small proportion of London's population owned stone-built mansions or palaces, mainly to the west of the City wall stretching in a line from Fleet Street to the Strand and Westminster, though none were of a similar design to the Parisian *hòtel* but most were as large or larger. The greatest lay mansion was the thirteenth century Savoy Palace, inherited by John of

Gaunt in 1361, and though it was rendered unusable as a consequence of the Peasants' Revolt in 1381 it was redeveloped as a hospital in the early sixteenth century. The construction of other great mansions followed such as the London residences of Lords Bandolf, Lovel and Scrope; the Earls of Northumberland, Ormond, Warwick and Westmorland; and the Dukes of Gloucester, Exeter, Norfolk and York (1)

The residences of ecclesiastical prelates were no less prolific, for example the Archbishop of York's residence, York Place in Westminster was first mentioned in 1245, and Ely Place in Holborn, the residence of the Bishop of Ely dates from the late thirteenth century. A plethora of less grandiose and largely timber-framed mansions or "inns" were developed on the north bank of the Thames to provide London homes for the Abbots of Cirencester, Faversham and Tewkesbury, and the Bishops of Bath and Wells, Carlisle, Chester, Durham, Exeter, Lincoln, St David's, Salisbury and Worcester. The residences of ecclesiastical prelates, however, were not confined to the north bank, witness the Bishop of Winchester's medieval palace in Southwark and the Archbishop of Canterbury's palace at Lambeth, with its formidable gatehouse of 1506. But even monasteries had imposing gatehouses, for example St. John's Gate (1504) was set within the walls of the Priory of St John of Jerusalem in Clerkenwell.

Lambeth Palace – gatehouse (1506)

St John's Gate, Clerkenwell (1504)

Even more than that of the Crown, the purchasing

power of the secular and ecclesiastical aristocracy created an enormous demand for goods and services produced or procured in the City and thus did much to stimulate the economy of late-Medieval London (2).

The Reformation and its Impact on London

Henry VIII (r.1509-1547)

Until the 1530s, Henry VIII was not only unwilling to champion the physical improvement of London, but was often disinclined to reside permanently in his capital. He was attracted to residences away from the medieval discomfort of his capital and where he could indulge in the excitement of the chase. Thus, instead of living predominately in the Palace of Westminster as most of his medieval forefathers had done, Henry had a penchant for spending much time at Greenwich and Richmond palaces and a host of other residences around the country that he would visit during his many progresses. Thus until the mid- to late 1520's, English foreign and domestic policy would not emanate from London but from locations comparatively remote from the former centre of royal power. Anglo-French relations would more often than not be determined in Greenwich or Richmond rather than in Westminster, and similarly relations with the Papacy would be influenced by decisions taken away from the capital.

From the outset of his reign, Henry VIII had allusions of emulating his royal ancestor, Henry V, victor of Agincourt and set his sights on waging a decisive war on Louis XII's France in the hope of regaining English possessions that had been lost during the final stages of the Hundred Years War. Although his father's privy councillors – William Warham (Chancellor and Archbishop of Canterbury), Richard Fox (Lord Privy Seal and Bishop of Winchester), John Fisher (Bishop of Rochester) and Thomas Ruthal (Bishop of Durham) remained in office, regarded peace as their primary priority and, on their own initiative, established a treaty of friendship with France, Henry was straining at the leash to embark upon a war with England's traditional enemy on the Continent. The moment was opportune in 1510 when the Holy Roman Emperor, Maximilian I, persuaded Henry to join the Empire, Spain and the Papacy in an anti-French Holy Alliance since it was feared that France was becoming too powerful in Italy and had already committed itself to deposing Pope Julius II. Thus, in June 1511, under Henry's orders, the Marquis of Dorset set sail from Southampton with a force of 12,000 men to retake Gascony, formerly an English possession. They reached the port of Fuentarrabia, intending with the help of the Spanish to attack Bayonne, but the Spanish never turned up. While the French rebuffed the English attack, Ferdinand of Spain sent his troops into Navare, occupied it, and declared the campaign at an end.

Two years later, Henry's involvement in a European was far more successful. To support the Papacy, and with the hope of securing for England her former possessions in northern France, an English army was dispatched across the channel on 28 June 1513. Under Henry's leadership, and with his "banners intertwined with those of the Pope" (3), it swept across Normandy and Flanders, assisted by a small contingent of Imperial troops, defeated the French at the Battle of the Spurs – so called since the French, after being ambushed, turned and fled. English and Imperial troops also captured important prisoners, and – after set-piece sieges – took two French cities, Therouanne on 24 August and Tournai a month later. In gratitude, Julius II stripped Louis XII of the title of 'Most Christian King' and conferred it instead on Henry VIII, and was also willing to sanctify Henry assuming sovereignty over the whole of France if the English army was able to conquer the whole country. Though this would have been impossible logistically, as the pope must have realized, England with her notable victory in the north became, for the first time since Agincourt, one of the three great European powers alongside the Holy Roman Empire and a much weakened France. But unlike most monarchs in Europe, Henry VIII lacked a royal palace `fit for a king' and matters got worse.

Though Greenwich, Richmond and particularly Westminster palaces were used by Henry VIII as London residences during the early years of his reign, Bridewell Palace became the principal abode of the king after Westminster Palace suffered severe fire damage in 1512. Built between 1515-23 on the banks of the Fleet River close to its confluence with the Thames, Bridewell Palace was a large rambling brick structure constructed around three courtyards and almost certainly devoid of Renaissance ornamentation. Between 1531-39 the palace was leased to the French ambassador and then it became a refuge for vagrants and homeless children and, after many different uses over three-hundred years, it was eventually demolished in 1863-4 .

By 1518, few men in England without noble birth exercised as much power as Wolsey in Early Modern Europe, and from the largess of his patrons, Henry VIII and Pope Leo X, and from his many ecclesiastical estates, Wolsey accumulated a vast amount of wealth, making him – rather than the king – the richest man in

England. Free from any restraint, he was thus able to indulge in the development of substantial properties, the most notable of which were Hampton Court in Middlesex and York Place in Westminster. He reached his moment of glory in 1520 when he was instrumental in organizing a major *rapprochement* between Henry VIII and François I at the Field of the Cloth of Gold, a lavish ceremonial meeting in the north-east of France. But, arguably he became too-clever-by-half by subsequently conducting an about-turn in foreign policy and formed an alliance with the Habsburg Emperor, Charles V in 1522, the outcome of which was an expensive and unsustainable war with France, that ended with a peace agreement in 1525. By now Henry's chief minister, had not only mismanaged foreign policy but had failed to secure an annulment of his King's marriage to Catharine of Aragon, an annulment that would have enabled Henry to have married Anne Boleyn in the hope of producing, what Catharine did not produce, a male heir.

Wolsey, however, must have been gratified when François I was held captive in Madrid after the Battle of Pavia in 1525. He saw this as an opportunity for Henry's army to march, in alliance with Charles V's forces, across northern France unopposed to Paris and to claim much of northern France as a reward for England's involvement. But although, for many years, Wolsey had planned for such a venture, Charles was not interested in a collaborative venture with England since saw no reason why England should benefit from the victory that he achieved almost entirely through his own efforts at Pavia. Thus after fifteen years' of ceaseless hard work and intrigue, Wolsey's European policy had not only proved cripplingly expensive but also in tatters. It must have been clear to both the Chief Minister and to Henry, that the Empire would never form an alliance with England, except when it would serve its own short-term and chauvinistic ends.

However, no sooner than François had been released from imprisonment in Madrid, he was determined to seek revenge for his defeat by Charles in 1526 and joined a conspiracy with England and Pope Clement VII to defeat the Empire, but Charles V immediately countered the anti-Imperial plot by ordering his German mercenaries to sack Rome, and – in effect-imprison the Pope. Charles's armies went on to defeat the French in 1529, and in the same year Francois – without consulting England – concluded a peace treaty with Charles. Unable to trust two of Europe's leading powers, England seemed impotent and while Wolsey was still among Henry's close circle of advisers his foreign policy was increasingly being called severely into question.

Two years earlier, Henry had embarked on proceedings to end his relationship with Catharine, and – despite some misgivings – employed Wolsey as the papal legate to rush through an annulment, prior to obtaining the Pope's approval as a *fait accompli.* However, on June 1 1527 news reached London that Rome had been sacked by Imperial forces, and it was recognised that since Charles was Catharine of Aragon's nephew it was out of the question that he would connive in a process that would involve Clement delegating powers to Wolsey's to authorize an annulment that would be merely confirmed by the pontiff on his release. However, in 1528, after the Emperor's departure from Rome, Clement accepted Wolsey's proposal that annulment proceedings should be heard in England by an extraordinary tribunal, and on October 9 a papal legate, Cardinal Campaggio arrived in London to represent the Pope. However, after much vacillation, proceedings began on June 18 1529.

After a summer adjournment in keeping with Papal practice, and in response to Catharine's request "that the case be heard in Rome by His Holiness himself" (4), Clement's legate announced that the whole annulment proceedings would have to take place in the Eternal City. Henry was enraged since under no circumstances would the king of England "go humbly to Rome and kneel at the feet of the Pope" (5), while Wolsey was publicly disgraced for his failure to secure an annulment and, on 21 September, was as Lord Chancellor, ordered by the Dukes of Suffolk and Norfolk to surrender his great seal. In the hope of avoiding the full wrath of Henry over his far-from successful foreign policy and his inability to secure an annulment, Wolsey presented the king with his sumptuous Hampton Court Palace. Situated on the north bank of the Thames at Hampton, 12 miles (19km) upstream from Charing Cross, Hampton Court Palace was largely Tudor-Gothic in style.

Hampton Court Palace - west facade gatehouse (1514-25)

Built for Cardinal Wolsey on a manorial site that he bought from the Order of St. John of Jerusalem for 200,000 gold crowns in 1514, the new edifice – Hampton Court- was developed over the following eleven years to become the finest residence in England. Wishing to live as graciously as any cardinal in Rome, Wolsey attempted to create a Renaissance palace, and according to Jonathan Foyle (6) he was inspired by Paolo Cortese's treatise, *De Cardinalatu,* that described the elements of contemporary Italian palatial architecture. However, although Wolsey's edifice featured rectilinear symmetrical planning with grand apartments on a raised *piano nobile,* all embellished with classical detailing, what emerged was a hybrid building that stylistically combined redbrick, Perpendicular Gothic with stone and terracotta Renaissance ornamentation, Giovanni da Maiano producing a set of eight relief busts of Roman emperors set in the Tudor brickwork. In total, the building was a far cry from an Italianate renaissance Palace.

The scale and grandeur of Wolsey's Hampton Court is even more remarkable when contrasted with Fulham Palace further downstream. Built for Richard Fitzjames, Bishop of London (1506-22), Fulham Palace it is much smaller in size reflecting not only the bishop's lower income than that of the Cardinal but his more modest ambitions. Nevertheless, the building is a fine example of early-Tudor architecture, its red brickwork exhibiting diaper patterns of dark purple seen best from its imposing courtyard.

Fulham Palace (c.1514)

Soon after being given Hampton Court by Cardinal Wolsey in 1529, Henry VIII attempted to create a palace which in scale would rival that of the Château de Fontainebleau in France. Over a period of ten years a series of internal courtyards was constructed "based on an analogous traditional scheme that presides over the colleges of Oxford and Cambridge" (7), Wolsey's Great Hall was rebuilt on the same site but on a grander scale than hitherto; the interior of Wolsey's chapel was enlarged and remodelled by the addition of a magnificent hammerbeam roof; royal lodgings surrounding Fountain Court were constructed; the Queen's gallery was erected at the rear of the palace overlooking a hunting park, a prototype of the many Elizabethan and Jacobean long galleries that were built in the years ahead; and to the north of the main complex, a substantial covered tennis court was constructed (8). Whilst the greatly enlarged building was essentially Gothic, some of the ornamentation, such as the *putti* and foliage in the spandrels of the hall roof were contemporary Italian.

Hampton Court Palace (Great Hall) (c 1530)

After 1529, Henry VIII's principal London residence was Whitehall Palace. Although we know very little about its development since most of it was consumed by fire in 1689, we do know that – as York Place – its ownership passed from Cardinal Wolsey to Henry VIII in 1529. Subsequently known as Whitehall – probably because its central feature, Wolsey's Great Hall, was built of white ashlar – its boundaries were greatly extended to enclose 23 acres (93 ha) stretching from present-day Downing Street in the south to the Admiralty and Whitehall Place in the north. Within its confines a plethora of new and disparate buildings were constructed, stylistically Gothic and largely red brick in composition. To the east of a north-south thoroughfare that intersected its site, Henry constructed a new hall and many royal apartments and offices, while, to the west, he built three tennis courts, a bowling green, a tiltyard for jousting and an octagonal cockpit. With over 1,500 rooms, the complex was the largest and busiest royal palace in Europe and at one time it was the largest building in the world. Much of the palace looked on to St James's Park to the east, a royal hunting ground of 90 acres (36.5 ha.) on land that Henry VIII acquired in 1531 from Eton College, the freeholders of St. James's Hospital for Leper Women (9). From here, Henry extended his London hunting domain over a further 390 acres (158 ha.) to the northwest in what later became Green Park and Hyde Park.

Across the northern part of the north-south thoroughfare that intersected Whitehall Palace, Henry built a gatehouse in 1532 to link the eastern and western sides of his palace. Often referred to as the Holbein Gate, though it is unlikely that the German artist had a hand in its design, the edifice had four corner turrets and was built of stone and flint intricately arranged in a chequered pattern. Like the entrance gateways to Hampton Court Palace, it was adorned with glazed terracotta roundels containing busts, a minor concession to Renaissance taste.

St James's Palace, gateway, north facade (1530s)

Built for Henry VIII between 1532 and 1540 on the site of the former St. James's Hospital, St. James's Palace remained one of several London residences of English monarchs until 1698 when – after the destruction of Whitehall Palace by fire - it became *the* principal residence of the monarch in London until 1809 when it too suffered severe fire damage. Almost certainly devoid of Renaissance ornamentation, the Tudor palace was a substantial redbrick edifice built around four courts. Today all that remains of it are its tall gatehouse flanked by octagonal turrets, its chapel reminiscent of the Watching Chamber at Hampton Court, and a few other parts of the original building (10). The current edifice dates largely from 1814.

Though Henry attempted to enhance his image as a strong and glorious Renaissance monarch, this carried little weight with the Papacy. For its part, Rome exacerbated the problems associated with Henry VIII's desire to rid himself of Catharine of Aragon by issuing a bill forbidding individuals from writing or speaking against the king's marriage to Catharine. Clement VII not only attempted to protect the queen but to reassert his authority over English churchmen.

Henry VIII therefore, in order to establish his authority over the church in England, summoned 15 clerics – including eight bishops – to the King's Bench to answer the charge of *praemunire,* a little used weapon dating from the fourteenth century that prohibited clerics from showing allegiance to Rome to the detriment of their allegiance to the King. Thereupon followed the Reformation Years (1530-1537). In September 1530 *praemunire* charges were levelled against the whole of the English church, and soon after Wolsey was arrested for high treason and died on 29 November at Leicester Abbey en route to his trial in London and certain execution at the Tower. With the loss of support from their Cardinal, the clergy were collectively found guilty of exercising their powers in the Church courts to the detriment of royal authority and duly fined £100,000.

Henry was clearly preoccupied with his break from Rome and in securing a male heir, and within four years from Wolsey's demise the King had completely severed his links with Rome, though he remained a Catholic until his dying day and remained antagonistic to the spread of Lutheranism in his kingdom. First, from January 1531, the English clergy were compelled to acknowledge the king as "sole protector and supreme head of the Church of England"; second, in 1533 the Act of Annates eroded Papal authority in England. English bishops would no longer pay fees to Rome when first appointed to their dioceses, and further legislation enabled bishops to be appointed by the king without Rome being consulted; third the Act of

Appeals of 1533 made the King, not the Pope, the final legal authority thereby enabling Henry VIII's marriage to Catharine of Aragon to be annulled and the King to marry Anne Boleyn (an act for which Henry was excommunicated by Pope Clement VII); and finally – under the Act of Supremacy of 1534 – Henry VIII is declared Supreme Head of the Church of England; the Anglican Church becoming the established church of England and Wales and the Channel Islands. However, the question of a male heir remained unresolved. While Anne Boleyn gave birth to a daughter, the future Elizabeth I, in 1533, in 1534 she bore a son, Henry, who died in infancy.

Whereas Wolsey was the architect of Henry's foreign and domestic policies from around 1515 to 1529, Thomas Cromwell became the king's principal minister in 1535 after Wolsey's successor, Sir Thomas More, was beheaded in the Tower of London for failing to take the Oath of Supremacy under the Act of 1534. Cromwell, aware of the relative meagreness of royal finance, immediately set forth to direct the compilation of the *Valor Ecclesiasticus* to provide details of the very considerable amount of wealth owned by the church. Consequently, in February 1536 a bill to dissolve the smaller monasteries went before Parliament, with the likelihood that the larger-ones would be picked-off at leisure. To be sure, "Henry's personal authority over the Church gave him access to incredible riches. There were around 500 monasteries scattered throughout England, some desperately poor but many rich and well run, and maintaining a thousand-year old tradition of prayer, work and learning. But changes of intellectual fashion away from monasticism made them vulnerable, and their collective wealth made them tempting. So in 1536, the process of dissolving the monasteries began" (11). Reaction to the dissolution was immediate. In October 1536, the Revolt of the Pilgrimage of Grace took place under Robert Aske, a popular rising by Roman Catholics in the north of England ending with 250 people being hanged. There was a brief lull in Cromwell's sequestration of monastic wealth during which Anne Boleyn was hanged on May 19 1536 on trumped-up charges of adultery, incest and sexual perversion (her principal fault in the eyes of Henry was that she had failed to produce a surviving male heir), and her successor as Queen, Jane Seymour, died on 12 October 1537 after the birth of her son, the future Edward VI.

Through the Act for the Dissolution of the Greater Monasteries in 1539, Henry's confiscation of Church wealth continued. Within a year, all remaining monasteries were closed down and their land sold-off. Even St Thomas's Hospital (once named St Thomas the Martyr after Becket's canonisation in 1173) ceased to function because of its monastic status, though St Bartholomew's Hospital (initially closed by Henry) was re-founded in 1544 in response to a petition by Sir Thomas Gresham, MP for the City of London. Though the land acquired by the king was worth £100,000 in its existing use, he often sold-off or leased the properties to his courtiers and gained nearly £1,500,000 for the royal coffers.

Nonsuch Palace (1538-46

Some of the proceeds funded the construction of
Nonsuch Palace, begun in 1538 and completed in 1546.
As many as 2,000 acres (810 ha) of prime Home
Counties estate land six miles south-east of Hampton
Court were swept clean to make way for the greatest
palace in England, a monument that would stand
comparison with the finest in Europe. Henry VIII's aim
was to rival François I's country chateau in Chambord,
the glittering monument to the French king. Intended as
a hunting lodge and guest house for distinguished
foreign visitors, the same functions of Chambord,
Nonsuch cost at least £24,000 to build (an enormous
sum at the time). Unfinished at the time of the King's
death (1546), the building was subsequently completed
by Henry Fitzalen, the 12th Earl of Arundel to whom
Mary I had sold it in exchange for estates in Suffolk.
Returning to royal ownership in 1592, the palace was
eventually demolished in 1687 soon after Charles II
had given it to the Duchess of Cleveland, and today no
trace of the palace remains. However, according to
three contemporary images of the edifice, - of which

the drawing by the Flemish artist, Jorus Hoefhagel is the most famous – the palace was about 150 yards (137 metres) long and built around two open courtyards each with a fortified gatehouse. While the outer courtyard was quite plain, the inner courtyard was heavily ornamented. Its lower walls were built of stone and the upper part was of half-timber work, and although the northern side of the court was fortified in the Gothic style, its southern side "consisted of a range of building between two very large octagonal towers whose upper parts developed into many-windowed pavilions crowned by pointed lead roofs and pinnacles with vanes" (12). While most of the structural work on the palace was almost certainly undertaken by local labour, there is no question that Henry employed foreign craftsmen to produce the ornamentation such as plaster statues and bas-reliefs between the timbers and – covering the timber themselves – a reventment of slates arranged in patterns (13). William Cure, a carver from Amsterdam, was at work on the palace from 1541, Nicholas Bellin of Modena (who was formerly employed by Francois I at Fontainebleau before escaping to England after being charged with fraud) was engaged on decorative slate work at Nonsuch also from 1541, and Gilles Gering (possibly from Flanders) was a moldmaker at Nonsuch around 1545. However, while Nonsuch was "renowned for its fantastical skyline and elaborate stucco decoration, inspired by the palaces of François I at Chambord and Fontainebleau" (14) it was very much a hybrid edifice combining a wealth of Renaissance motifs (more Flemish than Italian) with an "undisciplined amalgam of traditional elements" (15).

During the final years of Henry's reign very few other buildings of architectural merit were built in or near

London, or in England as a whole for that matter. His personal life and recurrent wars pre-occupied his attention. Following the death of Jane Seymour, Henry married three more times. First, his marriage to Anne of Cleaves in 1539 not only ended in divorce as Henry found her unattractive, but it also brought about the execution of his chief minister Thomas Cromwell whom Henry suspected of secretly linking the marriage to an alliance with German Lutheran prices. Second, his subsequent marriage to Catharine Howard in 1540 ended with her execution for treason in 1542, though in reality it was more likely because of her infidelity; and finally he married Catharine Parr in 1543 who outlived him. But freed from the problem of succession the latter years of Henry's reign were plagued by war with Scotland and France. During the Reformation years, foreign affairs had been no less tortuous than marital the intrigues but although Henry VIII, charged with a relentless nationalistic zeal, "had broken the power of the Pope, dissolved the monasteries, defeated rebellion, beheaded traitors and made himself supreme over the Church "(16), he was only moderately successful in enhancing the physical fabric of his capital city and its environs, partly because he was unwilling to adopt Classical architecture since, in his view, it was tainted by the Church of Rome.

Henry's very last contribution to the built environment of London - commenced during the last year of his reign (1547) – was a monumental gateway, the Whitehall Gate , built across the southern end of Whitehall. Though some of its attributes were traditional, for its example its comer turrets, its central opening for horses and side openings for pedestrians, and its Tudor lights in the windows, the style of the building was – to an extent- Classical. The main storey of the gateway exhibited two tall Ionic pilasters, while its central opening displayed secondary Ionic orders; the side openings of the gateway were flanked by Doric pilasters and capped by pediments; and above an entablature was surmounted by a semi-circular feature containing the signs of the zodiac framed by round towers with dominical caps (17). Both the earlier Holbein Gate and the newer southern gatehouse were demolished in the eighteenth century to improve the flow of traffic along Whitehall, the former gate in 1759 (after a successful appeal against its demolition in 1719) and the latter gate southern in 1723.

Edward VI (r. 1547-1553)

Though St. James's Palace was a western offshoot of Whitehall, Somerset House – developed some years later – became an eastern extension of the monarch's principal seat of power. Granted to Edward Seymour, Earl of Hertford, by Henry VIII in 1538, Chester Place – south of the Strand – became the location of an imposing new residence overlooking the Thames. After demolishing an old Inn of Chancery and other buildings on the site in 1549, Seymour – who on the succession of Edward VI had become the Duke of Somerset and Lord Protector – built one of the most influential buildings of the Tudor era, Somerset House. Possibly designed by Sir John Thynne, and with its Strand façade built of stone from the demolished Priory Church of St. John Clerkenwell and St. Paul's Charnel House and Cloister, Somerset House was a two storey edifice "built round a quadrangle which is entered from the Strand through a three-storey gateway. At either end of the front are bay-windows crowned with ornamental attics" (18). Though the plan of Somerset House is largely late-medieval, similar to that of an Oxford or Cambridge college, the symmetry and

124

ornamentation of its Strand façade is distinctly classical. Its gateway, reminiscent of a 'triumphal arch', is adorned by recessed windows framed by pairs of orders on pedestals on each of its three storeys, and a pier containing a niche in the middle storey. Either side of the gateway, the façade is pierced on the ground and first floors by windows surmounted by pediments, while coupled windows with wider pediments adorn each end of the building. In Italianate style, a continuous balustrade extends along the roof. Somerset House – or at least its Strand façade – is regarded as the first building in England with mainly Renaissance attributes. It is often said that its façade was stylistically modelled on contemporary French practice as exemplified by the frontispiece, to the Château d'Anet by Philabert de l'Orme (1547), Pierre Lescot's *Cour de Carre* at the Louvre (1547) or Jean Bullant's south portal at the Château d'Ecouen (1555). However, it does seem a little improbable that French designs would have been so quickly employed in the development of a major new building in London. After the execution of the Duke of Somerset in 1552, his partly-unfinished house reverted to the Crown and was occupied intermittently by Princess Elizabeth before her succession as Queen Elizabeth I in 1558. Thereafter – except during the Commonwealth (1649-1660) – it remained a royal palace until the late seventeenth century (see chapters 5 & 6). Following years of neglect, the old Somerset House, was demolished in 1775 and replaced by a Neo-classical building that has remained in use to the present day.

Somerset House (begun 1549), possibly by Sir John Thynne

Although Somerset might be applauded for importing Classical architecture into England, his political fortunes were discredited and short-lived which was remarkable since his army defeated the Scots at the Battle of Pinkie Cleugh and captured Edinburgh during his first year in power, and his administration authorised the use of Thomas Cranmer's English Book of Common prayer by the Act of Uniformity of 1549 – both popular achievements within his realm. However, his chief critic John Dudley, Duke of Northumberland, arrested Somerset in 1550 and the former Protector was subsequently condemned to death for treason and executed in 1552. During the rest of Edward's short reign, Northumberland, in his role as Lord President of the Council, showed little interest in developing buildings in London, possibly because he was pre-occupied with pushing through Parliament the Second Act of Uniformity that dismantled the Mass, and authorising Thomas Cranmer to publish the 42 Articles - the basis of Anglican Protestantism. However, he did ensure that St Thomas's Hospital was transferred to the City of London and re-opened (after its closure by Henry VIII), but ordered that its name was changed from St Thomas the Martyr , with its Catholic connotations, to St Thomas, the Apostle.

Following the death of Edward VI in 1553 at the age of only 16, Northumberland attempted to secure the Protestant ascendancy by proclaiming Lady Jane Grey Queen of England instead of the Catholic Princess Mary, Henry's eldest daughter. Mary, however, was able to engender sufficient support to effectively oppose Lady Jane Grey's claim to the throne and was quickly crowned Queen in her stead. Both Northumberland and Lady Jane Grey were consequently tried for treason and duly executed. Mary's reign was infamous for the manner in which she attempted to restore Catholicism as the `one and only' religion of England. She restored Catholic bishops, a celibate clergy, holy days and the Mass, and recognised the Pope as head of the English church. She also planned to marry the staunchly Catholic King Philip of Naples and Jerusalem, possibly as a ploy to consolidate Catholic rule in England, a provocation that led to a massive Protestant backlash across the country manifested particularly by a rebellion led by Sir William Wyatt that advanced on London in January 1554 in a failed attempt to ameliorate Mary's ambitions. The marriage duly took place in July 1554, and the union was reinforced by her husband becoming Philip II of Spain in 1556. Protestants were now being persecuted on an enormous scale, 300 being burnt at the stake in 1555 alone, including Thomas Cranmer, Archbishop of Canterbury, Nicholas Ridley Bishop of London, and the reformist Hugh Latimer. While a Counter Reformation' was proceeding, it is probable that Mary was suffering from severe depression resulting from two phantom births, continual childlessness, the absence of her husband Philip for eighteenth months while he visited the Low Countries and Spain , the loss of Calais in 1558 and worsening ill-health that caused her death in the same year at the age of only 42. Events were such that during the fifty years of her reign she showed little inclination to improve the built environment of London, or even to encourage others to enhance the fabric of her capital.

References

1. S. Inwood, *The History of London*, Macmillan, 1998. p 94.
2. Ibid, p 95.
3. D. Starkey, *Monarchy. From the Middle Ages to Modernity*, Harper Press, 2006, p 31.
4. R. Lacey, *The Life and Times of Henry VIII*, Book Club Associates, 1972, p 86
5. Ibid, p 87.
6. J.Foyle, `Hampton Court: The Lost Palace', *BBC-History*, 2011.
7. F. Prima and E. Demartini, *1000 Years of World Architecture*, Thames and Hudson, 2006, p 174.
8. Sir John Summerson, *Architecture in Britain 1530-1830*, Yale University Press, 9th Edit, 1993, pp 24-25.
9. B. Weinreb and C. Hibbert, *The London Encylopaedia*, Macmillan, 1993, p 738.
10. Sir John Summerson, *Architecture in Britain 1530-1830*, Yale University Press, 9th Edit, 1993Op.Cit., p 27.
11. D.Starkey, *Monarchy. From the Middle Ages to Modernity*, Harper Press, 2006, p 51
12. D Watkin, *English Architecture*, Thames & Hudson, 2001, p 85.
13. Sir John Summerson, *Architecture in Britain 1530-1830*, Yale University Press, 9th Edit, 1993, p 33.
14. D.Watkin, *English Architecture*, Thames &

Hudson, 2001, p 85.

15. R.Furneaux Jordan, A *Concise History of Western Architecture*, Thames & Hudson, 1969, p 220.

16. D.Starkey, *Monarchy. From the Middle Ages to Modernity*, Harper Press, p 55.

17. Sir John Summerson, *Architecture in Britain 1530 1830*, Yale University Press, 9th Edit, 1993, p 33.

18. Ibid, p 43

Chapter 4

Elizabethan London: Merchant developers take over

By European standards London was a relatively small city in 1550 accommodating no more than 120,000 inhabitants (1). At this time, the majority of Londoners lived within the old medieval walls, though beyond these confines the built-up area of the capital was expanding rapidly in most directions, westwards to Temple Bar and Holborn Bar, eastwards to Whitechapel Bar and the Minories (on the eastern edge of the Tower) and southwards across the Thames to Southwark (the borough was purchased by the City from Edward VI in 1550). In addition, Westminster remained a settlement in its own rite, spatially and administratively separate from the City, while there was little growth northwards because of the greater distance from the Thames, the City's main highway. From this relatively low base, London experienced a population explosion between 1550 and 1600, as the number of its inhabitants increased to 200,000 by the end of the sixteenth-century and its share of the total population of England and Wales rose from 4 to 5 per cent. As in Paris, population increase was attributable entirely to in-migration since pestilence ensured that mortality rates were greatly in excess of birth rates.

Economic activity was also moving outwards from the City, not only because of fewer space-constraints beyond its walls but also because of lax apprenticeship regulation and the absence of taxation in the expanding suburbs. As Peter Hall relates "leather manufacture moved out to Bermondsey, Southwark and Lambeth, sugar-refining and glassmaking to Stepney and Islington, alum and dye works to the north and east, shipbuilding to Rotherhithe and Deptford, brewing to Clerkenwell and Holborn, bricks and tiles to Islington, clocks to Holborn and Westminster, and so on" (2). But such activity, merely spread squalor from the city to the previously green and pleasant countryside to the east, south and north of the capital. Industry not only attracted entrepreneurs and labour to the expanding suburbs, but also property speculators and rapacious landlords "profiteering out of jerry-built dwellings and foul industrial premises" (3).

It was in the East End of London that population and industrial growth was particularly dramatic. Within the eastern wards of the City, congestion had grown severe. Though building-lots in, for example, Aldgate and the eastern suburbs had been freed by the Dissolution of the Monasteries earlier in the century, "within a generation the spaces gained by seizure and demolition had grown congested, and landlords resorted to throwing up hovels in side alleys, crowding the poor into cellars and dividing properties for multiple occupation" (4). As population and economic activity increased, particularly in relation to maritime trade, the East End and its low-grade housing expanded eastwards along three major route ways: to the north, from Aldgate East to Whitechapel Street; further south from Tower Hill along the Ratcliff Highway to Shadwell; and – skirting the river – from the Tower to Wapping. The City, apart from its eastern suburbs, remained a social mismatch. "Aldermen and a few aristocrats still lived within the walls, yet within spitting distance dwelt butchers, bakers and candlestick makers" (5). While timber and plaster high-density housing satisfied the needs of artisans and the urban poor, large high-quality merchant houses of stone, brick and timber were scattered across the city. However, from Temple Bar to Westminster, the West End of London became - like the western fringe of Paris – the most favourable location for high-value development. This was no accident. In both Paris and London the court was concentrated in the west, respectively in close proximity to the Louvre or Whitehall Palace. Thus, along Fleet Street and the Strand, gracious residences such as Essex House, Cecil House, Bedford House and York House were developed for the aristocracy; elegant tailors' and silk-ware shops were established in the vicinity, and – to an extent – goldsmiths' and silversmiths' businesses were relocated from the city. Clearly, in the words of Peter Hall, "London [in the late-sixteenth century] was starting to exhibit those familiar socio-geographical distinctions, above all the fundamental one between east and west, that have persisted ever since" (6).

However, although Elizabeth showed no little interest in using architecture to enhance her role as sovereign, the aristocracy showed no such reluctance to develop sumptuous properties albeit predominantly in the countryside, in order to escape from the pestilence and squalor of urban living, particularly in the summer months when government was often in recess.

The Security of the Crown in Elizabethan England and its Effects on the Development of London

Largely because of a substantial increase in overseas trade, London thrived throughout most of the later-sixteenth century, but sadly this was not reflected in a commensurate improvement in its physical fabric. In her youth, Elizabeth Tudor – the future Queen – resided mainly in the Palace of Greenwich or the Palace of Hatfield, and was accustomed to a physical environment that had changed little since the Later-Middle Ages.

Throughout her subsequent reign, Elizabeth's adopted policies carefully crafted to deal with different cause of concern. Within a year of her Coronation (1558-1559), Elizabeth's first priority was the establishment of a religious settlement. While she eschewed the Catholicism of her elder sister and predecessor, Mary I (r. 1553-1558), she was equally reluctant to embrace a radical form of Protestantism introduced into England during the reign of her brother Edward VI (r. 1547-1553). Like her father, Henry VIII, "Elizabeth wanted the middle way in religion – partly because she believed in it, and partly because she saw it as the best defence of Royal Supremacy, which she was determined to revive as her God-given right" (7). Though a policy of religious neutrality might initially have seemed the wisest course to pursue, by 1559 she recognised that – since her Catholic peers and bishops were entirely opposed to Supremacy – she had little alternative but to ally herself with her Protestant Commons and councillors, a change of direction encouraged by William Cecil, her Secretary of State. In this, and in return for accepting Cranmer's Protestant Book of Common Prayer of 1552, she secured the support of the Commons, but in the Lords her policy was accepted by only three votes (with a number of Catholic peers absent for reasons beyond their control). Shrewdly, Elizabeth rejected the title 'Supreme Head of the Church of England', in favour of the less contentious title: "Supreme Governor of the Church of

England". In the same year (1559), the Act of Uniformity was passed, which made attendance at church and the use of the revised 1552 Book of Common Prayer compulsory, though penalties for recusancy, or failure to attend or conform, were not extreme. Traditional ceremonies were retained, for example the clergy was obliged to wear the surplice and cope and to make the sign of the cross at baptisms. "[T]he Church of England was [thus] frozen in time. The result was a Church that was Protestant in doctrine, Catholic in appearance and which would , Elizabeth hoped, satisfy all but a handful of extremists on both sides" (8). With the publication of the *Thirty-Nine Articles* in 1563 and the Subscription Act of 1568 that made it illegal for the clergy not to subscribe to the Articles, the establishment of the Anglican Church was complete. As an exercise in the 'art of the possible', Elizabeth's religious settlement saved England from a doctrinal war that would soon devastate France.

Chronologically, Elizabeth's second main concern was the succession. From the outset of her reign, Elizabeth showed little interest in marrying and producing an heir. To be sure she initially developed close friendships with potential suitors, most notably Robert Dudley, Earl of Leicester and, for more than twenty years, turned down offers of marriage from Philip II of Spain (in 1558), Philip's cousin, the Archduke Charles of Austria (in1559), Henry, Duke of Anjou (in 1568) and his brother François, Duke D'Alencon (in 1572). But she never married. Elizabeth was clearly "determined that England would have one mistress and no master" (9) – and least of all a 'master' whose loyalty would be first and foremost to a foreign state. Of equal importance, and to the anguish of parliament, Elizabeth declined not to name a successor since, in her view, a named successor would – as "next in line" – become the focus of plots against her and bring about her demise. However, even though a successor was not named, this did not prevent supporters of Mary Stuart, Queen of Scots and cousin of Elizabeth, from furthering her claim to the English throne. Mary Stuart had become the widow of the French king, Francois II in 1561 and duly returned to Scotland as queen. But since Scotland was dominated by a Protestant parliament and a Protestant church, her reign was unstable. Lord Darnley, who she married in 1564, was murdered in 1567 possibly on the orders of Lord Bothwell, and in the same year Mary married Bothwell. Because of accusations of her complicity in the murder, Mary was forced to abdicate and – after being held captive in Lochleven Castle for eight months – fled Scotland in May 1568 and sought refuge south of the border. However, under the advice of Sir William Cecil, Elizabeth recognised that, if she was to safeguard her throne, she had no alternative but to imprison her cousin, a fate Mary endured for 15 years. In England, Mary played up her Catholicism, and Catholics in turn identified with her. In 1569, a rebellion in the north of England led by the Earls of Northumberland and Westmorland aimed unsuccessfully to put her on the throne of England and bring back Catholicism as the 'one true faith of the nation'. Despite being moved from one castle to another during her imprisonment, Mary was allegedly the focus of several plots against Elizabeth. However, throughout most of her time incarcerated, her involvement in conspiracies such as the Ridolfi plot of 1571, and Throckmorton plot of 1583 was never proven. Only when Sir Francis Walsingham, the Queen's spymaster, produced evidence that Mary was implicated in the Babbington plot of 1586 to kill Elizabeth and succeed her on the throne, was Mary put on trial and found guilty. She was executed at Fotheringay Castle on February 8 1587, soon after she had provocatively nominated Philip II as her heir. Though Elizabeth had signed the death warrant, it was implemented without her further command by her Privy Council as guided by its senior member, the arch-Protestant Secretary of State, Lord Burghley (as Cecil had become). Elizabeth's anger at Mary's execution knew no bounds partly because her ten councillors had taken a decision that she was reluctant to take – to execute her cousin – and partly because their action would almost inevitably provoke a threatening response from Catholic Spain, aided and abetted by the Papacy.

Though Elizabeth for nearly three decades was able to prevent Mary from deposing her from the throne of England, she was not so successful at combating the determination of the papacy on the one hand, and her Protestant Privy Council on the other from attempting to limit or eradicate her sovereign power. A Bull, known as *Regnans in Excelsis*, was issued by Pope Pius V in 1570 to confirm the Pope's right to rule 'all people and all kingdoms', and "for her defiance of this claim, it condemns Elizabeth, deposes and excommunicates her, and absolves her subjects from their oath of alliance"(10). In short, the Pope was in effect, declaring war on Elizabeth by calling for the assassination or murder of an errant ruler. Eventually responding in kind, Elizabeth's Privy Council in 1584 introduced a similarly violent Bond of Association by which those who subscribed to the bond would swear to band together to: prosecute to the death any person or persons assassinating the Queen in favour of any possible claimant to the throne; forbid anyone in whose name such an assassination had taken place from succeeding to the throne; and to leave the responsibility of nominating an heir to Elizabeth with and by the authority of Parliament (11). However, though the Protestant nobility and gentry subscribed to the bond in their hundreds, and an Act of Parliament legalised the bond, Elizabeth regarded the bond with almost as much disfavour as the Papal Bull since it also set religion above the Crown, and gave powers to her subjects – through the medium of Parliament – to approve a new sovereign. Clearly, the introduction of the bond marked a watershed in English history. It not only demonstrated that a fierce, nationalistic Protestantism had clearly emerged in England, but implied that if a monarch or an heir – fell too far out of step with the religious prejudices of the nation [he or she] would do so at their peril" (12), clearly a warning to future monarchs if ever there was one.

To ensure the security of her realm, it was not sufficient for Elizabeth to provide solutions to religious and succession problems at home, she had to – in addition – pursue a foreign policy aimed reactively at defending England against external threats, first from France and then from Spain, and proactively at extending the influence of her country abroad.

Though Elizabeth thwarted French ambitions to put Mary on the throne of England, her policy was somewhat calamitous when English armies were deployed in France, in part because she lacked control over her commanders once they were abroad, and in part because she was unwilling to provide them the supplies and reinforcements they required for successful campaigns. Eager to reclaim Calais (it had been lost to France in 1558), Elizabeth ordered her forces to occupy Le Havre with a view to exchanging the Norman port for Calais. But though her troops held Le Havre from October 1562 to June 1563, they were driven out by an unlikely coalition of Huguenot and Catholic forces, with Calais remaining a French city to the present day. After this debacle, a quarter of a century passed before Elizabeth's armies ventured into France again. During this time, and under the encouragement of William Cecil, Elizabeth conducted negotiations with her two French suitors, Henry of Anjou (in 1568) and subsequently his younger brother François D'Alencon, just as much to enhance diplomatic relations with France as to potentially produce an heir. However, following the Massacre of St. Bartholomew's Day in 1572, cordial relations with France were suspended until the end of the French Wars of Religion. In 1589, the Protestant Henri IV inherited the French throne, but this was opposed by the strongest Catholic power, Spain. There was thus a possibility that the channel ports would be taken by the forces of Philip II, possibility to provide launch-pads for an invasion of England. In an attempt to help prevent this eventuality, Elizabeth sent an army to northern France to support the French king against the possibility of Spanish encroachment, but also to help defend Henri against remnants of the Catholic League who were attempting to depose him. Unfortunately for Elizabeth, her army, under Lord Willoughby, roamed northern France to little effect and – having lost half its men – returned to England in December 1589. An even greater disaster occurred in 1591, when an English army of 3,000 troops under the command of John Norreys was defeated by the Catholic League army in Brittany, while later in the year another English force, under Robert Devereux, Earl of Essex, was routed at Rouen, and its survivors returned home in January 1592.

Whereas French foreign policy threatened the sovereignty of England in both the earlier and latter parts of Elizabeth's reign, it was only in the last twenty years of her long reign that Spain became England's dominant enemy. Following the suppression of Protestantism in Holland by the forces of Alexander Farnese, Duke of Parma and Philip's governor of the Netherlands, the Treaty of Nonesuch (1585) between England and Holland resulted in English troops being dispatched to the Netherlands to support Protestant Dutch rebels. However, the expedition led by the Queen's former suitor, Robert Dudley, Earl of Leicester, was an abject failure as it was under-resourced in terms of troops and money. However, more successfully, the English began attacking Spanish ports, and in 1587 Francis Drake destroyed part of the Spanish fleet in the Atlantic. In response, but also as part of a major campaign to depose Elizabeth from the throne, Philip set out to extend the war to England. On 12July 1588, the Spanish Armada set sail for the Channel to accompany the forces of Farnese in the invasion of England. *En route* to the Netherlands, the Armada was broken up and dispersed by English fireships, and returned to Spain severally depleted after being struck by gales while fleeing around the north coast of Scotland.

Although "[w]ith the defeat of the Spanish Armada, Elizabeth's reputation stood at a zenith at home and abroad" (13), the English victory was not a turning point in the war. Spain still controlled the Netherlands and could have invaded England at any moment, while English military engagements with Spain were far from successful. In 1589, an English expedition to Lisbon to liberate Portugal from Spain was an abject failure, and in 1591 an English fleet under Sir Richard Grenville was defeated by the Spaniards in a sea battle off the Azores. However, more as a demonstration of England's tactical audacity rather than an indication of her strategic prowess, in 1596 an English expedition, under Robert Devereux, captures and burns Cadiz.

Although at the beginning of her reign, Elizabeth had reason to believe that French troops would descend upon England from Scotland, towards the end of her reign she was concerned that Spain would establish bases in Ireland from which to attack her homeland. Despite the fact that Ireland was one of her two kingdoms, Elizabeth faced a hostile indigenous population, staunchly Catholic and virtually autonomous. In an attempt to safeguard her realm, she not only granted land to her Protestant courtiers to establish a stronger foothold on the island, but deployed more troops in Ireland to prevent dissidents from giving Spain bases to continue its war against England. Tension increased as English forces – using scorched-earth policies – put down a series of uprisings in the early 1580s, and from 1594 Hugh Neil, Earl of Tyrone waged a nine-year rebellion against the Crown. Throughout most of the conflict, English troops under the leadership of Sir |John Norris made little headway against Tyrone's rebels, and therefore in 1599, and in the expectation of a more positive outcome, Robert Devereux was appointed Lord Lieutenant of Ireland charged with the duty of putting down the rebellion. However, without permission from the Crown, he signed a truce with Tyrone, returned to England and was duly arrested. In contrast, his successor, Charles Blount, Lord Mountjoy, secured a victory over an invading Spanish army at Kinsale in January 1602, and accepted the surrender of Tyrone in 1603, a few days after Elizabeth's death. The final outcome was that Elizabeth's successor James I, immediately granted an amnesty in Ireland and, with Philip III, signed the Treaty of London that ended the Anglo-Spanish war.

Throughout her long reign, Elizabeth was pre-occupied – in chronological order – with establishing a religious settlement, dealing with what may have seemed an intractable problem of succession, and in counteracting the belligerence of the Papacy and Spain. Unlike many other monarchs on the Continent, and partly because of the circumstances of her upbringing, she had little propensity to commission great works of architecture. However, her undoubted pragmatism enabled her to recognise that the Crown could not afford expenditure on sumptuous ventures while simultaneously provide resources to safeguard the State from internal and external threats. It might also be suggested that because Elizabeth owned a plethora of palaces in, or in close proximity, to her capital – most notably Windsor, Richmond, Whitehall, St. James's, the Tower and Greenwich – she saw little need to expand her real estate. Of course, her failure to add a new Renaissance palace to her stock of assets might have been due to her lack of interest in architectural design. Unlike, for example, Catherine de Medicis or other contemporaries such as the Roman Popes, Florentine dukes and Milanese Gonzaga, Elizabeth was not born into a built environment imbued with the treasures of the Renaissance.

With her restless energy, and with her court in tow, Elizabeth undertook a succession of 'progresses' from one country mansion to another, motivated by the desire not only to maintain good relations with her nobility but also to ensure her security – a policy adopted to ensure that no one could predict where she might be sleeping in a week's time. While her wanders hither and thither, undoubtedly diverted her attention from building a royal palace worthy of her glory, it encouraged the nobility of England to construct magnificent residences in which to receive her and curry her favour. .

Burghley House (1552)

Theobalds (1564-74)

A number of country mansions were thus built within easy access of London during the Elizabethan period, the foremost of which was undoubtedly Theobalds in Hertfordshire. Having already commissioned Burghley House in northern Cambridgeshire in 1552, William Cecil, the Lord

Chancellor, recognised that a residential location much closer to the capital would facilitate greater access to the centre of political power, Whitehall. In 1564, he therefore purchased for his second son, Robert Cecil , Theobalds just off the London to Ware road in Hertfordshire – a mere 15 miles (25 kilometres) from the capital – and immediately commissioned the construction of a modest courtyard house. Subsequently, in anticipation of hosting visits by the Queen. William extended and then completely rebuilt the mansion to create [by 1574] one of the "greatest palaces ever built in England" (14). Much larger than Burghley House (itself an enormous pile), Theobalds was full of innovations and must be coupled with Longleat as a house of outstanding originality" (15). Its attributes were impressive. Theobalds contained five courtyards arranged symmetrically, with entry to the first courtyard being facilitated by an arch leading to a loggia, entry to the second courtyard being via another loggia, and entry into the third courtyard – the inner or Fountain Court – being through a hall passage and a further loggia. Though its plan might well have been based on that of Giulio da Maiano's Poggio Reale at Naples (1487), its Elizabethan towers and turrets were almost certainly surmounted by ogee-shaped caps. Theobalds was "prophetic of houses to come and with a special bearing on the two great houses of James I's reign, Audley End and Hatfield" (16).

Much closer to the capital than even Theobalds, Wimbledon House was a further mansion commissioned by a member of the Cecil family. In 1588, Thomas Cecil, William Cecil's eldest son, acquired the lease of Wimbledon manor – an estate only 7 miles (11 km) from Whitehall – and duly constructed a substantial house built on an H-shaped plan, "the first house of its size to use this plan in the form in which was to become so general in the next three decades" (17). However, unlike any other country residence in sixteenth and seventeenth century – England, Wimbledon House featured a terraced approach on its garden side, reminiscent of the steps of the Caprarola Villa Farnese near Rome, designed by Vignola (1559). Such a configuration, dramatically increased the recessional effect of the house, an effect that – without the use of steps – was not only in accord with current fashion but more importantly heralded the Jacobean style of domestic architecture of the following century.

Osterley Park, west facade (1572-6), possibly by Henryk van Paschen

Osterley Park in Middlesex was another imposing mansion built on the edge of London in the later-sixteenth century. Possibly designed by the Flemish mason, Henryk van Paeschen – and built for the prominent City merchant, Thomas Gresham, in 1572-6 on the site of a medieval manor, it is recorded that Queen Elizabeth visited the house twice. Built of red brick, with white stone details, and with turrets in the four corners, the substantial building consists of four wings of equal length and is arranged around a central courtyard, features that remain broadly intact despite Robert Adam adorning the edifice with Neo-classical features in the later-eighteenth century (see Chapter 9).

From the twelfth century, much of the riverside between the Strand and the Thames had been occupied by the residences of prominent churchmen and other ecclesiastics before being sold-off or given away by Henry VIII after the Dissolution of the Monasteries. Subsequently, the riverside and its periphery provided an attractive residential location for the London elite – courtiers, aristocrats, government ministers and occasionally royalty. Although in Elizabethan times, some of the properties such as Arundel House, Durham House and York House retained many of their original medieval features and were largely wooden-framed, residences such as Essex House (1563), Cecil House (. 1575), Bedford House (1586) and Salisbury House (1605) were entirely Tudor-Gothic in style and were almost certainly constructed largely of brick with an ample use of glass window panes. In the eighteenth and nineteenth centuries, all were demolished and their sites redeveloped for current use. One such edifice of this style not to have been demolished is the 'Old Building' of Harrow School, founded by Royal Charter in 1572 but not completed until 1616.

Harrow School (1572)

In the late sixteenth-century, Renaissance architect-ture was not much in evidence in the English capital. As in the Middle Ages, there was an adherence to half-timbered houses (new examples of which continued to be constructed in country towns till late in the seventeenth century). In London, most were destroyed during the Great Fire of 1666 or were demolished during the rebuilding of the City after the conflagration, but the seven wood-framed and gabled houses of Staple Inn in Holborn remain extant and, despite their renovation in the nineteenth century, they "represent the most outstanding example of sixteenth-century domestic architecture in London" (18). Like so many houses of the period throughout the capital (and in contrast to the new grand houses of The Strand), its façade is characterised by "a mesh of woodwork, rows of windows, projections on the first floor pillars and [a] double-slope roof (19). Half-timbered houses of this sort were ubiquitous across London and continued to be built until the late seventeenth century. Some remain today: notably St Bartholomews Smithfield (1595), the Inner Temple gatehouse (1610) and the George Inn in Borough High Street (1676) .

Staple Inn Holborn (1586)

Gatehouse, St Bartholomew's Church (1595)

Inner Temple Gatehouse (1610)

The Ascendancy of the Renaissance

At the beginning of Elizabeth's reign, the style of architecture in London was about to change dramatically – in large measure because of the development of international trade. Following the granting of royal charters to the Merchant Adventurers Company in 1552 and Muscovy Company in 1555 (during the reigns of Edward VI and Mary I), both being lucrative to the State and the merchant fraternity, Elizabeth sold charters to the Eastland Company in 1579, the Levant Company in 1581 and the East India Company in 1600 to allow them – in turn- to monopolise English trade with the Baltic, the Turkish Empire and India for many years ahead.

Resulting from London becoming one of the most

vibrant commercial cities in Europe in the second-half of the sixteenth century; a *bourse* was constructed in the English capital to provide a central market place for trading transactions. Sited between Threadneedle Street and Cornhill, it was built in the Flemish Renaissance style, putting the English capital at least on a par with Antwerp as the commercial hub of north-western Europe. The new London *bourse*, or Royal Exchange as it became known, was commissioned in 1566 by a successful City merchant, Sir Thomas Gresham, and was designed by a Flemish mason Henryk van Paeschen. Built on a site in Cornhill purchased by the Corporation of London and the Worshipful Company of Mercers, and following the clearance of 36 houses, the Royal Exchange was constructed with the invaluable assistance of Flemish craftsmen often using ready-cut Flemish materials.

Royal Exchange (1566), by Henryk van Paschen

Opened by the Queen in 1571, the Royal Exchange was the first stone-built Renaissance-style building in the City of London. It was constructed around a courtyard and was "surrounded by a loggia whose arches were carried on Doric columns, with an upper storey have Ionic pilasters and niches with statues of the English Kings" (20). Each of its four wings were covered by pitched slated-roofs pierced by dormer windows, while the east wing was dominated by a bell tower surmounted by a huge grasshopper, an emblem from the Gresham crest. At ground level as many as 4,000 City merchants had the opportunity of indulging in their commercial activities, instead of-as before-having to conduct their business while walking in Lombard street, while on the floors "above the arcades [there] were haberdashers, armourers, goldsmiths, drapers and glass-sellers" (21). The Royal Exchange remained in its original form until it was destroyed by the Great Fire of 1666, but it was replaced with a new, almost identical, building within three years, a measure of its importance to the economy of London (see Chapter 9) and the degree to which its design was considered fit-for-purpose.

Old Hall, Lincoln's Inn (1492)

Notwithstanding the emergence of Renaissance architecture, London was the centre of English Common Law still endowed with many fine medieval buildings, particular in the Inns of Court. One of the first of any prominence is the Old Hall in Lincoln's Inn (1492), but this is easy surpassed in its architectural magnificence by both the Great Hall in Grays Inn (1555 but reconstructed in the 1950s) and more particularly by the Middle Temple Hall, "the finest Elizabethan building in central London" (22). Constructed in 1562-1573, and used as a debating chamber for students under the guidance of a senior barrister, this amply-glazed Elizabethan brick building with stone-dressings is notable particularly for its internal features; a superb oak double-hammerbeam roof and magnificent screen.

Middle Temple Hall (1562-73)

Great Hall, Gray's Inn (1555), restored post-World War II

The downside of Elizabeth's reign was that the globalisation of world trade and the inflow of gold and silver from the Americas increased the money supply and resulted in price inflation. Capitalist entrepreneurs got richer and richer since inflation cheapened the real cost of labour, and the less well-off -on relatively fixed wages –got poorer and poorer, particularly when a spate of poor harvests in the 1590s led to famine. The population of London, however, continued to increase at a pace, largely because migrants from the countryside thought that they could escape poverty and the strictures of the Pool Law Act of 1598 by seeking work in the capital. With the expansion of prosperous areas in the west, and the development of more and poorer housing in the east, the spatial growth of London was phenomenal during the last decades of the sixteenth century and appeared to be out of control. Responding to the Crown's concern, " in 1580, at the mayor's request – and to avert threats to law and order, food supplies and health – the Queen issued a proclamation prohibiting new building within three miles of the City gates on any site vacant in living memory" (23). This was followed by Privy Council orders in 1590, parliamentary legislation in 1593 and a royal proclamation in 1602 all aimed at curbing the growth of London, but there was little evidence to suggest that these measures were successful, indeed their main effect was to increase congestion within the existing built-up areas adding to squalor and the incidence of disease.

References

1. P. Hall, *Cities in Civilisation. Culture, Innovation and Urban Order*, Weidenfeld & Nicolson, 1998, p 1155.
2. Ibid, p 121.
3. R. Porter, *London. A Social History*, Penguin Books, 2000, pp 79-80.
4. Ibid, pp 55-6.
5. Ibid, p 57.
6. P. Hall, *Cities in Civilisation. Culture, Innovation and Urban Order*, Weidenfeld & Nicolson, 1998, p 122.
7. D. Starkey, *Monarchy. From the Middle Ages to Modernity*, Harper Press, 2006, pp 76-7.
8. Ibid, pp 78-79.
9. Ibid, p 79.
10. Ibid, pp 63-64.
11. Ibid, p 94.
12. Ibid, p 86.
13. Ibid, p 321.
14. Sir John Summerson, *Architecture in Britain 1530-1830*, Yale University Press, 9th Edit., 1993, pp 67 & 69.

15. Ibid, p 69.
16. Ibid, p 69.
17. Ibid, pp 70-71.
18. A. Bahamòn, *London. Atlas of Architecture*, Batsford, 2006, p 15.
19. Ibid, p 15.
20. Sir John Summerson,_*Architecture in Britain 1530-1830*, Yale University Press, 9th Edit., p 171.
21. R. Porter, *London. A Social History*, Penguin Books, 2000, p 60.
22. S. Bradley and N. Pevsner, *London 6: Westminster*, Yale University Press, 2004 p 348.
23. P. Hall, *Cities in Civilisation. Culture, Innovation and Urban Order*, Weidenfeld & Nicolson, p 121.

Chapter 5

Early-Stuart London: Inigo Jones and the Emergence of the Renaissance

As a thriving centre of commerce without rival in Europe, London with a population of around 200,000 in the early seventeenth century "was not merely expanding, it was bursting out of its shell, ceasing to be the familiar old walled city" (1). Eastward from the main west-east axis of the City, Cheapside, the eastern expansion of London was characterised by "an industrial suburb, dominated by shipping, wharves and boat-building and swarms of artisans, mariners and migrants" (2). However, westward, the expansion of London took the form of new prestigious development in Covent Garden and Lincoln's Inn Fields, while, further west still, Westminster with its early-Medieval origins became a town in its own right imperceptibly merging with the newly-to-be-developed 'West End' in general. Thus, by around 1660, only about a quarter of London's population lived within the city walls (compared to around 75 per cent in 1560), while the eastern dockland suburbs contained a third of London's inhabitants, and Westminster and the suburbs south of the Thames each accommodated a quarter (3).

Stuart Absolutism and the Growth of London

James I (r.1603-1625)

Although the early-Stuart kings of England superficially eschewed French absolutism, no doubt because of the centuries' old practice of the monarch having to defer to Parliament on matters of taxation, this did not prevent James I, and later his son Charles I, from developing the concept of the "Divine Right of Kings", whereby deference to Parliament could be selectively abandoned when the monarch considered that such action would be justified to ensure the realisation of royal objectives.

Soon after his coronation in Westminster Abbey in 1603, James I of England, therefore attempted to put into practice the ideology that he had set-out in his treatises *The Trew Law of Free Monarchies and Basilikin Doran* of 1597-8. His belief in the necessity of a strong monarchy had evolved after he had acceded to the throne of Scotland as James VI in 1567 when his kingdom became riven by rebellious nobles and a hostile Calvinist Kirk.

James also reigned over a comparatively austere and economically insular country with a narrow tax base. Thus when he inherited the throne south of the border, he rather foolishly perceived that England would provide eminently suitable conditions for the introduction of his brand of absolute monarchy and, that with political stability and a benign Church of England, his rule would be trouble-free, while its wealth generated by rapidly expanding trading links with the rest of the world and distributed amount a rapidly emerging merchant class would provide rich pickings for a tax-raising monarch.

To centralise many of the sources of taxable wealth, Robert Cecil – as Lord Treasurer to James I – built a *bourse* in the Strand in 1608 as a western counterpart to Gresham's Elizabethan exchange which it might have resembled. However, it was demolished in 1737 and its more detailed architectural attributes are largely unknown.

Despite the growing prosperity of the merchant classes, the financial position of his Treasury was dire. Under Elizabeth I, war with Spain and hostilities in Ireland had left a debt of almost £400,000. To cut state expenditure, he immediately introduced an amnesty in Ireland, and in 1604 invited Spanish delegates to a conference at Hampton Court, the outcome of which – later in the year- was the Treaty of London that secured peace between England and Spain. 1604 also saw the opening of James's First Parliament, and the unification of the crowns of England and Scotland, but although relations with Catholic Spain had ameliorated and political stability at home seemed to have been generally assured, there was a measure of unease among Catholics in England since they feared that their religious freedoms would be seriously impaired by a Puritan parliament – a fear that found its full expression in the unsuccessful Gunpowder Plot of 1605.

James was still on good political terms with Parliament, but cash was in short supply, and although Parliament granted the Treasury £450,000 in 1606, the Treasury debt still amounted to £280,000 four years later. Clearly, state expenditure continued to exceed the proceeds of taxation and thus, in an attempt to create more of a fiscal balance, Robert Cecil, Master of the Court of Wards, drew up a list of comprehensive proposals that were incorporated into the "Great

157

Contract" of 1610. However, negotiations between Parliament and James over the details of the Contract failed and, exercising his assumed right to tax without Parliamentary consent, dissolved Parliament. For four eventful years, James and his court ruled alone. On the credit side, the publication of the Authorised Version of the Bible ('King James's Bible') in 1610, reinforced the role of the Church of England in the nation's psyche, and enhanced James's profile as "defender of the faith". Less successfully, James presided over an increase in the Treasury debt (it rose to £500,000 in 1612), and he married-off his daughter Elizabeth to the German Protestant Leader, Frederick V of the Palatinate, a union that ultimately led England to unwittingly commit troops to war on the Continent (see below). Financial constraints led James to recall Parliament in 1614, but the "Addled Parliament", as it became known, refused to consider his financial concerns and was duly dissolved.

Throughout the first eleven years of James's reign, the financial debt – inherited from Elizabeth I – was not reduced despite an effort to cut expenditure on foreign adventures, and because of fiscal constraints imposed by Parliament, James was in no position to fund the construction of new buildings for his own or his family's needs. He either did not have the money or it would have been inexpedient to draw upon Treasury funds for this purpose. This did not deter Thomas Hutton. 'The richest commoner in England' from purchasing the former monastery of Charterhouse in 1613 and rebuilding it as a boys' school and hospital for the needy.

Charterhouse (1611)

But, from the dissolution of Parliament in 1614 to
its reopening in 1621, James too had few scruples in
funding the development of new buildings, despite the
Treasury debt rising to £900,000 in 1618.
Parliamentary criticism of profligate expenditure for a
while was in abeyance. Throughout contemporary
Europe, royal palaces were not only being
commissioned by a ruling monarch for his or her use,
but also for his or her spouse. Thus, in 1616, James I
commissioned the Queen's House at Greenwich as a
residence for his wife, Queen Anne of Denmark.
Designed by Inigo Jones, the Queen's House was the
first truly Classical buildings in Britain, and is one of
the most important houses in the country's architectural
history. To meet the wishes of Queen Anne of
Denmark, it was built to supersede her former
residence, the rambling, mainly red-brick Palace of
Greenwich, which since Tudor times had been known
as the Palace of Placentia. Inspired by Italian
precedents such as Sangallo's Villa at Poggio a Catano

(1480s), Andrea Palladio's Villa Chiericati at Vicenza (1550-7) and Scamozzi's Villa Molini at Padua (1590s), the Queen's house would have appeared revolutionary to English observers accustomed to the medieval or Elizabethan vernacular. However, in specific terms, it does not replicate any Classical building elsewhere. The house initially consisted of two rectangular blocks either side of the west-east London to Dover road, and these were joined to each other by a first-storey room – effectively a bridge – across the road, a unique concept. Work on the house ceased in 1617, only one year after it had begun. James I was financially constrained limiting the amount of resources that could be allocated to the further development of the residence and, because Queen Anne of Denmark died in 1619, the resumption of work was not a priority. However, in 1629, and under James's successor Charles I, work began on completing the house to meet the accommodation needs of the new queen, Henrietta Maria. When completed in 1635, two further rooms, flush with the earlier bridging-room, had been constructed across the London-Dover road to form an integrated first floor and consolidating the whole structure of the building. In its completed form, the northern block of the house, contains a centrally-situated double-height entrance hall, while the southern block boasts a central loggia on its upper floor. Its tripartite façade is rusticated at ground floor level, finished in plain stonework on the upper floor, and surmounted by a cornice and stone balustrade. While its northern elevation is rather austere, its southern elevation "makes more than a passing reference to the Palazzo Chierciati, echoing the proportion and the general mood, and simply reversing Palladio's pattern of solid and void" (4).

160

Queen's House, Greenwich (1616)

It is very probably that, very early in his reign, James I was disenchanted with the rambling Tudor Palace of Whitehall with its jumble of brick buildings of varying style and function, and was unwilling to spend much to modernise the complex. In 1619, the king therefore commissioned Inigo Jones to design a new building to replace the old Elizabethan banqueting suite of the palace that he disparagingly referred to as an "old rotten, slight-builded shed" (5). What emerged in 1622 was the new Banqueting Hall, Palladian in style, faced with Portland stone and, above its highly rusticated base, its ground floor façade is punctuated by Ionic columns, pilasters of the same Order, and pedimented windows; its upper floor windows are separated by Corinthian columns and pilasters; and its cornice is surmounted by a balustrade. On both floors, the edges of the façade are framed by double pilasters. Internally, the building is dominated by an immense two-storey double cube, 110 ft (33.5 m) in length, 55 ft

(16.7 m) in width and 55 ft (16.7 m) in height, and is decorated by a Rubens ceiling, commissioned by Charles I, and painted in 1635. Arguable Inigo Jones's masterpiece, the Banqueting Hall was the first purely Classical building in central London.

New Banqueting House (1622), by Inigo Jones

From 1623 to the end of his reign in 1625, James commissioned no further buildings. With a downturn in foreign relations, state expenditure was escalating rapidly. In 1619 Frederick V of the Palatinate – son-in-law of James – had assumed the crown of Bohemia, despite it being claimed by the newly elected Holy Roman Emperor, Ferdinand II, and in 1620 at the Battle of White Mountain, Frederick's army was defeated by the Catholic League under Count Tilly. Eventually, in 1624, following the Parliament willingly granting £300,000 for a war against Spain (and indirectly against the Empire) an expedition of English troops under

Count Mansfeld was sent to support Frederick in the Palatinate in his war against Ferdinand. In the same year, an Anglo-French Treaty, ensured the subsequent marriage between Charles Prince of Wales and Henrietta Maria, daughter of Henri IV and Marie de'Medici. Although at the time of war with Spain the marriage was intended to cement relations between England and France and thus create a balance of power in Western Europe, the unpopularity of Henrietta in England, because of her Catholic faith, heralded a period of political and religious instability in England that ultimately led to the Puritan Revolution a quarter of a century later.

During the early-seventeenth century far more buildings of merit were developed by private patrons than by the monarch himself, and numerous examples of these are to be found in both central London and in its outer environs. This was possibly because attractive sites for the development of palaces and sumptuous town houses such as those on the river side of the Strand had been acquired and fully built-up by noblemen and prelates in Medieval and Tudor times, and their properties remained intact and sometimes enhanced. A completely new venture, however, was Northumberland House, the London home of the Percy family from 1640 to 1866. Commissioned by Henry Howard, 1st Earl of Northampton in 1605, on a site adjacent to Charing Cross the building was first known as Northampton House. Its exterior was distinctly Jacobean being loosely embellished with Classical ornamentation. Its façade, noted for its elaborate four-storey carved stone gateway, was 162 ft (49 m) in width, while its depth was even greater. There was a turret in each corner of the building, and the house contained a large central courtyard enclosed by the four wings – in contrast to the normal Parisian practice of employing only two or three wings and a masking wall or dummy frontage. Soon after completion, the property passed to the Earls of Suffolk, relatives of the Howard family, and in the 1640s the house was bought by the senior member of the Percy family, the Earl of Northumberland who, through marrying a Howard, was able to obtain the building at a discounted price of £15,000. After numerous alterations over the following two hundred years such as the placement of the emblematic Percy lion above the gateway, Northumberland House was demolished in 1866 to make way for the development of Northumberland Avenue.

Northumberland House (1605)

The only other residence of any note to be developed along the Strand in the Jacobean period was Salisbury House. Funded by Robert Cecil at the turn of the seventeenth century, the house was built on the waterfront opposite Exeter House on the northern side of the Strand, the Elizabethan property of his father Lord Burghley. Of comparatively little architectural merit, and in no way similar to a *hôtel*, neither house withstood redevelopment at the end of the seventeenth century (see chapter 4). Away from the Strand, and with royal consent, Robert Cecil during the years 1609-12 funded the development of substantial residences for the affluent in an area bounded by Leicester Fields and St Martin's Lane. The houses, however, soon fell into disrepair because their tenants were unwilling or unable to maintain them in good condition, but the area was redeveloped again as a prestigious neighbourhood in the eighteenth century (see chapter 6).

Cloth Fair (early 1600s)

Sir Fulke Grenville's House (1619-20) – facade relocated in
the Victoria and Albert Museum

With the economic and social ascendancy of the merchant in the early sixteenth century, the number of grand houses constructed in London was undoubtedly dwarfed by a proliferation of less prosaic dwellings of traditional Gothic design particularly on the edge of the City of Bishopsgate, Fleet Street, Holborn and around Charing Cross (6). Buildings similar to these were constructed in Cloth Fair, adjacent to St Bartholomew, and of eleven built, one remains today – the oldest house in London. However, other dwellings of the period exhibited elements of Classical design, albeit to a limited extent. There was, for example, the development of brick and stone town houses such as those owned by Sir Fulke Grenville and Lady Coke in Holborn. Both dwellings – dating from around 1619-1620 were surmounted in the Dutch fashion by "a gable with scrolled sides rising to a pediment, triangular in

Grenville's house, segmental in Lady Cook's" (7). With James I's proclamation of 1605 that prohibited the use of timber in the construction of house fronts (to reduce the risk of conflagration, to conserve the national timber supply, and to create greater uniformity in street design), and the undoubted influence of Inigo Jones, the stage was now set for a transformation in the style of domestic architecture across London.

Cope Castle (later Holland House), Kensington (1605)

It was, however, the outer-environs of London that attracted the development of resplendent Jacobean mansions. Located in Kensington only 9 km (6 miles) from the City of London, Holland House could have been regarded as a country residence rather than, in an Italian sense, a *villa suburbana,* Kensington was not only beyond the walls of the City but outside of the increasingly built-up western suburbs of Holborn, Westminster and Marylebone. Commissioned in 1605 by Sir Walter Cope, James I's Chancellor of the Exchequer, and named initially as Cope Castle, Holland House gained its present name when it came under the Earl of Holland through marriage after the Civil War. Possibly designed by John Thorpe, Holland House was a massive edifice of Jacobean design rising above an "H" shaped plan to four storeys, with a façade featuring a proliferation of towers and gabled pavilions, side wings in each of the four corners, tall arcades stretching across all but the central portion of the ground floor facade, and a profusion of strapwork and pierced crestings. During the Second World War, the house was very severely damaged and has only partly been restored.

Charlton House (1607)

Also located only 9 km from the City, but to the south-east in what was rural Kent, Charlton House, is regarded as one of the best-preserved Jacobean mansions in England. Built between 1607 and 1612 for Sir Adam Newton, Dean of Durham and tutor to the eldest son of James I, Prince Henry, and designed by John Thorpe, the house is particularly noted for the symmetry of its three-storey façade with its two side wings and ogle-domed towers; its heavily –fenestrated *Ditterling* central section; and its roofline balustrade. Built largely of brick, its elevations are enhanced in appearance by the use of stone quoins, and the use of stone in its central section where a rounded portal is framed by double engaged columns. Of broadly similar design to Charlton House, Ham House near Richmond on Thames and only 12 miles (18 km) to the south west

168

of the City of London, was commissioned in 1610 by Sir Thomas Vavasour, Knight Marshall to James I. The architect is unknown, though the pattern set by Thorpe appears to have been broadly adhered to. The three story façade has two projecting arcaded side wings that were later extended (without further arcading) in 1672 by its then owner, the Duke of Lauderdale. Like other Jacobean houses, Ham House was constructed mainly of brick, though the corners of its elevations are outlined by stone quoins.

Ham House, Richmond (1607)

Hatfield House in Hertfordshire has somewhat different origins from those of other Jacobean mansions on the fringe of London. Not entirely liking the late-fifteenth century Royal Palace of Hatfield, James I gave it to his chief minister Robert Cecil in exchange for Theobalds, Cecil's ancestral home, also located in Hertfordshire. Demolishing much of the palace, Cecil rebuilt the edifice on a nearby but somewhat higher site in 1611 using its bricks to create a new residence. Located 20 miles (30km) north of the City, and constructed on an inverted U-shaped plan, Hatfield House consists of: a three storey 230 ft (85 m)

169

northward-facing façade with unobtrusively projecting wings and central section (formerly its garden front); two southward facing wings ornamented at their extremities by ogee-capped corner towers; and connecting the two wings, a ground floor loggia, 120 ft (36 m) in length surmounted by a gallery and central frontispiece of three storeys (8). While the loggia and the frontispiece were undoubtedly Classical in style, and the work of Robert Lyming, much of the rest of the building might have been designed by Robert Cecil himself, who, like his father William Cecil, Lord Burghley, "took an active part in his own building works" (9).

Hatfield House, Hertfordshire (1607)

Built between 1603 and 1616, Audley End in Essex was the earliest and perhaps the grandest Jacobean house constructed in the early-seventeenth century. Located some 50 kilometres (30 miles) from central London, though still only a half-day's journey from the capital by coach, Audley End was designed by Bernart Jannsen for Thomas Howard, the 1st Earl of Suffolk and Lord Treasurer, while its construction was supervised by Suffolk's uncle, the 1st Earl of Northumberland. With an inner and outer courtyard designed so that its stone buildings gradually decreased in height, the main three storey core of the house was arranged round an inner court, with its west wing comprising, at its centre, a lower block accommodating the great hall with its oriel window and ornate two tier portals, with two lateral wings to its left and right. Externally there is little ornamentation except for Ionic and Corinthian orders in the portals and ample decorative balustrading – the only Classical elements incorporated into the building. The East wing of the main block was demolished in 1712, along with the large outer-court – 130 ft (40m) square – projecting from the west wing. This was lined on its north and south sides by two-storey wings with open arches at ground floor level and by windows and niches above, punctuated at each side by a central tower. The middle of the outer side of the court contained a gatehouse with a "triumphal arch" sandwiched between twin lead-capped towers reminiscent of Tudor times. Being on such a vast scale and costing £200,000 to build, Audley End was very probably "the most ambitious composition of [its] kind ever built in England [so much so that James I is alleged to have remarked that it was] too great a house for a King but was very well for a Lord Treasurer's" (10). Since Thomas Howard had responsibility for Royal finances, profligate expenditure on his part soon provoked accusation of embezzlement, and he was duly convicted of this offence in 1619 and sent to the Tower of London but was released some years later after paying a huge fine.

Audley End, Essex (1603)

Charles I (v.1625-1649)

Though the Renaissance continued to have an impact on architecture during the reign of Charles I, many buildings of merit were constructed during the second quarter of the seventeenth century with only scant regard to Classicism.

Smaller residences in close proximity to London, for example, exhibited the artisanal 'style of architecture' whereby a master bricklayer or other skilled craftsman rather than a professional architect took full responsibility for the construction of the building in liaison with its patron. Dating respectively from 1631 and 1638 the 'Dutch House' at Kew and Swakeleys near Uxbridge were two such examples. Because of the quasi-classical treatment of their gable ends, they were – to an extent – stylistically derived from Sir Fulke Greville's and Lady Cook's houses in Holborn (see above) though they used pediments, both triangular and segmental, more extensively. Cromwell House on Highgate House is another residence constructed in the artisanal tradition. Built for Richard Springwell in 1637-1640, the resplendent redbrick building with its street façade is pierced by six window bays and a central portico on its ground floor, seven window bays on its *piano nobile* and seven dormer windows in its attic. Despite its name, there is no reliable evidence that Cromwell ever lived there. York House in Twickenham was also built in the 1630s. Commissioned by Andrew Pitcairn, a courtier of Charles I, the seven-bay, three storey residence was extended by the addition of a west wing and east wing in the eighteenth century.

Dutch House, Kew (1631)

Swakeley's Middlesex (1638)

Cromwell's House, Highgate   (1637-40)

York House, Twickenham (1630s)

These buildings were, however, four of the last houses near London to be designed in this style , but the first houses subsequently built in the *avant guard* Palladian style in and near the capital normally also used brick rather than stone as their main building material, and therefore their construction – like that of the 'Dutch House', Swakeleys or Cromwell's House – was dependent more on the expertise of bricklayer-contractors than on the skills of stonemasons, a dependency that continued throughout the seventeenth century and in the early years of eighteenth .

The adoption of Palladian architecture:

Artisanal architecture was not, of course, appropriate to the needs of the monarchy and the Church. Therefore, soon after his coronation, Charles I ordered the completion of the Queen's Chapel at St James's Palace, the first church in London (and indeed in England) to be constructed in the Classical style. Initially commissioned by James I in 1623, and designed by Inigo Jones, the chapel was intended as a place of worship for the Catholic Infanta Maria of Spain, the prospective wife of the future Charles I . However, when the wedding plans were abandoned in late-1623, so did construction work on the chapel. However, it was resumed in 1626 and completed the following year following the wedding of Charles to Henrietta Maria of France, another Catholic. The chapel was Jones's first ecclesiastical commission and, using his knowledge of Palladian theory, he designed a single-chamber building of double-cubed proportions reminiscent of a *cella* or main body of a Classical temple (11). Although an ecclesiastical building, it could be mistaken externally as a residential property since the exterior of its ground floor is rusticated and, like a Palladian house, displays strong horizontal divisions. Its west facade was based loosely on the former Prince Charles's Lodging built by Jones in Newmarket. Of two tiers, the chapel is pierced by a central doorway and two flanking windows at ground floor level, while its upper tier contains a trio of windows, the central one of which is round-headed. Its east facade is illuminated by a Venetian window of the sort that Scamozzi occasionally used. A corbel cornice in the style of the Roman Pantheon surmounts the upper tier of the building (12).

Queen's Chapel (1626), by Inigo Jones

But Charles's recognition of Henrietta's faith did not stop at the Queen's Chapel. He further developed Somerset House for her use. Situated between the Strand and the Thames, Somerset House had been constructed in 1547-50 for Thomas Seymour, the Lord Protector of England, but thereafter until the seventeenth century it was the residence of Princess Elizabeth (the future queen) in 1552-60, Queen Anne of Denmark (intermittently between 1603-17) and then by Henrietta Maria (frequently between 1625-36). Despite its scale, Somerset House remained a `house' and was never declared a `palace'. During the early-seventeenth century, although the original three-wing residential structure with its Great Court was not substantially redeveloped, Anne of Denmark had commissioned a number of expensive improvements and additions some of which were designed by Inigo Jones in the Classical style, and later in 1630 Charles I funded the construction of a large new chapel in 1630 for the use of his Catholic queen. Also designed by Jones, the building – completed in 1635 – was constructed on a site to the south-west of the Great Court and it too was Classical in style. However, because the chapel was designed to serve the spiritual needs of a Catholic and was tended by the Capuchin Order, it was wrecked by Puritans after the Queen's departure for the Netherlands in 1645. But since Somerset House had been founded by a Protestant, Thomas Seymour, the building itself was considered to be of great significant importance to the Puritan Revolution and it was within its walls that Cromwell lay in state in 1658.

During the first few months of Charles I's reign, relations between England and France rapidly deteriorated, notwithstanding the king's recent marriage to a French princess. Only a year after an unsuccessful military expedition to Cadiz led by the Duke of Buckingham, Charles declared open war on France in 1626. Buckingham this time was put in command of an expedition to the Ile de Rhe (off La Rochelle) to provide support for the Rochellaise Huguenots in their rebellion against Louis XIII, but English intervention into what was, in effect, a French religious war, similarly failed to achieve its objectives. Throughout this time, relations between Charles and his Parliament were antagonistic, partly for financial reasons but partly because of religious controversy. Charles's First and Second Parliaments, in respectively 1625 and 1626, were increasingly concerned that the king's propensity to spend necessitated an increase in the level of taxation and therefore, during the Third Parliament in 1628, the House of Commons presented Charles with A Petition of Right to protect the subject from any future increase in taxation without the consent of Parliament. Although Charles signed the petition, albeit reluctantly, he resorted to raising money through 'forced loans' for the continuing war with Spain. But Charles' first minister, Buckingham, was not personally constrained from investing in his London residence, York House, where in 1626, he commissioned the construction of the York Watergate, possibly to the design of Inigo Jones.

York Watergate (1626-7)

Despite previous support for the Huguenot cause in France and war with Catholic Spain, Parliament was increasingly concerned that Charles was intent on transforming England from a Protestant to a Roman state, after all, his wife Henrietta Maria was a Catholic and enjoyed freedom of worship. In 1628 matters came to a head when William Laud (an Arminian) became Bishop of London, while Richard Montagu (similarly an Arminian and Charles's personal chaplain) was appointed Bishop of Chichester (Arminians, it should be noted, stressed the importance of the priesthood and particularly the episcopacy – the institution of bishops, and emphasised the importance of ritual in church services and the symbolism of the altar. They represented the High Church and, although they did not recognise the Pope as head of the Christian faith, were almost indistinguishable from Catholics). Relations between king and the largely – Puritan Commons were almost at rock bottom, and therefore Charles dissolved Parliament in March 1629 and it did not meet again until April 1640. Thus, during the first four years of Charles's reign conditions were not favourable for any form of property development in the capital. Financial constraint in government and political instability clearly had a debilitating impact on construction activity. Between 1625 and 1629 few if any buildings of any importance were built in London.

Absolute rule: 1630-1640

In complete contrast to the earlier years of his reign, during the 1630's Charles funded, promoted or presided over major development schemes aimed at improving the built environment of London. The conditions could not have been more favourable for a major hike in royal expenditure. At home, he had a free-hand to raise revenue without Parliamentary consent, and abroad he could secure peace with Catholic France and Spain without incurring the ire of Protestants at Westminster. With Parliament dissolved, he continued to collect tonnage and poundage (import duties) at will, sold knighthoods to all landowners for £40 a year, with the imposition of fines for non-compliance, and in 1633 revived the obsolete Forest Laws that imposed fines on the encroachment of illegal enclosures and buildings. The reintroduction of ship money in 1635 provided a further source of revenue (when, following medieval precedent, seaports were obliged to contribute to the cost of the fleet). In the following year, the tax was extended inland, raising the total yield from these sources to over £200,000 annually. In relation to foreign policy, peace abroad was a royal priority. This would not only curb expenditure, but would enhance the security of the realm. In 1629, the Peace of Suss ended the war between England and France, and in 1630 a peace treaty was signed with Spain.

It, was thus, within this context that Charles now had the financial resources to commission the completion of the Queen's House at Greenwich in 1635 (construction having been abandoned in 1618). The house was a delayed gift to Henrietta Maria since it would have been unthinkable for the king to have funded work on the completion of this residence during the 1626-1629 war with France.

Other construction activity also occurred in the peaceful 1630s. The first and foremost project was the development of Covent Garden. Almost a century earlier in 1536, a convent and its garden occupied a site north of the Strand, but with the dissolution of the monasteries in that year, ownership passed from Westminster Abbey to Henry VIII. The land was subsequently bestowed on John Russell, 1st Earl of Bedford, and on a site within the garden, one of his successors built Bedford House, close to the present Southampton Street. Later the 4th Earl of Bedford, eager to turn his estate into profit, obtained for a fee of £2,000 a licence from the monarch, Charles I, to develop housing "fit for the habitations of gentlemen and men of ability" (13). However, the most important building constructed in Covent Garden (and the only seventeenth-century building to remain on the site) is St

Paul's Church. Although the proposed housing was intended to be speculative, Charles – eager to counteract his alleged Catholic sympathies – was only willing to give his consent to its development if the Earl of Bedford incorporated a church for Protestant worship at the western end of the *piazza*. From the outset the Earl was reluctant to incur a high level of expenditure on the church. He advised his architect, Inigo Jones, to keep it cheap and "not much better than a barn", to which Jones's reputedly replied "You shall have the handsomest barn in Europe". But what Jones produced was an austere church in a primitive or vernacular style (14) . Begun in 1631 and completed in 1633, its eastern façade is dominated by an enormous portico supported by four Tuscan columns and pillars, surmounted by an unadorned pediment, and it is flanked by gateways and two houses. Although its original entrance was at the east-end, the doorway was re-sited at the west end and framed by pavilions below a strong pediment (15). With little effective control over the cost of construction, the Earl undoubtedly paid more for the church than he anticipated. Whereas the total cost of developing the piazza amounted to £13,000 (15), the cost of constructing the church alone was disproportionately as much as £4,000. Consecrated in 1638, the edifice was subsequently known as St. Paul's, Covent Garden.

St Paul's Covent Garden (1631-8), by Inigo Jones

The rest of Covent Garden was henceforth developed as a prestigious residential precinct incorporating tall three-storey arcaded houses along the northern and eastern sides of a paved rectangle, with the church – St. Paul's – on its western side, and Bedford House and its terraced garden on its southern side. Because of the scale of this innovative scheme, the Privy Council insisted that the Royal Surveyor, Inigo Jones, should be responsible for the design of the project and, inspired by the Place Royale in Paris, and possibly the Piazza Grande in Livorno, Tuscany, Jones produced the first of the regularly-planned London squares that were to dominate the residential development of much of London for another two-hundred years. But the cost of development was high, £13,000. Thus, in the later seventeenth century, the 5th Earl of Bedford obtained a licence to hold a fruit and vegetable market on the site to supplement rental incomes. However, the piazza (as the residential component of the scheme was erroneously known) at first proved a great success among residents, and within the immediate vicinity soon led to the planned development of King Street, Henrietta Street, Russell Street, Bedford Street, Maiden Lane and James Street, that by the end of the seventeenth century had degenerated from a prestigious residential neighbourhood into a seedy run-down area of squalor, and poverty. The social elite had migrated to St. James, Mayfair and Bloomsbury while Covent Garden became rife with prostitution. In the 1830's, Covent Garden was transformed by the construction of a large market hall at its centre and, later in the nineteenth century, the arcaded houses on the northern and eastern sides of the rectangle were demolished, though Bedford Chambers built on the north side of the square in 1887-1889 to an extent replicates their former appearance. Thus, unlike the Place de Vosges in Paris, the appearance and use of Covent Garden today differs vastly from its original planned form.

A nineteenth century replica of the piazza, Covent Garden (started 1631), by Inigo Jones

The development of Covent Garden in the early 1630's was echoed further east by the construction of town houses in Lincoln Inn's Fields in 1638-43. Located to the west of Lincoln's Inn, Lincoln's Inn Fields was developed by a speculator, William Newton, who obtained licences from the Commission of Buildings to construct 32 houses around a newly-laid out square. Although evidence is lacking, it is assumed by many architectural historians that Inigo Jones, as commissioner, exerted a considerable influence over the development of at least the western side of the square with its more or less identical houses, most of which were adorned with Ionic pilasters. Among this row of houses, however, one majestic building stands out, Lindsey House. Designed by Inigo Jones c. 1638-1640, it is the tallest and most ornamented house on the western side. Faced with stone and stucco, its rusticated ground floor serves as a podium for six Ionic pilasters that frame the tall rectangular pedimented windows on the *piano nobile* and the smaller unpedimented windows on the top floor, while across the full width of the façade a balustrade surmounts a deep cornice. Palladian in style, Lindsey House became a model for a plethora of town houses throughout the English-speaking world from the second half of the sixteenth to the early nineteenth century. At long last, Gothic architecture and its Jacobean and Dutch mutations had been largely superseded by Classicism, but few buildings in the square exemplify this development today because Lincoln's Inn Fields was redeveloped piecemeal in the eighteenth, nineteenth and twentieth centuries and only part of its western side – including Lindsey House – remains as a reminder of its innovative architecture.

Lindsey House, Lincoln's Inn Fields (c.1640), by Inigo Jones

Providing a direct route from Lincoln's Inn Fields in the east to Long Acre in the west, Great Queen Street was also developed by William Newton in the late 1630's and early 1640's, possibly to designs of Inigo Jones, Peter Mills (a City of London bricklayer) and John Webb. All the houses in the street were built of fine redbrick, and their generously-fenestrated facades were adorned by Corinthian pilasters rising from the podium of the ground floor to the heavy wooden eaves above the second floor. Above, in contrast to the flat roofed residences in Lincoln's Inn Fields, the houses in Great Queen Street had steeply-pitched roofs pierced by gabled windows. However, although Great Queen Street was reputedly the first regular street in London, and by putting an end to gabled individualism of former styles "provided a discipline for London streets which was accepted for more than two hundred years" (16), it was soon demolished and replaced by individually-designed houses of variable merit in the eighteenth century. The street suffered a final blow when it was severed by the construction of Kingsway in 1906. Possibly of even more importance than the houses in Great Queen Street, and also dating from the late 1630's-early 40's, were a block of buildings in Lothbury, in the City of London, commissioned by Lord Maltravers and designed by Inigo Jones. The significance of the houses was that they "were the first example of a classical uniform astylar urban terrace" (17) and were thus the forerunning of the unified Georgian terrace of future years. However, they were unfortunately destroyed by the Great Fire.

During his work on Covent Garden and Lincoln's Inn Fields, Inigo Jones began to undertake a much more substantial commission: a programme of transforming the western façade of Old St. Paul's. Since the reigns of Elizabeth I and James I the cathedral had been in a poor condition, and although Jones had produced some tentative plans for restoring the edifice as early as 1608 and again in 1620 (18), it was not until 1628 that work on the cathedral was feasible. William Laud had just become Bishop of London and, recognising the need for his cathedral's restoration, encouraged Charles I to meet its costs from the Privy Purse. In 1634 Inigo Jones was appointed as surveyor of a commission established to undertake the necessary work and, together with his deputy Edward Carter, demolished and cleared the incongruous dwellings and shops. They entirely recast the Romanesque parts of the cathedral in rusticated masonry, restored the Gothic choir, attached Ionic transepts doorways, and most strikingly of all added a Corinthian portico, 565 ft (172 m) in height and ten columns in width, to the west end of the cathedral, "the only portico on such a scale north of the Alps" (18). Restoration was completed by the construction of two symmetrical towers flanking the portico, the southern

187

tower being a replica of the old tower of St. Gregory-by-St. Paul's, and a northern tower of similar design to maintain symmetry. With restoration completed in 1640, the west front of Old St. Paul's anticipated the Neoclassicism of the eighteenth century (19) and might have hastened its general appearance had it not been for the destruction of the cathedral in the Great Fire of 1666.

Old St Paul's (1640), Classical extension by Inigo Jones.

The 1620s-30s showed that Inigo Jones was not only very prolific but that he had the ability to work on a number of major projects simultaneously. Thus, under the direction of both James I and Charles I, Inigo Jones drew up a succession of plans for the rebuilding of Whitehall as a magnificent Italianate palace that, if completed, would stand comparison with the Louvre and, later, the palaces of Versailles. According to Sir John Summerson, historically the most important plan – dating from 1638 – would, if implemented, have involved abandoning the Banqueting House and incorporating a Vitruvian forum in the manner of Palladio as set out in his third book. Jones's 'forum' would be a large central court 300 ft (91 m) square, colonnaded in two storeys. On the park side to the west, it would lead to a chapel royal adjacent to the King's Court to the north and Queen's Court to the south, and to the east it would connect with the Great Hall – based on Constantine's basilica in Rome – followed by a circular court flanked by the separate private apartments of the King and Queen facing the river. The only palace comparable in size and magnificence would have been Philip II's Escorial (outside of Madrid) but even that would have been smaller in scale than the new Whitehall. To critics, Inigo Jones appears to have mastered the application of Classical motifs to a single bay and could extend his expertise to the design of a whole façade, but on a larger canvas his ideas were far less satisfactory. Since Jones "trained himself to think not in mass but in detail" (20), it was probably fortuitous that his gargantuan Whitehall Palace never got built. With the political upheavals of the 1640s-50s, the king simply ran out of funds and was more intent on saving his throne than on embarking on a grandiose building project.

The Short and Long Parliaments: 1640-1653

To raise money for an effective campaign against the Covenanters, Charles – in April 1640 – had no alternative but to recall Parliament but, since it refused to vote him the necessary funds for a Scottish campaign he dissolved it after less than a month. The Short Parliament, as it was called, was superseded by the Long Parliament that lasted from November 1640 to 1653. From the outset, parliamentarians were critical of Charles's past and current policies. Passed by Parliament in December 1641, the Grand Remonstrance condemned Charles's conduct throughout his entire reign, and in the same year Charles had to forgo tonnage and poundage, an important source of revenue. In an attempt to pacify Parliament, Charles marched into the House of Commons in January 4 1642 to arrest five of his principal opponents, but learning that they had already made their escape, Charles and his family fled to Hampton Court and Maria Henrietta escaped to Holland. Thereafter, the Civil War (1642-1648) divided the nation, and divided families for nearly seven years. "On one side was Charles I, insisting on his supremacy over Church and state. And on the other, parliamentary forces that believed the king's powers should be limited and that religion was a matter for individual conscience (providing it was Protestant), rather than royal decree" (21). In England, throughout the six years of the war, supporters of the monarch fought-it-out with Parliamentary troops, whereas in Scotland in 1648 Presbyterian forces took on the English Royalists. With both sides exhausted, hostilities ceased and at the beginning of 1649 Charles was put on trial and, from the Banqueting Hall of his Whitehall Palace was executed on January 30th.

Unfinished business

Both during the last nine years of Charles's reign and throughout the Commonwealth and Protectorate (1649-1660) very little, if any, buildings of architectural merit were constructed in London. The financial constraints of Parliament, the Civil Wars, and other priorities of government militated against investment in the built environment. The outbreak of Civil War in 1642 had put an end to Charles's dream of commissioning Inigo Jones to rebuild Whitehall and it was not until after the Restoration that redevelopment in due course became feasible (see chapter 6). Despite a substantial rate of economic growth in London, there were no attempts during the early seventeenth century either to replace London Bridge or to construct a second bridge over the Thames, say from the City or Westminster to the south bank. The medieval London Bridge measuring around 860 ft (260 m) in length and completed in 1209 thus remained in existence, despite its 20 small arches being unsuitable for easy river navigation and its 12 ft (4 m) width (after allowing for housing) being too narrow for uncongested traffic flows. Although the bridge could hardly have been conducive to economic development, London had to wait until the 1740's before a second bridge (Westminster Bridge) was built across the Thames, and until 1831 before the New London Bridge replaced its ancient predecessor (see chapters 7& 8). Neither were any new hospitals built in London during the early seventeenth century despite a succession of plagues and other endemic diseases. The English capital also had to make do with the ancient facilities of St. Thomas's and St. Bartholomew's hospitals (both of which - modernised over the centuries - remain in use today).

References

1. R. Porter, *London. A Social History*, Penguin Books, 1996, p 82.
2. Ibid, p 83.
3. Ibid, p 83.
4. B. Risebero, *The Story of Western Architecture*, Herbert Press, 3rd Edit., 2001, p 151.
5. R. Porter, *London. A Social History*, Penguin Books, 1996, p 8.
6. Sir John Summerson, *Architecture in Britain 1530-1830*, Yale University Press, 9th Edit., 1993, p 93.
7. Ibid, p 93.
8. Ibid, p 81.
9. Ibid, pp 81-2.

10. Ibid, p 77
11. Ibid, p 117.
12. Ibid, p 117.
13. Sir John Summerson, *Georgian London, Penguin, pp 31-32*I, pp 31-2.
14 D.Watkin, *English Architecture*, Thames & Hudson, 2001, p 100.
15 S. Jenkins, *Landlords to London. The Story of a Capital and its Growth*, Book Club Associates, 1975, p 424.
16 Sir John Summerson, *Architecture in Britain 1530-1830*, Yale University Press, 9th Edit., 1993, p 134.
17 D.Avery, *Georgian and Regency Architecture*, Chaucer Press, 2003, p 17
18 Sir John Summerson, *Architecture in Britain 1530-1830*, Yale University Press, 9th Edit., pp 122-4.
19 D. Watkin, *English Architecture*, Thames & Hudson, 2001, p 100.
20 Sir John Summerson, *Architecture in Britain 1530-1830*, Yale University Press, 9th Edit., p 128.
21. D.Starkey, *Monarchy. From the Middle Ages to Modernity*, Harper Press, 2006, p 117.

Chapter 6

Later-Stuart London: Wren and the rebuilding of the capital

Throughout the seventeenth century and into the eighteenth Stuart monarchs, both absolutist or constitutional, played a pivotal role in enhancing the urban fabric of London, which with its population of about 400,000 in 1650 was second only to Paris as the largest urban area in Europe. By 1700, with a population of 575,000, London had become the largest metropolis in the Christian world and was expanding rapidly beyond its ancient walls. As vividly described by Roy Porter "the east side was assuming a character all of its own, as an industrial suburb dominated by shipping, wharves and boat building; and [to the west] Westminster ….was coming into its own as a town, as distinct from being greensward planted with an abbey, a royal precinct and a lustrous border of palaces. Indeed, regarding developments west, West End begins to be a more apt term than Westminster" (1). By the mid-seventeenth century, the capital's extra-mural population was three times as great as the number residing in the City itself. However, like demographic change in Paris, the increase in population was not attributable to any significant change in birth and death rates but was due exclusively to migration. However, in contrast to Paris and all other cities in the *ancien régime*, London was both a national capital and a major centre of commerce and industry. It duly attracted an inflow of an enormous population from the rest of southern England seeking employment in administration, the law, the church, in commerce and industry, and in a host of semi-skilled and unskilled manual occupations. London, though every bit as environmentally squalid as Paris, differed from the French capital by experiencing not only the Great Plague of 1665 in which around 80,000 of her population perished, but also a major conflagration (the Great Fire) in 1666 which destroyed about four-fifths of the medieval city within three days.

The Spatial Growth of London in the late-Sixteenth Century

After the Great Fire of London 1666 development was of two distinct forms. First, in the West End and on the outer fringes of the City unaffected by the Great Fire, there was a spate of development involving the construction of royal palaces, town and suburban mansions, squares and terraced housing in response to the fashionable predilections of the monarch, aristocracy and merchant classes. Second, in the City, redevelopment often took pride of place over new development largely as a result of economic necessity rather than aesthetic or environmental appeal. There was a desperate need to rebuild as much of the capital as possible in the aftermath of the Great Fire, but redevelopment was not in response to the requirements of the monarch, aristocracy and other wealthy patrons, but was intended to satisfy the needs of the church, the Corporation of the City of London and the growing bourgeois class of bankers and merchants, and was promoted, though not necessarily funded by the Crown.

The French and Dutch Connections

In England, the relationships between the monarchy and the church, and the monarchy and its subjects during the second-half of the seventeenth century to some extent replicated those in France. Both Charles II and James II – like their French cousin Louis XIV - believed in the "divine right of kings" and were not immune from suspending Parliament when they were unable to gain support for their more contentious policies. It might have been expected, therefore, that Charles II (r. 1660-1685) – following the execution of his father and eleven years of commonwealth government (1649-1660) – would be willing to rule as a constitutional monarch and not push through contentious policies that would fail to have the support of parliament. However, although Charles was checked by a stronger parliament than English monarchs had been accustomed to, in exasperation he took over the reins of government himself to ensure the succession of his Catholic brother James. Under James II (r. 1685-1688) England became a far more absolute state than hitherto and, with a Catholic king on the throne, it was thought that it would not be long before it would closely resemble Louis XIV's France. To avert this possibility, William of Orange and his Stuart wife, Anne, were invited to take over the throne in 1688 when it was deemed that James had abdicated after fleeing to France. Constitutional monarchy was introduced and the rights of Protestants secured, though the reign of William and Mary took England into major wars on the Continent on a scale not matched for centuries. Constitutional monarchy was well established by the time Anne came to the throne in 1702, but almost the whole of her reign (1702-1715) was inflicted by a deliberating war against Louis's France and her allies.

The Slow Road to Constitutional Monarch and the Shaping of London

The Convention Parliament, 1660-61

After eleven years of Commonwealth rule, an elected Convention Parliament was constituted in March 1660 to oversee the return of monarchical government. It soon became aware that, while still in exile in the Netherlands, Charles II (as he was known by his followers since his father's execution in 1649) issued the Declaration of Breda on April 4 promising – among a raft of detailed concessions – an amnesty for life, a just land settlement, liberty of conscience, and the payment of arrears to the army. On May 1, parliament declared Charles rightfully king since 1649, and on 25 May Charles landed in Dover and entered London on May 29. Through the medium of Acts of Indemnity and Oblivion, the Convention Parliament duly implemented most of the pledges that Charles had made at Breda but, with regard to religion, Parliament – packed with Presbyterians – was unwilling to legitimise the Church of England (as Charles had demanded) let alone the Church of Rome (as he might secretly have desired). After the election of 1661, the Cavalier Parliament came into existence but, in contrast to its predecessor, the House of Commons was now dominated by members supportive of the monarch and faithful to the Church of England.

Somerset House (1661-2), Strand entrance based on designs by Inigo Jones possibly inspired by Bramante.

Soon after Charles returned to England, and before he had time to give serious consideration to the development or redevelopment of royal palaces, the Queen Mother, Henrietta Maria - having recently returned from exile in France – re-occupied her old riverside home, Somerset House, and funded the construction of the building's New Gallery, quite possibly based on designs by Inigo Jones although there is no reliable evidence to support this. Built in 1661-1662, the gallery was in the style of Bramante and was supported by rusticated arches, replicated in Sir William Chambers' reconstruction of the Strand front of the building in 1778 (2). Following the Queen

Mother's return to France in 1665, Catharine of Braganza – betrothed to Charles in 1662 – often retired to Somerset House and it was there that she permanently resided after the king's death in 1685.

The Clarendon Parliament, 1661-79

Throughout most of the reign of Charles II, religion and foreign affairs were pre-eminent political issues, and no more so that during his first few years on the throne when Edward Hyde, the Earl of Clarendon and Lord Chancellor, exercised considerable influence over the development of policy. In religious matters, three Acts constituted what is often referred to as the "Clarendon Code" first, the Act of Uniformity of 1662 stipulating that the holder of a church office must have been ordained by a bishop, must use the Book of Common Prayer, and must obey the canons of ecclesiastical law; second, the Conventical Act of 1664 prohibiting all assemblies of worship other than those of the Church of England; and third, the Five Mile Act of 1665 forbidding expelled (non-conformist) ministers from settling within five miles of any corporate town, or earning their living by teaching in any private or public school.

In foreign policy events were more troublesome than religious issues largely because Clarendon enthusiastically embraced the policy of the Common-wealth in being pro-French and anti-Spanish. He sold Dunkirk to France for £250,000 and, to unsettle Spain which had lost the suzerainty of Portugal in 1640, oversaw the marriage of Charles to Catharine of Braganza of Portugal in 1662 in return for a dowry of £350,000 plus the island of Bombay, Tangiers and the coast of north-west Africa. Clarendon also played a major role in establishing hostile relations with the

Netherlands. Motivated almost entirely by colonial and commercial considerations (and in the trail of the First Dutch War of 1652-1654), the Second Dutch War was waged from 1664 to 1667 in which New Amsterdam was taken by the English in 1664 and renamed New York, and the English navy defeated the Dutch fleet off Lowestoft in 1665. However, later in the same year, Dutch ships under the command of De Ruyter, entered the Medway River at Chatham, burnt English warships and carried-off the English flagship, The *Royal Charles*, as a prize. Overall, Clarendon's policies were unpopular and it was widely believed that he had acquired much of his wealth by all sorts of dishonest means. Possible unfairly, he was even believed, through his ineffectual administration, to have been responsible for the Plague of London that claimed 120,000 lives in 1665 and the Fire of London that rendered 200,000 people homeless in 1666. More pertinently, he was increasingly disliked by Charles, and in 1666 was duly dismissed and fled to France where he died seven years later.

King Charles's Block, Greenwich (begun 1662), by James Webb

Despite religion and foreign affairs dominating the attention of the Cavalier Parliament during the early years of Charles's reign, the king was determined to downplay policy weaknesses and present an image of pomp and grandeur to his subjects in the hope that this would enhance the popularity and legitimacy of his rule. In 1662, Charles was therefore eager to reconstruct Greenwich Palace and thus commissioned James Webb, a disciple of Jones, to produce plans for an arrangement of new buildings that would replace the old and deteriorating palace, Placentia that had been built for Henry VII, c. 1500-6. The proposed building was intended to consist of "a main block with an applied portico in the centre surmounted by a drum and two wings, and two wings extending [northwards] to the river" (3). Inspired by Palladio's design for the Villa Tressino at Meledo or the Villa Rotunda at Vicenza, the composition of the main block with its central dome would have been something new for England had it been realised (4). However, a shortage of resources after the Great Fire of 1666 forced the abandonment of most of the project by 1669, but what was built is truly distinctive. The west wing, later known as King Charles's Block, is a "large scale single unit, tied together at the centre and ends by a giant order, and no part could be added or taken way without destroying the conception of the whole" (5). Truly a Renaissance building, the west block "is beyond question the most accomplished building, in its mastery of architectural forms, to be erected in England in the 1660's" (6).

Although Charles showed a desire to decentralise his court to Greenwich during the early years of his reign, Webb at this time made many drawings for the rebuilding of Whitehall Palace, some derived from proposed rebuilding schemes drawn-up prior to the

Civil War. At the time of the Restoration, the palace consisted of little more than the Banqueting House connected to a number of rambling Tudor lodges and galleries running down to the Thames. Inspired by plans left by Inigo Jones, Webb proposed that the east façade of the Banqueting House (facing the river) would be connected to a central portico which in turn would be joined to a replica of the Banqueting House which would, with appropriate internal fittings, serve as a chapel. From the eastern side of this north-south block, two wings either side of an open courtyard would extend to the river, but on the western side two smaller enclosed courtyards would occupy a stretch of Whitehall enabling private apartments to extend from the main block to a secondary north-south block overlooking St. James's Park.

Proposed Whitehall Palace (1660s), by James Webb. It was intended to rival Louis XIV's Louvre in Paris

Whilst Webb's proposals were not accepted largely because of the high cost of developing Whitehall, the improvement of the park itself had preoccupied the king since his accession. He not only extended it by 36 acres, but greatly enhanced its attributes in accordance with the designs of Louis XIV's landscape gardener, Andre le Notre. Fruit trees were planted, the park was stocked with many deer and exotic birds, an aviary was added that was to become Birdcage Walk, and a broad avenue, the Mall, was laid out, 0.6 miles (1 km) in length and 54yds (50 m) in width. Though shorter and narrower than its French equivalent, the Champs-Elysees, and essentially a tree-lined promenade rather than a general or ceremonial thoroughfare, it was nevertheless one of the very few new streets of any length to be developed in a straight line in Restoration London.

Eltham Lodge (1663-4), by Hugh May

Not only is it clear that religious issues and foreign affairs had little adverse impact on the development of royal palaces during the Restoration, but the accumulation of private wealth resulting from service to the Crown and from the expansion of commercial activity at home and overseas fuelled the construction of sumptuous mansions in the capital and its environs. Eltham Lodge in southeast London was built for John Shaw in 1663-1664 on land leased from the Crown. It was designed by Hugh May who combined elements of Dutch Palladianism with the style of Sir Roger Pratt. While simple and refined in design, Eltham Lodge is neither Classical in the manner of Inigo Jones nor vernacular. It is a double-storey brick house with stone dressings, Ionic pilasters, an architrave cornice, and a central pediment in stone (7). Burlington House on the north side of Piccadilly was commissioned by Sir John Denham and work began on its construction in 1664. With its anachronistic H-plan, the building was reminiscent of a Tudor or Jacobean mansion, but before it was completed in this style it was sold to the 1st Earl of Burlington in 1667 who employed Hugh May to take over the design work from a relatively minor architect and complete the building according to Classical parameters.

Clarendon House (1664-7), by Sir Roger Pratt.

Possibly even more imposing, Clarendon House - opposite St. James's church Piccadilly - was built for Edward Hyde, Lord Clarendon and Lord Chancellor, and masterfully designed by Sir Roger Pratt. Built between1664-1667, Clarendon House was the architect's most influential house. With wings projecting forward at right angles from the main building, two storeys of roughly equal height, a roof concealed behind a balustrade extended around the front facades, and a domed lantern crowning the central face, "Clarendon House was among the first classical houses in London and easily the most striking of them" (8). However, it was unfortunate that, after being dismissed as Lord Chancellor, Lord Clarendon vacated his house and fled to France in 1667. The building thenceforth became inadequately maintained and was demolished in 1685 making way for the development of Bond Street, Dover Street and Albemarle Street in the early eighteenth century (see chapter 7). Also on the northern side of Piccadilly, Berkeley House was commissioned by Lord Berkeley of Stratton, a Royalist commander in the Civil War. Designed by Hugh May and built in 1665, the mansion was quintessentially Palladian in style, with its quadrant colonnades connecting the main block to its service wings that protruded at either end outward towards the street, and its pedimented centre piece crowning its nine-window fain façade (9). As influential on the design of town mansions as Pratt's Clarendon House, it too has not survived to the present day having been burnt down in 1733, but strips of land either side of the mansion – sold-off after the death of Lord Berkeley in 1668 – were subsequently developed as Berkeley Street and Stratton Street (10).

Despite differences in scale and design detail, the

204

Piccadilly mansions of the Restoration shared the principal attributes of the Parisian *hôtel*. Each had a forecourt, each had a main block with projecting side wings, and each had a gated-wall across the street-side of the forecourt to provide privacy and security. Notwithstanding the magnificence of the stand-alone urban mansion or even the prestigious residential street, the most visually imposing form of planned development is the square, developed partly to increase the wealth of speculative landlords and partly to enhance the quality of life of the urban resident. Although the Earl of Bedford and William Newton were active in developing their estates north of the Strand in the 1630's (see chapter 5), it was not until after the Civil War that large areas in present-day Bloomsbury and St. James's became the focus of urban expansion. The first such development was Bloomsbury Square (then known as Southampton Square) and its surrounds. As early as 1636, Thomas Wrothesley, 4th Earl of Southampton, had intended to undertake profitable development on his Bloomsbury manor, but his plans were thwarted by his failure to obtain a licence from Parliament. However, during the latter years of the Commonwealth, he was permitted to build a mansion, somewhat in the style of Inigo Jones – in the midst of his estate and, in the early 1660's obtained consent to lay out a square to the south of it. With rows of distinguished brick houses, surrounding a semi-public garden in the centre, Southampton Square was "the first open space in London to be so designated" (11), and set the pattern for the development of other squares across the western edge of London throughout the rest of the seventeenth century and beyond. To fund development, the 4th Earl granted building licences to lessees at low ground rents, on condition that they build a house, or houses of

205

character, at their own expense with the proviso that, at the end of the lease, the property would revert to the ground landlord. Recognising that the square was not enough in itself, the 4th Earl pioneered adjacent development to demonstrate that it was both financially feasible and socially desirable to include, within his overall plan, a market and a number of smaller less-expensive residential streets, undoubtedly an example of contemporary planning at its best.

The Cabal: 1667-77

In 1667 Charles decided that, instead of conferring enormous power on any one individual minister and risk unpopularity himself if policies failed, it would be politically more expedient to spread responsibilities among different high-status parliamentarians. He thus looked to the Cabal (the acronym for his leading ministers; Clifford, Arlington, Buckingham, Ashley and Lauderdale) to frame and implement governmental policy. With each minister being responsible to the king and to him only, new policies evolved within the areas of religion and foreign affairs, though their implementation often led to unforeseen circumstances. In religious matters, Ashley recommended the enactment of the Comprehension Bill of 1670 to accommodate some Presbyterians in the church and tolerate other non-conformists, and the king concurred since the Bill, if enacted, might have paved the way to the toleration of Catholics to whom he was empathetic. However, the Bill was not only rejected by Parliament but Parliament renewed the conventicle Act of 1664 and made its conditions more stringent.

In 1672 Charles, on his own account, therefore side-lined Parliament by using the royal prerogative to implement a Declaration of Indulgence. Charles, after all, had a Catholic mother (Henrietta Maria), he had married a Catholic (Catharine of Braganza) and now wished to prepare the ground for his brother James's reception into the Roman Catholic Church and duly suspended all acts that imposed political or religious restrictions on Catholics and – for that matter – Protestant non-conformists. Not only was this unpopular, but arguably unconstitutional and illegal. It was now becoming clear that both the king and his Cabal was having little effect on religious and constitutional policy, and this inability to control events became more pronounced in 1673 when Parliament voted against the suspension of penal statutes in matters ecclesiastical, and requested the king to withdraw his Declaration of Indulgence. Although all ministers, except Arlington, advised Charles to stand his ground, the king was fully aware of the extent of Parliamentary opposition to the declaration, and therefore complied with Parliament's request. A further blow to the king's authority was the Test Act of 1673. This countered Charles's increasing tendency to approve the appointment of Roman Catholics to offices under the Crown by stipulating that no person would be employed in such a capacity unless he had taken the sacrament according to the rites of the Church of England and made a declaration against transubstantiation. The Act not only led to Clifford resigning as Lord Treasurer and Buckingham being dismissed from the Chancellorship, but Charles's brother, James, Duke of York, was relieved of his position as High Admiral. Arlington, meanwhile, took little part in public affairs, and only Lauderdale retained his influence but this was almost entirely confined to

207

Anglo-Scottish affairs.

All members of the Cabal, nevertheless, stamped their mark on foreign policy. In the 1670, Clifford and Arlington, together with Lord Arundel of Wardour and Sir Richard Billings, signed – on behalf of Charles – a secret Treaty of Dover, a document counter-signed by Colbert on behalf of Louis XIV. Under the treaty, Charles would declare himself a Catholic, receive £100,000 from Louis and 6,000 troops in the pay of France, and both countries would wage war on the Netherlands. If successful, England would gain the islands of Wallcheren and Cadsand and the port of Sluys as spoils of victory. Buckingham – like Ashley and Lauderdale – knew nothing of this agreement, but was nevertheless in favour of an alliance against the Netherlands. Therefore, to further his war-aims and without any reference to Charles becoming a Catholic or to French largesse, he negotiated a second and open treaty with France that was not only signed by Colbert but approved by the whole of the Cabal. The Third Dutch War eventually broke out in 1672 and lasted to 1674. Following an indecisive and bitter engagement between the English and Dutch navies off Southwold, a French army under Louis XIV – in coalition with 6,000 troops of Charles's illegitimate son, the Duke of Monmouth, resoundedly defeated the Dutch and occupied three of the seven provinces of the Netherlands. However, the situation was soon countered when Charles's nephew, William of Orange – having only just gained power in the Netherlands – opened the dykes and forced the French to flee for their lives. Following this debacle, Charles prorogued Parliament for 15 months ruling temporarily as an absolute monarch.

Although Charles's religious and foreign policies may or may not have been popular at the time of the

Cabal, it was certain that – with the government's debt amounting to £1,300,000 – his financial policy was a cause of major concern. Normally, the debt should not have been so great since it was customary for the government to anticipate its annual tax revenue, and against this borrow from goldsmiths to fund ongoing expenditure prior to the receipt of revenue. In acting as banks, goldsmiths accepted money at a given rate of interest and lent it to borrowers at a higher rate. At the beginning of the 1670's, the rate of interest paid to goldsmiths was 5 per cent, and by the government 12 per cent, but in 1672 against the advice of Ashley, the Chancellor, but supported by Clifford and Lauderdale, Charles – in attempting to reduce the possibility of national bankruptcy – issued a royal order allowing goldsmiths only 6 per cent, which in turn meant that depositors would receive only 1 per cent. Although this action might have been seen by some to have been financially expedient, it also struck a severe blow at the credibility of government out of all proportion to any gained achieved.

Despite the very great problems relating to religion, foreign affairs and particularly finance, the King, his Cabal and Parliament – to their credit – were willing to lay down the ground rules under which London would be rebuilt after the Great Fire and to fund a spate of construction activity in the capital for a number of years after the conflagration. They recognised that destroyed or damaged buildings needed to be replaced or repaired as soon as possible if the economic, religious and social life of the capital was to regain its stability let alone its vibrancy. Very soon after the four-day fire had died out on 5 September 1666, rebuilding schemes came flooding in. In his master plan, Christopher Wren – Savilian Professor of Astronomy at Oxford (1661-1673) – proposed that the whole of the burnt area should be cleared and re-built – almost in stellar fashion – to provide "wide streets and large open spaces, with new St. Paul's and Royal Exchange serving as the principal of several focal points" (12).

Other schemes by Dr Robert Hooke and John Evelyn also called for a system of vistas and square, but none of these grand projects – however much they might have appealed to the king – were acceptable to the Corporation of the City of London. The corporation's first priority was to encourage each property – owner to rebuild as soon as possible on their existing sites to enable businesses to resume trading with minimum delay. The alternative – complete redevelopment – would have been too costly and too time-consuming, and would have involved a massive redistribution of property, with inevitable disputes over rights of ownership. Though Haussmann was commissioned to undertake the large scale redevelopment of Paris two centuries later, the time was not ripe in London to embark on such a major exercise. Unlike mid-nineteenth century Paris, seventeenth-century London could not draw upon the resources of an Industrial Revolution to reconstruct its built environment, but Wren's plans nevertheless provided the inspiration for the layout of Washington in the early nineteenth century.

It should not be assumed, however, that *in situ* development across the City of London went hand-in-hand with a *laisser-faire* approach to urban renewal. Under the Act for the Rebuilding of London, 1667 – drawn-up jointly by the Privy Council and City authorities – three important courses of action were implemented: first, the rearrangement of some of the worst features of the layout of London as it was before the Great Fire; second, the partial standardisation of new buildings particularly to reduce the risk of fire; and

210

third, the raising of money for the development and redevelopment of public buildings by a tax on coal (13).

Under the provisions of the 1667 Act, commissioners opened-up the congested but fire-damaged quayside from Blackfriars to the Tower, stipulated that new river warehouses must be pitched-back from the waterfront; and transformed accessibility in the City by creating a new north-south thoroughfare – New Queen Street – that linked the Guildhall to the Thames; and widened west-east routes such as Cheapside, Poultry and Cornhill. Also, to facilitate accessibility, fire-damaged gateways through London Wall, notably Ludgate, Newgate and Aldersgate, were reconstructed in 1672, and although Temple Bar – marking the boundary between the City and Westminster – escaped the ravages of the Great Fire, it too was rebuilt in 1672. With plans drawn-up by Christopher Wren, Temple Bar was not only built from Portland stone (in contrast to brick employed in the other reconstructed gateways), but was designed in the Baroque style, whereas the other gateways continued to be essentially Gothic. Though Temple Bar was demolished in 1880, and reconstructed by the wealthy brewer Sir Henry Meux as a gateway to his estate at Theobalds Park, Hertfordshire, the building was acquired by the City of London Corporation and Temple Bar Trust in 2003, and reconstructed once again in the City at the entrance of Paternoster Square, north of St. Paul's Cathedral.

Temple Bar (1672), by Sir Christopher Wren

Apart from enhancing accessibility, it was also necessary to prevent construction from proceeding in a disorderly and hazardous manner. Building regulations and safety standards therefore demanded that new houses should have external walls built from brick and stone (rather than timber and plaster), fixed the precise thickness of walls at various heights, and regulated both the height of ceilings and the height of the whole building. Only houses of four storeys could be constructed in "high" and "principal" streets, while three-storey dwellings were confined to secondary streets, and two-storey dwellings were hidden away in side streets. A further class of house, one that did not front the street but which lay behind it, was also restricted to four storeys (14). However, such regulations did not lead to conformity in design. The stylistic attributes of the house were determined by the taste of owner and the skills of the builder and whether he was essentially a bricklayer, mason or carpenter (15).

A plethora of further measures introduced by Parliament brought much improvement to the London environment and the safety of its citizens. The Sewage and Paving Act 1671 introduced the cambering of streets and raised pavements that brought about the end of central drainage ditches in favour of side drainage, and later – to further reduce the risk of fire – legislation prohibited the construction of overhanging buildings, while the minimum width of side streets was set at 14 ft (4.3m) and alleys 10 ft (3.1m), measures also designed to avert the risk of fire.

As with most large scale renewal schemes, the availability of finance presented problems. Thus in order to collect revenue and fund the redevelopment of the infrastructure after the Great Fire, the Corporation of London, as a matter of priority, set up its Excise Office in Southampton Fields, its Hearth Tax Office in Leadenhall Street, its Post Office in Brydges Street, and the Custom House in Mark Lane (16). However, it was a source of revenue authorised by central government, the sea coal levy, which probably had the greatest long-term effect on the built environment of the City. Initially, at one shilling per ton, the levy facilitated the reconstruction of wharves, warehouses, markets and prisons but, when trebled, it funded the reconstruction of the City churches and St. Paul's. Notwithstanding the plethora of regulations that was introduced, and the very great need to raise substantial sums of money for development, it is remarkable how quickly the City of London was rebuilt. By 1668, 1200 new houses had been completed, in 1669 around 1,600 more were under scaffolding, while work was already underway or was soon to begin on a range of commercial and ecclesiastically buildings.

Of considerable importance to the economy of London, Thomas Gresham's Royal Exchange (built 1566-1571) was reconstructed between 1667 and 1671 by the City's surveyor Edward Jarman assisted by Thomas Cartwright. Funded by the City, the building retained the essential attributes of its Elizabethan predecessor, namely a two storey arcaded courtyard in which merchants and financiers could go about their business. In reconstructing the Exchange, the opportunity was seized to increase the size of the building. Donated by City livery companies the upper arcade, comprising a series of niches containing statues of monarchs, was constructed around the courtyard, and, funded by the Merchant Adventurers, a statue of Charles II by Grinling Gibbons was placed centre stage. On the east-side of the building, facing the street, the architects gave the Exchange "a grand entrance façade, with a triumphal arch, rising through two storeys, [and] at its centre over the arch [there] was a three stage tower recalling Gresham's original" (17). Although the Royal Exchange was burnt down again in 1838 and subsequently rebuilt, its entrance façade retains many of the features of the former building.

Custom House (1669-71), by Sir John Denham and Hugh May

With reconstruction managed by the Royal Office of Works, and with the design traditionally attributed to Wren, a new two-storey Custom House was built between 1669 and 1671, possible under the supervision of the office's Surveyor, Sir John Denham and its Comptroller, High May. With Wren just beginning work on St. Paul's, he may not have had the time or inclination to fully focus his attention on a new Custom House. Indeed, "the handling and proportion of the orders [of this building]... Tuscan and Ionic... appear to be rather fumbling" (18), and since its three-sided courtyard (with its wings running back to Thames Street) is reminiscent of Jacob van Campen's town hall in Amsterdam (1655), its style is arguably more-Dutch than early-Wren. Thus, it would not be surprising had the Custom House not been designed by the master himself but by one of his deputies (19).

Apothecaries Hall (1672), by Thomas Locke

Because as many as 45 company halls were burnt down during the Great Fire, and since a great amount of corporate capital had been invested in these buildings, the halls that replaced them were, externally, simple

215

and typically 'artisan', but relied on private munificence to provide them with lavish interiors. In the process of reconstruction, companies – in order to keep wealth in the City – tended to rely overwhelmingly on local architects and craftsmen to undertake design-work, for example Edward Jarman probably designed the Drapers', Fishmongers', and Haberdashers', Halls; John Oliver produced the design for Skinners' Hall; Thomas Lock built the Apothecaries' Hall; and John Caine designed Brewers' Hall and Tallowchandlers' Hall. The reconstructed Fishermans' Hall was stylistically alone in boasting a Dutch rather than an artisanal façade. Over time, most company halls have been either altered beyond recognition or destroyed (not least during the Second World War). Similar in some ways to the company hall, the Herald's College (or College of Arms) identifies with the world of commerce as well as with hereditary imagery. Designed by the bricklayer Maurice Emmett, and built between 1646 and 1694, the college is a somewhat crude building with old-fashioned pilasters adorned by Flemish brooches. Originally a rectangular structure around a central courtyard, the riverside façade was demolished during the building of Queen Victoria Street in the nineteenth century, leaving an open courtyard exposed to the street, with three wings.

College of Arms (1646-94), by Maurice Emmett

Four years after the Great Fire, Parliament passed the Rebuilding Act authorising the reconstruction of 52 of the 85 churches destroyed in the conflagration, an enormous project facilitated by funds derived from a £3 per ton tax on sea coal and from the parishes by means of donations from individuals or City companies. Without having any Protestant churches on which to base their designs, Christopher Wren (appointed Surveyor-General of the King's Works in 1669) and his associate, Dr Robert Hooke, built a variety of churches in the City and on its western fringe between 1670 and 1682, of which only 26 complete or partly damaged buildings remain (20). Because of the need to protect existing land ownership after the fire and to facilitate high density development, churches could only be rebuilt on their existing – often cramped – sites and this constrained innovation; indeed some church facades were invisible from the street.

Wren's church plans fall into three main groups:

fairly large rectangular buildings, smaller buildings that are entirely centralised, and buildings that are partly rectangular and partly centralised. The former group usually contains a nave and aisles, often with side galleries setting a fashion that was to last for over two centuries in keeping with Protestant practice, and while some longitudinal churches have a clerestory, others do not.

Table 6.1

Wren's extant London Churches

Church	Built	Steeple
St. Vedast, Foster Lane	1670-71	1709-12
St. Mary-at-Hill	1670	-
St. Edmund King and Martyr	1670-76	1708*
St. Mary-le Bow, Cheapside	1670-79+	1678-80
St. Michael Cornhill	1670-80	1715-22*
St. Bride, Fleet Street	1670-72	1701-02
St. Magnus Martyr, Lower Thames Street	1671-76	1705
St. Lawrence, Jewry	1671-77	-

St. Nicholas, Cole Abbey	1671-77	-
St. Stephen, Wallbrook	1672-79	1717
St. James, Garlickhythe	1676-83	1714-17*
St. Anne and St. Agnes, Gresham Street	1677-80+	-
St. Benet, Paul's Wharf	1677-83+	-
St. Martin, Ludgate	1677-84+	-
St. Peter, Cornhill	1677-84	-
Christ Church, Newgate Street	1677-87	1704
St. Mary, Abchurch	1681-86	-
St. Mary, Aldermary	1681-90	1702-04
St. Alban	1682-88	-
St. Margaret Lothbury	1683-92+	1700
St. Andrew, Holborn Circus	1684-86	-
St. Margaret Pattens	1684-89	1698-1702*
St. Andrew by the Wardrobe	1685-94	
St. Mary, Abchurch	1681-86	-

St. Michael Paternoster Royal	1686-94	1698-94

To the west of the City:

St. Clement Danes	1680-82	1719
St. James, Piccadilly	1682-84	-

Source: M.T.Whinney. `Wren', Thames & Hudson, 1998

+ Designed by Wren in collaboration with Robert Hooke

*Steeple influenced or designed by Nicholas Hawksmoor

The more prominent longitudinal churches commissioned during the Cabal are St. Dunstan, a damaged Gothic structure delicately patched-up by Wren (1670-71, St. Vedast, (1670-73), St. Michael Cornhill (1670-77), St. Edmund King and Martyr (1670-79), St. Brides (1670-84), St Magnus the Martyr, St Nicholas Cole Abbey (1671-77) and St. Lawrence Jewry (1671-77), the last- named being a particularly large parish church, devoid of aisles and in contrast to the other churches in this group, with an east façade adorned with four Corinthian half columns supporting a pediment, with pilasters at the angles (21). The second group represents Wren's desire to construct centrally-planned churches. Except for St. Mary at Hill (1670-76) and St. Mary le Bow (1670-80) all of his centrally-planned churches were started after the construction of St. Paul's had commenced (1676) and were doubtless inspired by it. The third group of churches includes

220

those in which Wren experimented with the application of a centralised plan, very probably in anticipation of the reconstruction of St. Paul's. In St. Benet Fink (1670-75, demolished 1842), columns arranged in the shape of an hexagon supported an oval dome with its lantern, and its plan was that of an elongated decagon, its design being possible modelled on that of Bellini's Sant'Andrea al Quirinale in Rome. However, only in the case of St. Stephen Walbrook (1672-80), was there a complete fusion between a rectangular and centrally – planned church. It was a costly building to construct because of its complexity. "Its diaphanous interior space in which a dome floats on eight arches and eight columns is a miraculous combination of two planning types, the aisled nave and the centralised plan" (22).

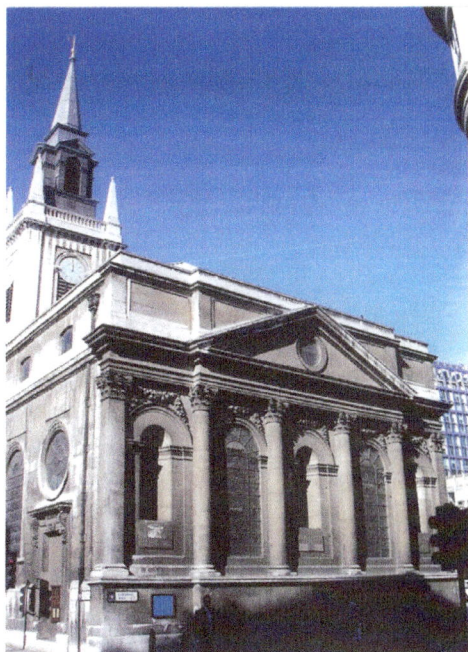

St Lawrence Jewry (1671-7), by Sir Christopher Wren

St Mary-le-Bow (1670-80), by Sir Christopher Wren

The time was now ripe for Wren to finalise his plans for the reconstruction of St. Paul's. Six years earlier before a start was made on St. Stephen Walbrook, the Great Fire had left the choir of St. Paul's in ruins but part of the old Romanesque nave, cased by Inigo Jones earlier in the seventeenth century, was still standing as was Jones's great portico at the western end, albeit badly calcinated. In May 1668, Dean Sancroft wrote to Wren in Oxford (where he was still Professor of Astronomy) informing him that the third pillar from the west had collapsed, suggesting that Jones's casing of the exterior had not been properly keyed to the old wall. Thenceforth Wren became responsible for work on St. Paul's, the commission being given to him by the Dean and Chapter, though the money for rebuilding would be sourced by the tax on sea coal. Wren immediately reported that St. Paul's was in a completely ruinous condition, and in July 1668 a Royal Warrant ordered the final demolition and clearing of the east end, the old choir and the central tower, while the west end was to be taken down carefully and its stone retained in the event that it could be used again (23).

In 1669, Wren produced his First Model for the reconstruction of St. Paul's. It consisted of a rectangular choir with a large domed square vestibule at the west end and, submitted in 1670, it immediately received the king's approval (24). However, its design was highly controversial, it related to a relatively small and curious building planned with the knowledge that not much money was available. A rectangle, which was intended for worship, was flanked by loggias on the ground floor, making the interior narrow and dark, but at first floor level it widened with galleries occupying the space above the loggias and lit by round-headed windows. The design was particularly criticised, not least, by Sir Roger Pratt, a fellow architect, who pointed-out that space was wasted on useless porticoes, the dome was in the west and not over the centre of the building, it significantly deviated in other ways from the traditional cathedral form, and suggested that it was not a grand enough replacement for Old St. Paul's. In response to these criticisms, Wren submitted further drawings to the king.

As an outcome, Wren was re-commissioned in 1673 to resume work on the rebuilding of St. Paul's. His new proposal – illustrated by his wooden Giant Model - was partly based on Michelangelo's unexecuted project for St. Peter's, and partly on Francois Mansart's abortive design for an extension to the Cathedral of Saint-Denis. But in the words of Margaret Whinney, "the plan was a complete novelty, for the building was in essence in the form of a Greek cross with four equal arms plus an extension to the west, the arms were joined by concave walls, and over the centre of the church was a dome carried on eight piers" (25). Its dome, with a diameter of 120 ft (36 m), would have been only 17 ft (5m) smaller than that of St. Peter's while, at the western end of the building, a substantial pedimented portico dominated by giant Corinthian columns lead to a vestibule with a smaller dome, echoing Sangallo's design for the Roman basilica (26). The Great Model – that for long has been on display in St Paul's - would undoubtedly have produced a stunning masterpiece, and Charles was so impressed with the proposed cathedral that he rewarded Wren with a knighthood.

The Protestant clergy, however, though that the proposed building was unsuitable for their liturgical needs since it was too closely modelled on a style of architecture that had evolved in Catholic Europe: the Baroque. "To them, the essence of a cathedral lay in the traditional Latin cross form, in which daily services could be held in the choir, and those for a larger congregation could use the nave" (27), and this would have been impossible in a cathedral with a centralised plan derived based on the Great Model. Also, money was scarce. It would have been prudent to have funded a building that could be built in stages, for example, the choir first and, then as more money became available, progressing gradually westwards toward the nave, but Wren's plans were not suitable for this form of construction" (28).

Ever persistent, Sir Christopher Wren submitted yet a third plan for the king's approval in 1675 and, on 14 May of that year, his designs were approved by both royal warrant and, more crucially, by the Dean and

Chapter of St. Paul's. In essence, the Warrant Design was predicated on a Latin-cross, with a choir of three bays and a nave of five. At the west of the nave there was a large projecting portico, and to the east of the choir, a small apse was incorporated into a half-bay. Between the choir and the nave, porticoed transepts – each of three bays – were projected to the north and south, while at the crossing, eight piers supported a tall colonnaded drum, a small ribbed-dome and a tall steeple (29). It is quite probable that, in order to obtain the approval of the clergy and to get work underway, the Warrant Design was very much a copy of a plan that predated his assembly of the Great Model. In accordance with the warrant, Wren was free to undertake piecemeal changes to his design during the cause of construction and thus, in an attempt to regain some of the flavour of the Great Model, he dispensed with the planned steeple and shortened the nave to three bays. With the foundation stone laid on 21 June 1675, work continued for three decades until the cathedral was completed in 1710.

St Paul's Cathedral (1675-1710), by Sir Christopher Wren

From soon after the completion of St.Paul's, the cathedral has been administered by its Dean whose department is accommodated in the Dean's Court in St Paul's Churchyard. Dating from 1670, the wide redbrick three-storey building has unusually large windows, more Dutch than England, and although some have argued that it is based on designs by Wren the evidence is far from conclusive.

Dean's Court (1670), attributed to Wren

Not only to provide a memorial of the Great Fire, but also to stimulate the reconstruction of the City of London after the conflagration, Parliament commissioned the erection of the Monument close to the source of the fire in Pudding Lane. Built between 1671 and 1676, the structure was designed by Sir Christopher Wren and Dr Robert Hooke, while the responsibility for its construction was placed in the hands of the Land Committee of the Corporation of London. Preceding the erection of a similar stand-alone monumental columns in other great cities such as Paris more than a century later, the Monument is a great

Doric column constructed of Portland stone and is 202 ft (61.6 m) high. After a great amount of controversy about the design of its summit, the Corporation settled on Hooke's flaming urn of bronze gilt symbolising the Great Fire, as opposed to a statue of King Charles II or a great copper ball surrounded by flames as preferred by Wren.

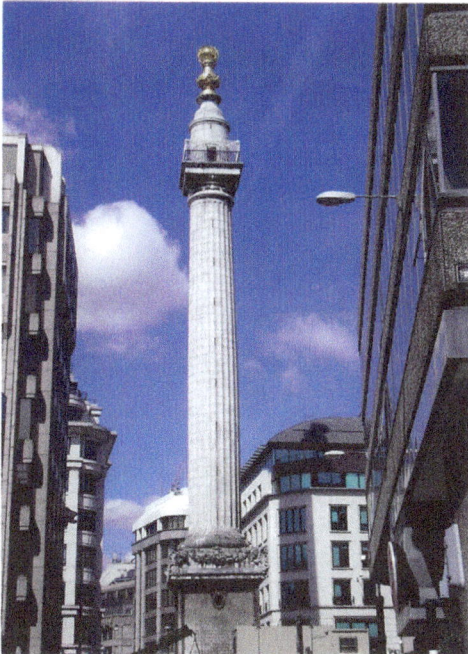

The Monument (1671-76), by Sir Christopher Wren. Much taller that the Nelson Column

While the City was being reconstructed during the aftermath of the Great Fire, London was expanding in all directions. In Westminster, St. James's Square was developed by Henry Jermyn, Earl of St. Albans after acquiring a site on a 65 year lease from the Crown in 1662, and its freehold in 1666. Since the site was in close proximity to St. James's Palace and a centre of court life, he envisaged that the square would become far more aristocratic than that of the Earl of Southampton's counterpart in Bloomsbury (see above), but after the Plague and the Great Fire there was a huge increase in the demand for housing away from the hazards of the City, and he raised the number of plots within the square from 12-16 to 22. Possibly designed by Sir John Denham, Surveyor General, the square was broadly based on that of the Place Royale (the Place des Vosges) in Paris. Like its Parisian antecedent, its houses were "plain, redbrick with stone dressings, of three storeys and an attick" (30). However, unlike the Place Royale, St. James's Square was not entirely enclosed since it was only developed on its west, north and east sides. To fund development, the Earl of St. Albans followed the Earl of Southampton's lead in Bloomsbury by letting plots on building leases, thereby setting in train the rapid development of the square. He also developed mixed uses on adjacent land, for example a market and residential streets such as King's Street, Charles II Street and Duke of York Street. Other squares of the same genre soon followed: Leicester Square in the early 1670's and Golden Square in 1675. Some famous streets were also built during this period. In 1670, for example, and acting for the Crown, Sir George Downing acquired a site between Whitehall and Green Park and built a cul-de-sac of plain red brick houses in what later became known as Downing Street , the residence of future Prime Ministers and Chancellors of the Exchequer (see chapter 7).

To the east of the City, Greenwich witnessed the construction of the confusingly-named Morden College on the edge of Blackheath. It was funded by Sir John Morden, a wealthy member of the Levant Company, to provide a home for other "Turkey Merchants' who had

228

fallen on hard times through no fault of their own. Begun in 1669, and with its design attributable to Wren, its chapel and colonnaded square courtyard lined with Doric columns is masked externally by its wide brick-façade, giant pediment and imposing portal. Since its foundation, it has been administered by charity trustees, and for generations has been used as a home for elderly people who pay according to their means.

Morden College (1669), attributed to Wren

In Richmond, Ham House was developed on the east bank of the Thames. Though essentially Jacobean in origin dating from 1610 (see chapter 5), the building was extensively refurbished and enlarged in 1672. Following the marriage of its then-owner, the Countess of Dysart, to the Earl of Lauderdale, one of the most influential ministers of Charles II and a member of his Cabal, a new wing was constructed across the rear of the whole of the building, transforming its original 'H' plan into a rectangular block with its short protruding wings restricted to its front. In keeping with the rest of its exterior, the rear three-storey façade is built of brick with stone dressings, and is intensively fenestrated, and in addition contains a central portal and looks on to a large formal garden.

Ham House, east facade (1672)

Greenwich again became important in the 1670's. The Scientific Revolution was well under way in Western Europe, and advances in astronomy – possibly more than in any other branch of science – were taking place. Galileo (1564-1642), born in Pisa, was the first astronomer to use the telescope, and what he saw in the universe convinced him of the truth of Copernicus's view that the earth rotates on its axis and revolves around the sun. Thus, to develop the science of astronomy further, Charles II ordered the construction of the Royal Observatory in Greenwich in 1675, for the use of the Astronomer Royal, John Framstead. Designed jointly by Sir Christopher Wren (an astronomer in his own right) and Dr Robert Hooke, the observatory was located on a hill overlooking Greenwich Park, Inigo Jones's Queen's House and Greenwich Palace, and in its construction made use of recycled bricks and other materials derived from an old castle on its site and other nearby-sources. Its central building, far from being Classical in style, is particularly notable for its one great octagonal room on the first floor, while Jacobean-style dominical turrets surmount each of its four corners and large scrolls link the centre to the side blocks (31).

Royal Observatory (1675), by Sir Christopher Wren and Dr Robert Hooke

Moorfields, north of London Wall, provided a suitable location for the development of Bethlehem Royal Hospital (Bedlam) when its former premises outside of Bishopgate – that it had occupied since 1377 – became obsolete. Designed by Dr Robert Hook, a new hospital was constructed in 1674-76 to provide accommodation for the mentally ill. With its lengthy façade comprising two long pedimented blocks separating three protruding pavilions with high roofs and domes, the new hospital was compared by John Evelyn to the Tuileries in Paris, or more latterly to the work of Lemercier or Le Vau at the Louvre though neither of these buildings were hospitals but royal palaces. Because of severe structural problems, Bedlam was demolished at the beginning of the nineteenth century, and its patients were transferred to a new building in Lambeth in 1815 (to become the premises of the Imperial War Museum in 1935).

Bethlehem Hospital (1674-6), by Dr Robert Hooke

Danby's administration: 1677-78

By the late 1670's, there was popular support in England for a war with France, and in 1678 parliament even voted £300,000 to strengthen the fleet for this purpose. Despite being commercial rivals, the Dutch were more natural allies of England, with their Protestantism and representative government. Nevertheless, there was a further Secret Treaty with

France whereby, in return for a payment from Louis XIV of £300,000 a year for three years, Charles would dissolve parliament, disband the army, and not assist the Dutch if they continued the war against France. These arrangements were negotiated on the English side by the Earl of Danby (who had replaced Clifford at the Treasury) and Sir Ralph Montagu, ambassador at Paris. However, because of parliament's anti-French stance, Danby was duly impeached of high treason, and to save him Charles dissolved parliament.

Despite his influence and wealth, Danby had not been interested in developing property, but the same could not be said of Ralph Montagu, who, assisted by the wealth of his wife Elizabeth, daughter of the Earl of Southampton and widow of the Duke of Northumberland, built a sumptuous residence in London on the present-day site of the British Museum. Designed by Robert Hooke, and built between 1675 and 1679, Montagu House, consisted of a central block and two service blocks flanking a large courtyard, broadly in the French style but with Dutch detailing. Burnt down soon after its completion, it was immediately rebuilt with even greater French attributes (see below).

A number of other notable development projects, both secular and ecclesiastical   took place in London in the late-1670's, Of the former, King's Bench Walk in the Inner Temple is the most impressive. Constructed in 1677-78, largely to the design of Sir Christopher Wren. It consists of five storey unadorned, though elegant, brick-built terraces containing the chambers that originally included living accommodation as well as office use. But since the nineteenth century they have exclusively satisfied professional demands.

King's Bench Walk (1677-8), by Sir Christopher Wren

More prolifically, Wren continued to work on the reconstruction of City churches as well as working on the reconstruction of St. Paul's. St. Benet Paul's Wharf, St. Peter Cornhill and Christ Church Newgate – all rectangular churches – were begun in 1677; while in the same year building work started on the centrally-planned churches of St. Anne and St. Agnes Gresham Street, St. Martin Ludgate, and St. Mildred Bread Street and St. Swithin Cannon Street (both destroyed in 1941). In 1676, work commenced on the hybrid church of St. James Garlickhythe, and in 1678 work on a further rectangular centrally-planned church, St. Antholin, was begun. The former church, though essentially rectangular, displays a strong element of centralisation. With a nave and aisle of five bays, it is crossed mid-way by a transept without a gallery, whose end windows are as large as those above the altar (32), whereas St. Antholin (demolished 1873) – like St. Benet Fink – had an oval dome, but in its case was supported by columns arranged as an octagon rather than an octagon with an oblong instead of a decagonal plan. Though Classical or Baroque architecture was none-too-evident in the main fabric of City churches (other than St. Paul's), Dutch architecture had quite a substantial influence on the external appearance of a number of churches built in the city in the late 1670's. However, whether the design of the longitudinal church of St. Benet's Paul's Wharf, and the centrally-planned churches of St. Anne and St. Agnes Gresham Street, and St. Martin's Ludgate came from published Dutch sources or from elsewhere it is difficult to say.

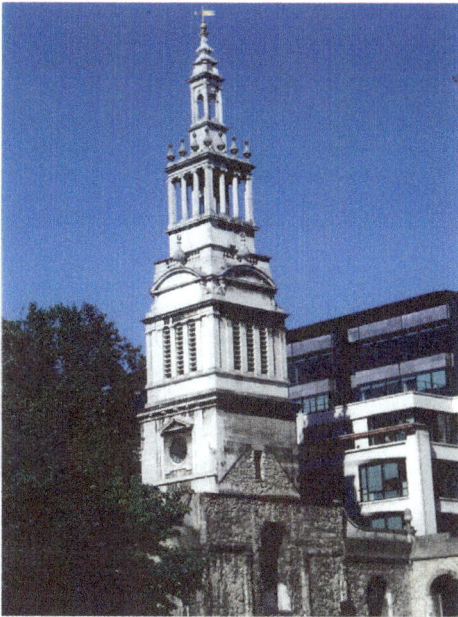

Christ Church, Newgate (1677), by Sir Christopher Wren

St Benet, Paul'sWharf (1677), by Sir Christopher Wren

Governance by Privy Council, 1678-81

By 1678, three administrations, those of Clarendon, the
Cabal and Danby, had been overthrown by votes of
parliament. Whether or not at the time it was
appreciated that this was seriously detrimental to
efficient administration is not known, but what was
understood was that, in the struggle between king and
parliament, parliament ultimately got its way.
Following the downfall of Danby, Charles established
an enlarged privy council (of 15 royal officials and 15
independent members of parliament) to act as a buffer
between king and parliament. However, this did little to

prevent behind-the-scenes chicanery that Charles favoured when faced with opposition to his policy aims and objectives.

Although it was widely known that Charles's brother, James, was a Roman Catholic, it was rumoured in the late 1670's, if not before, that Charles, too, had become a Catholic and that if he were able to restore Catholicism in England there would be a French invasion in support of the English king and his new faith. Though unsubstantiated, such a rumour fuelled an even less credible allegation. A former clergyman of the Church of England came forward with a story in 1678 that the Jesuits were plotting to murder both Charles and his brother, James, and establish Roman Catholicism by force. Although the Popish Plot, as it was later called, was unsupported by reliable evidence, the allegation was widely believed, and tellingly Oats was never prosecuted. With rumours abounding, parliament thought, as a matter of urgency, legislation was required to reduce the possibility of a Catholic seizing the crown, and therefore an Exclusion Bill was introduced in parliament in 1679 that would not only exclude James from the throne, but banish him from the country for life and place his Protestant daughter, Mary, and her husband, William of Orange, on the throne. Finding these proposals unacceptable, Charles duly dissolved parliament to prevent the Bill from being enacted.

Although elections had taken place in 1679 immediately after the dissolution, Charles postponed the reassembly of parliament until October 1680 as he was aware that the majority of elected members were in favour of legislation on exclusion. He was assured that, in the meantime, he could be sustained by money from Louis XIV. However, Charles could not indefinitely quell the tide of opposition. Within weeks of the

237

reassembling of parliament, the Exclusion Bill was passed in the House of Commons with its large "Country" (Whig) majority but was vigorously rejected in the Lords with its "Court" (Tory) majority. In their determination to block a Catholic succession, the Whigs declared that they would never grant the king any further financial resources to maintain his rule until the Exclusion Bill was enacted, and in response Charles dissolved parliament, yet again. A further election took place in 1681 and the Whigs were returned, as before, with a large majority. In an attempt to isolate Whig members of parliament from their supporters in the City of London, Charles moved his parliament to Oxford in an attempt to avert a crisis, but almost immediately the relocated parliament was dissolved since it continued to oppose Charles's proposals regarding the succession.

Despite the religious and political denouement, the further development of London streets and squares, the Inns of Court and London's churches continued apace. In 1670, and acting for the Crown, Sir George Downing acquired a site between Whitehall and St James's Park and build a cul-de-sac of plain redbrick terraced houses in what later became Downing Street, and in the 1680s work started on King's Square (later known as Soho Square) in the 1680's. Developed by Richard Frith, a bricklayer, and to an extent based on the plans of Gregory King, the square soon became a fashionable place containing residences of the nobility and gentry such as Carlisle House and Fauconberg House on the east side, and Monmouth House on the southern side.

New Square, Lincoln's Inn (1685-97)

Gray's Inn Square (1680s, restored post World-War II).

After the development of the Inner Temple in the previous decade, New Square in Lincoln's Inn was developed by the barrister and speculator Henry Serle between 1685 and 1697, and Gray's Inn Square was developed by the administrators of Gray's Inn throughout much of the 1680's. (The square, largely destroyed by bombing in 1941, was faithfully restored in the 1960's).

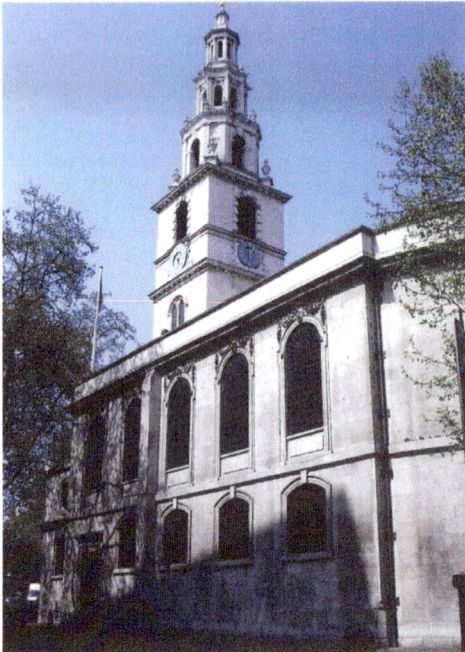

St Clement Danes (1680-2), by Sir Christopher Wren

St James's Piccadilly (1682-4), by Sir Christopher Wren

Of the several Wren churches begun in the early 1680's, only one, St. Mary Abchurch (1681-1686) had a centralised plan. The remainder, St. Clement Danes (1680-1682), St. Mary Aldermary (1681-1690), St. James's Piccadilly (1682-1684), St. Alban (1682-1688), St. Margaret Lothbury (1683-1692), St. Andrew, Holborn Circus (1684-1686), and St. Margaret Pattens (1684-1689), were all rectangular. Not all of Wren's London churches were replacements of those damaged in the Great Fire. St. Andrew, Holborn Circus – Wren's largest parish church – escaped the conflagration entirely, and so too did St. Clement Danes. Both were rebuilt because they were falling seriously into disrepair, whereas St. James's Piccadilly was a new church on a new site located on the northern edge of the estate of Henry Jermyn, the 1st Earl of St. Albans, who incurred the cost of construction. Most of Wren's churches were damaged by the blitz of 1941 but – except for St. Alban's where only its tower remains – all have been fully restored in recent years.

Absolute Rule, 1681-85

For the final four years of Charles's reign, the king managed to rule without a parliament. Antipathy to his increasingly tyrannical rule was both specific and general. With his brother, James, he narrowly missed being murdered by a number of adversaries when passing Rye House in Hoddesdon, *en route* from Newmarket to London in 1683, while in the same year there was widespread and angry concern within the boroughs when Charles recalled their charters, if under Whig control, and restored them after nominating new corporations of Tories. Through remodelling the corporations, he would be able to determine who would sit on the benches of the Commons, but for the time being could rule without a parliament.

Through manipulating the constitution to keep the exclusion issue at bay, Charles was now an absolute monarch and, through the goodwill of Louis XIV, received a permanent revenue so long as he did not recall parliament and adopted "a passive foreign policy that gave France a free hand in Europe" (33). If not before, England was now about to become a client-state of Louis's France. However, on February 6 1685, following his alleged conversion to the Roman Catholic faith, Charles unexpectedly expired before the full ramifications of absolute rule and subservience to France would be demonstrated. It was only three years before his demise in 1685, that Charles commissioned one of the finest architectural legacies of his reign,

Chelsea Hospital. Second in grandeur to St. Paul's and inspired by Louis XIV's Hôtel des Invalides in Paris, the vast complex was designed to provide a retirement home for some of the nation's most loyal subjects, army veterans who for generations to come strove to advance the interests of Britain in countless theatres of war. As a gesture for being the first English king to have a regular army, Charles met part of the cost of developing the hospital from the Privy Purse but – under the authority of Sir Stephen Fox, Paymaster of the Army – the remainder was funded from deductions in soldiers' pay, and consequently the total cost of construction was not funded directly by the Exchequer.

Chelsea Hospital (started 1682), by Sir Christopher Wren

With its riverside site and design attributed to Sir Christopher Wren, the plan for Chelsea Hospital was to an extent derived from that of Webb's Greenwich Palace abandoned some fourteen or fifteen years earlier (see above). The building consists of long and narrow blocks arranged around three sides of a large central courtyard, the fourth side being open and facing the Thames to the south. Built mainly of brick with stone dressings, the three main blocks are of equal height. However, the middle section of the northern and longest block that separates the hospital's main hall and chapel with their large rounded-windows, is marked on its north-facing façade by a flat pedimented portico supported by engaged columns of the giant Doric order, and on its south-facing façade by a projecting pedimented portico supported by giant Doric columns. The centres of the three-storey western and eastern blocks are adorned by flat pedimented porticoes with giant Doric pilasters, while their walls are pierced by square-headed windows. The three blocks are covered by a single sloping roof above a unifying cornice, and, except for the central block, are lit by dormer windows. Following the construction of an inappropriately small domed-tower in 1689, midway across the central block, the hospital was eventually finished in 1692 during the reign of William and Mary.

From the outset, the construction of Chelsea Hospital was under-funded, money was short. The use of stone was kept to the minimum, and because the hospital "was Wren's first large secular building, it is not surprising that it was experimental, both in plan and elevation ...... the long ranges of plain brick are a little bleak, and the accents are not quite strong enough for the size of the court" (34). Nevertheless, in its "use of the giant order [it] foreshadows the Baroque of Queen Anne's reign .... While the grand simple lines of the composition as a whole [are echoed] in many of the finest collegiate and hospital buildings of the [eighteenth] century" (35). More specifically, in rejecting the plan for Les Invalides in Paris, with its small and dark side courts, Wren's arrangement of the wards was notably humanitarian. To ensure that the older men would have as much light as possible , the "wards are reached by staircases at their inner end, [and] have a middle wall with cubicles on both sides opening on to a wide passage running the length of the lock behind large windows" (36). On balance, the hospital not only advanced architectural design in England but served, and still serves, its function admirably. One can only speculate what other public buildings and infrastructure projects he would have commissioned as absolute monarch had, like Louis XIV, he lived to 77 instead of meeting his death at 55.

James II (re. 1685-1688)

In February, 1685, a Roman Catholic succeeded to the throne of England for the first time since Mary Tudor was crowned Queen in 1553. What was particularly remarkable was that, despite the concern of Protestant exclusionists and the possibility of absolute rule, the accession of James, Duke of York, was quietly celebrated. As James II, the new king's first acts were aimed at minimizing political instability. First, he attempted to ensure that his finances were secure and ordered that customs duties, voted to Charles for life, should be collected as usual, though they would not be renewed until parliament met. He was, of course, grateful to Louis XIV – his cousin- for continuing to 'subsidise' the English monarchy to the extent of £67,000 for a further year, but much of the money was arrears due to Charles, and James received an insignificantly small proportion for his own use. Second, he released a number of prisoners such as Danby, four Roman Catholic lords and 1,200 Quakers to reduce discontent amongst their supporters. Third, to

245

further appease a segment of his subjects, he ensured that Titus Oats was indicted for perjury and duly fined and imprisoned for life. To begin with, parliament treated James favourably. Assembling in May 1685, it agreed that the king could continue to receive customs duties for life (a sum amounting to around £500,000 a year) and, in addition, granted him an annual sum of £900,000 together with the revenue from new taxes on sugar, tobacco, wine and vinegar for eight years, and on foreign linen for five years.

Although the Protestant rebellions in the summer of 1685 against James's rule (the unsuccessful risings of the Duke of Argyll in Scotland and the Duke of Monmouth in the West Country) were forcibly put down and their perpetrators cruelly punished, James attempted to demonstrate that he was even-handed in matters ecclesiastical. He set his sights on emancipating Catholics by aiming to abolish religious tests as a qualification for office, and authorising freedom of worship. After the Revocation of the Edict of Nantes (1685) and the resultant inflow of Huguenots from France, James appeared to be just as tolerant to Protestant dissenters as he was sympathetic to Catholics, though Protestants and especially Anglicans regarded this policy with suspicion. Their concern might well have been justified. James soon used his dispensing power to advance several Catholics to office despite the Test Act of 1673 while, in the Hales' Case, the decision of the king to appoint a Catholic, Sir Edward Hales, as Constable of Dover Castle (an important post in the defence of the realm), was uphold by Chief-Justice Herbert.

During the first year of his reign – possibly through a show of grandeur intended to enhance his position as monarch – James facilitated the large scale extension to his principle residence and seat of power, Whitehall

Palace. Though Sir Christopher Wren had produced drawings for the expansion of Whitehall soon after he had become Surveyor General in 1669, Charles II did not commit himself to enlarging Whitehall Palace throughout the 25 years of his reign, notwithstanding a substantial increase in national wealth during this period. However, during his short four-year term as monarch, James ordered the demolition of many of the obsolete Tudor buildings on the site and made substantial changes to the fabric of the palace. Wren duly designed and supervised the construction of a long Privy Gallery at right angles to the Banqueting House – extending towards the river in the east – with its frontage overlooking a new private garden to the south. Of three main storeys in height with dormer windows in the roof, the gallery was but one of several new buildings constructed on the site. Set within the palace, a chapel reminiscent of Inigo Jones's work at St. James, protruded into the garden and, behind the gallery in a courtyard and to the rear of the Banqueting House, Wren built a three-storey council chamber supported by open stone arches (37). Finally, the Queen's apartment was constructed parallel to the Thames, a fairly large building with a riverside terrace. Whereas the exterior of the Banqueting House was built entirely of stone, Wren mainly used brick (with stone dressings) to extend and reconstruct the palace because the material was readily available, comparatively inexpensive and it enabled construction to proceed speedily (38). Although in many ways vernacular, the proportions of the extended palace were basically Classical.

With his power-base at Whitehall being strengthened, James considered that the time was ripe to raise Roman Catholicism to a position of dominance in public affairs. He established an Ecclesiastical Commission under Lord Jeffreys to secure the king's hold over the church and universities. Ecclesiastical promotions consequently saw Catholic sympathisers appointed as bishops, for example Samuel Parker was appointed as Bishop of Oxford while, also at Oxford, Obadiah Walker was allowed to remain Master of University College after his conversion to Rome, and a Catholic, Bonaventura Gifford, was forced on Magdalene College as President against the wishes of the fellows. At Cambridge, the vice Chancellor, Peachell, was dismissed for excluding Catholics.

The established church was still, of course, Anglican, but in 1687 and 1688 James's First and Second Declaration of Indulgence granted new freedoms to Protestant Dissenters and Catholics alike. In angry response to an order that the Second Declaration had to be read at all Anglican churches, a bishops' petition – led by the Archbishop of Canterbury and Archbishop of London – urged the king to withdraw the declaration, an act of defiance that led to the bishops being charged with seditious libel. Although they were acquitted by jury, an act that over the course of time safeguarded Anglicanism, it was becoming increasingly clear to many of the king's opponents by 1688 that he aimed to establish a Catholic state in England and that by granting freedoms to Protestant Dissenters as well as to the Catholics he was employing a clever ruse in order to promote the ascendancy of the Church of Rome.

Since it appeared that James was in no mood to respond to the religious and constitutional views of many of his subjects, a group of influential Englishmen approached William of Orange to persuade James, his uncle, to respect the traditional influences in the government of England. William, for his part, was concerned that James might be drawn ever-closer to Louis XIV and, against the interests of the Netherlands,

248

form an alliance with France. William was antagonistic to James since his own Protestant wife, Mary (James's daughter from his first marriage, to Anne Hyde) had been deprived of her right of succession to the English throne – as Mary II – because James's second wife, Mary of Modena, allegedly barren, had disputedly given birth to a male heir, James Edward Stuart. William, consequently, received a letter from an illustrious group of English aristocrats inviting his armed assistance and, on October 19 1688, William and his forces sailed from the Netherlands and landed at Torbay on November 5 (ironically 83 years to the day after the Gunpowder Plot had failed to remove the first Stuart monarch of England). Meeting little resistance, William and his army marched on London and reached the capital on December 19, where he "promised to free the English from the Absolute tyranny instituted by his uncle" (39). Meanwhile, on December 11, James fled the capital but his attempt to escape was foiled. However, on December 23, he fled again, this time successfully, and lived for most of his remaining life in France as Louis XIV's guest in the Chateau St-Germain-En-Laye, where he died in 1701 at the age of 68.

While it might be said that James was tolerant to Protestants (both Anglicans and Dissenters), his opponents were fearful that no Catholic state in Europe (France, Spain or Austria) showed similar tolerance, and predicted that there was a real danger that James's experiment might lead to absolute monarchy and the dominance of Catholicism as exemplified by Louis XIV's France. It might be suggested, however, that had James not escaped to France and instead had established absolute power in England, there might well have been – in the French manner – the construction of a number of grandiose public buildings throughout London – such as the completion of the Whitehall Palace – as visible manifestations of the supreme authority of the monarch.

However, in the early 1680's, a plethora of non-governmental projects were undertaken in the capital, for example Montagu House was rebuilt, much speculative development was undertaken in the West End, and the City churches of St. Andrew by the Wardrobe and St. Michael Paternoster Royal were restored.

Burnt down in January 1686, Montagu House – under the direction of the 1st Duke of Montagu – was immediately rebuilt to the designs of a French architect, Pierre Puget. Considered by some to be the grandest private residence built in the capital in late seventeenth century, its cost of construction was enormous, and might have bankrupted the 1st Duke had he not married the extremely wealthy Duchess of Albemarle after the death of his first wife, Elizabeth, a woman also of considerable means. The house very much assumed the form of a contemporary Parisian *hôtel*. It consisted of two main storeys, together with a basement and a prominent mansard roof with a central dome. Its main façade was of 17 bays, with a projecting three bay centre and three bay ends. At right-angles to the main block, the protruding service wings of the original house flanked – as before – a large gated courtyard.

Montagu House (1686), Pierre Puget

Throughout much of western fringes of the City, large scale speculative development occurred during the last two decades of the seventeenth century. Major developers either acquired the freehold or leasehold of a piece of land, divided it into plots and either developed the land themselves or allocated the plots to smaller speculators on building leases, and ultimately sold the properties as investments with ground rents attached; or alternatively land would be developed by small speculators – normally builder-craftsmen – who would acquire a building lease on somebody else's freehold land, build the house or houses, and dispose of them leasehold. The former type of developer is best exemplified by Nicholas Barbon "a first-class financier, economist and big businessman" (40). Barbon's activities were widespread and diverse. He built housing in Denmark Street, Villiers Street, Buckingham Street, Essex Street and in Newport

251

Square in Soho; he developed Devereux Court on the edge of the Temple; and in the Temple itself he built New Court and, after a fire, several blocks of chambers. However, he was best known for developing Red Lion Square to the west of Grays Inn (1684-1698), together with a large number of houses on the adjoining Harpur and Rigby estates and in Ormond Street north of the square, but most notably in Bedford Row (1684) to the east of the square. Although his development projects were not always constructed within the context of a town planning scheme, his main contribution to planning in London was that he demonstrated that the extensive development of profitable standardised housing could provide the most viable basis for the development of streets and squares across the capital, a relationship that only came to fruition in the eighteenth and early-nineteenth centuries. Many amateur speculators also stamped their mark on the London property scene in the late seventeenth century: Sir Thomas Bond developed Albemarle Street and Bond Street, Sir Thomas Clarges built Clarges Street, Richard Frith built Frith Street (in addition to developing King's Square), Sir Thomas Neale and Groom Porter developed Seven Dials, and Panton Street was named after its developer Colonel Thomas Panton (41). Like Barbon, all laid the ground for the planned development of the Great Estates across the capital in the years that followed

Bedford Row (1684), by Nicholas Barbon

St.Andrew-by-the-Wardrobe (1680s), by Sir Christopher
Wren

Apart from ongoing work on St. Paul's Cathedral, the development of ecclesiastical property took place on a smaller scale than hitherto since most of the churches damaged during the Great Fire had now been restored. Rectangular in shape, and built of red brick, St. Andrew by the Wardrobe (1685-1694) and St. Michael Paternoster Royal (1686-1694) were Wren's last city churches, and were relatively unadorned. Like all the other churches reconstructed after the Great Fire, the cost of construction was met by Coal Tax. However, in the case of St. Andrew, the poverty of its parish was so severe that the cost of furnishing the interior also had to be met by the Coal Tax, whereas in the case of St. Michael, construction was suspended during the Glorious Revolution of 1688 because of the drying up of funds. In the following reign of William and Mary, London and its environs experienced a very different pattern of development, both in terms of its secular *and* ecclesiastical architecture.

Seven Dials (1690), by Thomas Neale

William III and Mary II (r. 1689-1694)

On January 2 1689, soon after William of Orange's arrival in London, a Convention Parliament passed two resolutions: first, that James II had endeavoured to subvert the constitution and, second, that it was inconsistent to have a Protestant kingdom governed by a popish prince. While Parliament initially favoured making Mary sole ruler it was eventually agreed that William and Mary could rule jointly but, to ensure that the kingdom was governed according to the fundamental principles on which the English constitution was based, Parliament drafted the Declaration of Right that was duly accepted by William and Mary, who were only then declared king and queen on February 18, 1689. Stemming from the Declaration, the Bill of Rights of 1689 destroyed the Stuart theory of the divine right of kings (and thus blocked any move towards absolute monarchy), reasserted the principles of the English constitution that the Stuarts had attempted to set aside, and began the rule of Parliament.

In the wake of the Bill, the issue of royal revenue was settled. Whereas the income of James II was a little under £2 million per annum, William and Mary's ordinary revenue was fixed at only £1.2 million, but this sum was enhanced by special grants, for example, the joint-monarchy received £700,000 for the improvement of the navy and £600,000 to defray the costs of the Dutch invasion. During the first parliamentary session of William and Mary's reign there were two other acts of importance. The first was introduced to quell popular opposition to the idea of a standing army (first introduced by James II) since it was believed that, in a moment of crisis, it could be used illegally by the monarch to suppress the will of

Parliament. Therefore, under the Mutiny Act of 1689, the army – in effect – became de-politicised since its members were obliged to comply with martial law or face severe penalties. The second act came into being to guarantee, within limits, the freedom of worship. Under the Toleration Act of 1689, Protestants – both Anglicans and nonconformists, were permitted to exercise their religious beliefs, but non-protestants received no such freedom, in contrast to James II's policy of extending toleration to Protestants and Catholics alike. Aside from the Act of Grace of 1690, that granted a general indemnity for a range of offences committed prior to the accession of the new sovereigns, and the Triennial Act of 1694 that fixed for three years the maximum term that any parliament could sit, few further domestic measures were introduced throughout the rest of William and Mary's joint reign to consolidate the ascendancy of the Protestant parliament.

Kensington Palace (1689), by Sir Christopher Wren

It was during this period of political stability that work started on the construction of Kensington Palace (1689) and the further development of Hampton Court (1689) to suit the private needs of the joint monarchs, and in 1691 the queen's apartments in Whitehall Palace were completed to facilitate her state functions in the capital. But Whitehall remained out of favour and "was abandoned for all save ceremonial occasions. Neglected and forlorn, like so many underused buildings, it burnt down in 1698 and was never rebuilt" (42). Only James I's Banqueting House survived the conflagration of what was England's inadequate answer to the Louvre.

Hampton Court, the Queen's Apartments (1689), by Sir Christopher Wren

Hampton Court, the King's Apartments (1689), by Sir
Christopher Wren

Hampton Court, Fountain Court (1689-94), by Sir
Christopher Wren

The political agenda of William and Mary's joint reign, however, was not confined to religious and constitutional issues in England. It was taken-up substantially by military campaigns in Ireland, Scotland and on the Continent, and – in response to the huge cost of war – by the foundation of the Bank of England. By means of ships and troops, Louis XIV assisted the exiled James II to head an expedition to Ireland in 1689 to reinforce the hold of Roman Catholicism on the island in the face of Protestant insurgence. After landing in Kinsale in March 1689, James made his way to Dublin and summoned a parliament to meet on May 7. With its large Catholic majority in the Commons House, the parliament declared the legislative independence of Ireland, forbade the assembling of Protestants in churches and elsewhere on pain of death, handed Protestant churches to Catholic priests, restored all schools and colleges to Catholicism, and forcibly expelled English and Scottish colonists. Since April 30 1689, Londonderry had become a refuge for Scottish and English settlers who had flooded into the city to escape from the threat of extermination but, following a three month siege by James's followers, the city was relieved by the arrival of English naval support on July 30. Earlier, on July 1, William III and his army defeated the combined Irish-French forces at the Battle of the Boyne, and secured Dublin and the centre of Ireland. At the time of the battle, James had been relying on the military support of a French fleet landing in Ireland but, under its commander Tourville, it had been defeated in a sea battle by an Anglo-Dutch fleet off Beachy Head. James had hoped that the fleet would intercept William's return from Ireland, and cover an invasion of England led by James, but this was not to be and James was forced to flee to France on July 14.

William's commanders went on to take the rest of Ireland and, on their completion of their task, the Treaty of Limerick of 1690 granted Roman Catholics the same privileges in the exercise of their religion that they enjoyed under Charles II.

In Scotland, a very different religious scenario prevailed. Under both Charles II and James II, the Episcopacy (broadly equivalent to the Church of England) had become established by law in opposition to the wishes of a large majority of the people. No one but an Episcopalian was permitted to sit in the Scottish parliament or vote in elections and, while Presbyterians during James II's reign were subjected to severe persecution, Roman Catholics were placed in high offices. After James fled England, the law was set aside and a Convention assembled whose members, chosen mainly by Presbyterians, accepted William and Mary as king and queen. However, supporters of James fought back. At the Battle of Killiecrankie (1689), Viscount Dundee with his Jacobite Highlanders initially defeated General Mackay and his royal sympathisers, but eventually the uprising was put down when Dundee met his death after Mackay had rallied his forces. Subsequently, in 1690, the first General Assembly of the Scottish Church since 1653 was convened by Presbyterians, an occasion which resulted in the Presbyterian Church becoming the established church in Scotland (a situation that still prevails). There were, however, still recalcitrant Jacobite's who were reluctant to accept the official status of the Presbyterian Church, and therefore to minimise the likelihood of serious unrest, William agreed to pardon all Jacobite chieftains if they swore an allegiance to the Crown by January 1 1692. Unfortunately for the Macdonalds of Glencoe, they were six days late in taking the oath and therefore, in his frustration, Sir James Dalrymple (Secretary of

State for Scotland) persuaded the Campbell's to massacre the Macdonalds, their old enemies.

Since warfare until comparatively recently was normally confined to the summer months, William tended to spend many summers after 1690 on the Continent to protect his Dutch territorial interests, and the winter months in England when Parliament was sitting. As head of a great European coalition during the War of the Grand Alliance (1688-1699), in which the forces of England, Holland, the Empire and Spain were united against France, William was successfully involved in wars against Louis XIV's forces in Flanders, Catalonia, on the Rhine and in Lombardy between 1691 and 1697. However, a victorious outcome of a battle was not always certain or immediate. Although William's Anglo-Dutch fleet fought a successful naval battle off Cape La Hogue in 1692 to avert a French invasion of England, his armies suffered defeat by Louis at the land battle of Steenkerke, but this was ultimately avenged by William at the Battle of Landen in 1693, though not overwhelmingly.

Warfare was getting not only more sophisticated but more costly. Until 1694, it had been customary for the king to borrow only in advance of the receipt of tax revenue but, as a consequence of festering warfare on the Continent, royal expenditure had risen to around £4 million per annum, whereas estimated revenue amounted to only £3 million a year. To offset this deficit, the Chancellor of the Exchequer, Charles Montagu, therefore established the Bank of England as a joint-stock company by an Act of Parliament to lend money to the state. Established by a group of London merchants, the bank initially supplied the government with a loan of £1.2 million at 8 per cent interest, and in return issued promises to pay on demand in the form of

262

bank notes. Since the principal need never be repaid provided interest was regularly paid-out, it formed the origin of the National Debt.

Despite high levels of expenditure on military campaigns, 1689-1694, William and Mary were willing to continue to fund from their allocated revenue the development of the royal palaces of Kensington and Hampton Court on the west fringes of the capital, and the Queen's Apartments in Whitehall, while building work on St. Paul's Cathedral proceeded apace, similarly facilitated by taxpayers. Meanwhile, the increase in the private wealth of the nation provided the context for the construction of a number of imposing mansions in the capital such as Fenton House (1693).

Fenton House (1693)

The Reign of William III as a Sole Monarch: 1694-1702

In December 1694, Queen Mary II died of smallpox, leaving the king to reign alone until his own demise eight years later. War on the Continent continued, and in October 1695 William captured Namur from the French after a three-month siege. France was now exhausted and sued for peace. Under the subsequent Treaty of Ryswick (1697), Louis agreed to give up all conquests except Strasbourg and Landau, and acknowledged William as King of England.

There was a respite in hostilities, and of course it was unknown that it would last for only three years. During this time William commissioned Wren to design a new Whitehall Palace (the former palace having been accidentally burnt down in 1696 by the carelessness of a Dutch laundry women). Wren duly set to work on the project and proposed that the Inigo Jones's Banqueting House (having survived the fire) should be converted into a central portico of the new palace and, using giant Corinthian columns on the portico and lesser Corinthian columns along new north and south wings , a new facade would adorn much of Whitehall and purvey a sense of awe for the monarch and his successors to balance the increase power of Parliament, a short distance to the south in Westminster. However, the palace was never rebuilt since financial resources were limited because the costly War of the Spanish Succession broke out in 1700 and lasted thirteen years (and more importantly the Early-Georgian kings of the eighteenth century had no intrinsic desire to flaunt their wealth by building a new mega-palace).

Through their descent from Phillip II (d.1621) there were three legitimate claimants to the Spanish throne and its possessions in succession to the last of the Hapsburg kings of Spain, Charles II. Initially, William and Louis opted for the Elector Joseph of Bavaria as the least contentious claimant, leaving the other contenders – Louis, dauphin of France and the Archduke Charles of Austria – with little support. However, on the death of the Elector Joseph in 1699, preferences changed. William hoped that Spain, the Spanish Netherlands, Sardinia and the colonies would collectively ally with the Austrian Archduke Charles, while the dauphin was likely to receive support from Naples and Sicily, the Duchy of Milan, the provinces of Guippuscoa and Elba. However, these proposals were not implemented because the Austrians would do nothing to ingratiate themselves with the Spanish, while Louis XIV took every opportunity to better the position of France.

Like the Elector Joseph before him, King Charles II of Spain also died in 1700 and left a will bequeathing the whole of the Spanish dominions not to the dauphin but to the dauphin's son, Philip of Anjou. This was supported wholeheartedly by Louis XIV (Philip's grandfather) but opposed by William and the Austrians. The first major incursion of the subsequent war – France seizing the Spanish Netherlands in 1701 – marked the beginning of a long struggle across much of Europe that eventually settled the question of the Spanish Succession in 1713.

But even the British succession was by no means clear-cut. Although Anne, James II's youngest daughter, would undoubtedly succeed William, all her 17 children had pre-deceased her and there was therefore a possibility that James Edward Stuart (later known as the Old Pretender) would attempt to succeed to the British throne on the Queen's death. In an attempt to forestall this eventuality, Parliament decreed by the Act of Settlement of 1701 that, on the death of Anne, the throne would pass to Sophie, the Electress Dowager of Hanover and granddaughter of James I, the nearest acceptable descendent of the Stuart line.

Greenwich Royal Naval College, Chapel (1694-1702), by Sir Christopher Wren

Greenwich Royal Naval College, Hall (1694-1702), by Sir
Christopher Wren

Despite the political traumas of insurrection in
Ireland and Scotland, and a long period of warfare on
the Continent and its surrounding seas, William and
Mary's reign "turned England from a feeble imitator of
the French absolute monarchy into the most powerful
and aggressively modernising state in Europe" (43).
This was reflected in the development of buildings both
small and large. On a comparatively small scale, Joseph
Avis, a Quaker, was commissioned by the local
Spanish and Portuguese community to build a
synagogue in Bevis Marks adjacent to Bishopgate.
Constructed in 1700-1, the rectangular redbrick
building shares many of the same features as a
Protestant church of the period: it has three galleries, a

flat ceiling and two rows of windows. On a large scale, there was the development   of substantial grandiose edifices such as Hampton Court (completed in 1702) and Greenwich Royal Naval College (constructed mainly between 1694 and 1702). The skyline of the City of London was soon magnificently transformed by the continuing development of St. Paul's Cathedral (begun during the reign of Charles II) and by the addition of steeples to the City churches of St. Vedast (1694-1697), St. Dunstan-in-the-East (1697) and St. Bride Fleet Street (1701-1703).

Spanish and Portuguese Synagogue, Bevis Market (1700-1)

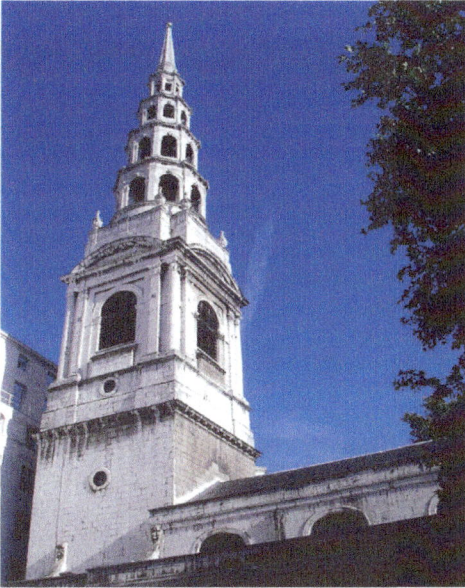
St Bride's Steeple (1701-3), by Sir Christopher Wren

Schomberg House, Pall Mall (1698)

Greycoat Hospital (1701)

In the private sector, an increase in wealth provided the resources for the construction of a number of mansions in the West End and beyond such as Schomberg House in Pall Mall (1698), though the latter property was commissioned by a German aristocrat rather than an English merchant. Philanthropic bodies also funded the development of property, for example in Victoria the Greycoat Hospital School was founded from charitable funds in 1695 to provide education for children with limited family means, a function that anticipated the development of the near-by Blewcoat School founded a few years later (see below).

The Reign of Queen Anne (1701-14)

On March 8 1701 William died following a hunting accident, and Anne the staunchly Protestant daughter of James II succeeded to the throne in 1702. From the outset she was very much aware that her Whig government, under its leading minister Lord Sidney Godolphin, recognised that without the parliamentary union of England and Scotland there would always be a risk that the Scottish parliament would pursue an independent foreign policy detrimental to the interests of England. Already the Scottish parliament did not accept the Act of Settlement of 1701 that promised the throne to the Hanoverians on the death of Anne and, in due course, could instead support James Edward Stuart's claim to the throne of Great Britain, even though he was a Catholic. The Scottish parliament was so intent on maintaining its integrity that in 1704 it passed four acts to safeguard its independent political and religious powers – the fourth act (the Act of Security) giving the Scottish parliament the right to choose Scotland's future monarch if Anne died without an heir (and that seemed a certainty). Antagonised by the Scottish approach to the succession, the English parliament passed the Alien Act in 1705 which would apply if the Scots failed to pass legislation whose contents were very similar to those of the Act of Settlement. If the Scots refused to acknowledge the eventual Hanoverian succession, they would be deemed aliens of England and there would be a cessation of free trade not only between the two countries but also between Scotland and the colonies, over the following century.

However, in Anne's relatively short but eventful reign, there was a virtual cessation of large scale development projects in the capital, undoubtedly because continual warfare was putting a substantial strain on public resources, notwithstanding the role of the National Debt. Although St. Paul's Cathedral was completed in 1710 it was started some 40 years earlier and, apart from some minor additions to the Royal Naval Hospital at Greenwich, the only other publicly-funded projects of any note were the erection of steeples on their City churches of St. Magnus Martyr (1705), St. Edmund King and Martyr (1708), and St. Michael Paternoster Royal (1713).

Buckingham House (1702-5), by William Wynde

Marlborough House (1709-11) by Sir Christopher Wren

In the increasingly-wealthy private sector, however, financial constraints were largely absent, although in 1707 a Building Act was passed prohibiting the use of decorative wooden eaves and cornices as a safeguard against fire spreading from one building to another across the capital, and it also required that the façade of the house should be raised above the eaves and party walls by at least 18 in (450 mm) to create a parapet to protect the roof timbers. Further legislation in 1709 insisted that window sash boxes should be set back at least 4 in (100mm) into the façade of a house (44). Within these constraints, private development nevertheless continued apace. Apart from the increasing development of terraced housing, a number of sumptuous houses were constructed during Anne's reign, for example Buckingham House (1702-5) was constructed for John Sheffield, the 1st Duke of Buckingham and Normanby; Marlborough House (1709-1711) was built for Sarah, the eponymous duchess and favourite of the queen; Roehampton House in Wandswoth (1710-1712) was built for Thomas Carey; and a number of substantial houses in Laurence Pountney Hill (1703) and Wardrobe Place (1710) were constructed for City merchants while to the east of Fleet Street, Gough Square contains a number of smaller terraced housing of the period, No. 17 becoming the residence of Samuel Johnson (1748-59).

Roehampton House (1710-12), by Thomas Archer

Laurence Poultney Hill (1703)

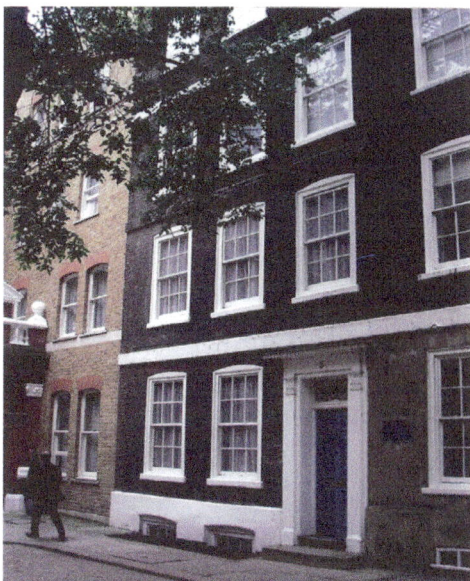

Wardrobe Place (c 1710)

Gough Square (c 1700)

Not only was there no shortage of private finance for the development of residential property in the early years of the eighteenth century, funds from wealthy benefactors also found their way into construction. Such was the case of the development of Blewcoat School in Victoria. Though the school was initially founded for poor boys in 1688, in 1709 - with funds provided by the owner of the Stag Brewery, William Greene - it relocated from its original site near the church of St.Margaret to Duck Lane in Victoria, with girls being admitted in 1713.

Blewcoat School (1700)

References

1. R. Porter, *London. A Social History*, Penguin Books, 2000, p 8.
2. Sir John Summerson , *Architecture in Britain 1530-1830*, Yale University Press, 1993, p 176.
3. Ibid, pp 176-7
4. Ibid, pp 176-7
5. M. Whinney, *Wren*, Thames & Hudson, 1998, pp 16-17.
6. Ibid, pp 16-17.
7. Sir John Summerson, *Architecture in Britain 1530-1830*, Yale University Press, 1993, p 174.
8. Ibid, pp 140-1.
9. Ibid, p 174.
10. B. Weinreb and C. Hibbert, *The London*

Encyclopaedia, Macmillan, p 58.

11. Sir John Summerson , *Georgian London*, Penguin Books, 1969, p 39.
12. R. Porter, *London. A Social History*, Penguin Books, 2000, pp 109-10
13. Sir John Summerson, *Architecture in Britain 1530-1830*, Yale University Press, 1993, pp 52-3.
14. R. Porter, *London. A Social History*, Penguin Books, 2000, p 110; Sir John Summerson, *Architecture in Britain 1530-1830*, Yale University Press, 1993, pp 53-4.
15. Sir John Summerson, *Architecture in Britain 1530-1830*, Yale University Press, 1993,. pp 53-4.
16. R.Porter, *London. A Social History*, Penguin Books, 2000, p 110;
17. Sir John Summerson, *Architecture in Britain 1530-1830*, Yale University Press, 1993 (A), p 188.
18. M. Whinney, *Wren*, Thames & Hudson, 1998, p 42.
19. Sir John Summerson, *Architecture in Britain 1530-1830,* Yale University Press, 1993, pp 189-90.
20. M. Butler, *London Architecture*, Publications, 2006, p.50
21. M. Whinney, *Wren*, Thames & Hudson, 1998. p 59.
22. D. Watkins, *English Architecture*, Thames & Hudson, 2001, p 108.
23. M. Whinney, *Wren* Op. Cit., p 81-4.
24. D. Watkins, *English Architecture*, Thames & Hudson , p 109
25. M. Whinney, *Wren*, Thames & Hudson, 1998, p 89-90.
26. Ibid. pp 89-90
27. Ibid, pp 90-1.

28. Ibid, pp 90-91.
29. Ibid, pp 93.
30. B. Weinreb and C. Hibbert, *The London Encyclopaedia*, Macmillan, p 740.
31. M. Whinney, *Wren*, Thames & Hudson, 1998, pp 144-5.
32. Sir John Summerson, *Architecture in Britain 1530-1830*, Yale University Press, 1993, pp 328-9.
33. D. Starkey, *Monarchy, From the Middle Ages to Modernity*, Harper Press, 2006, p 172.
34. M. Whinney, *Wren*, Thames & Hudson, 1998, p 149
35. Sir John Summerson, *Architecture in Britain 1530-1830*, Yale University Press, 1993, p 222.
36. M. Whinney, *Wren*, Thames & Hudson, 1998, p 147.
37. Sir John Summerson, *Architecture in Britain 1530-1830*, Yale University Press, 1993, pp 224-5.
38. M. Whinney, *Wren*, Thames & Hudson, pp 154; 156-8.
39. D. Starkey, *Monarchy. From the Middle Ages to Modernity*, Harper Press, 2006, p 174.
40. Sir John Summerson, *Georgian London*, Penguin Books, 1969, p 45.
41. Ibid, p 45
42. D.Starkey, *Monarchy. From the Middle Ages to Modernity*, Harper Press, 2006, p 198.
43. Ibid, p 171
44. D.Avery, *Georgian and Regency Architecture*, Chaucer Press, 2003, p 14.

Chapter 7

London during the Early-Hanoverians: the ascendance of the Palladian and Neo-Classical styles

Had it not been for a massive migration of population from smaller urban areas and the countryside to London the English capital would have experienced a major reduction in the number of its inhabitants throughout the eighteenth century because of high mortality rates. According to the best available estimates, the population of London increased from 575,000 in 1700 to 675,000 in 1750, while the first official census shows that the British capital contained 1,097,000 inhabitants by 1801. The population of London had now overtaken that of Paris, making the British capital the largest city in Europe. London also accommodated a considerably higher proportion of the national population than Paris, and – unlike the French capital – its share increased rather than decreased towards the end of the eighteenth century. With the population of England doubling from 5 million in 1700 to 10 million in 1801, London's share of the national population rose very slowly from 11.5 per cent to 12.3 per cent over the same period (1).

High densities in the eighteenth century cities went hand-in-glove with appalling living conditions and London was no exception. To the south and east of the City (and also in isolated parts of the West End), housing conditions were little better than they had been in the seventeenth century or earlier and often comparable to the worst found by Edward Chadwick or Charles Booth in the nineteenth century. As is so vividly described by Stephen Inwood, London's slums were characterised by "[j]erry-built and patched-up houses, sub-divided tenements let to families unable to afford a proper rent, common lodging houses which fostered crime and disease, stinking alleys and courtyard, wet, airless and fully occupied cellars, [and] sheds and hovels thrown up on waste ground" (2).

While the spatial growth of London in the eighteenth century was substantial, it was greater in some directions than others. To the west and north, expansion was the result of the well-to-do seeking an "escape from the growing hazards of inner-city life – air pollution, disease and street violence" (3). New buildings, developed at relatively low density. "Sprawled over the fields of Westminster, engulfing the earlier settlements of Holborn, the Strand and Whitehall" (4), while to the south and east, migrants from other parts of the British Isles were accommodated in Southwark, Shoreditch and Stepney, and towards the end of the century settled in Whitechapel, Wapping and Limehouse. During the course of the eighteenth century, London's population spread even further afield, westward along the Thames to Chelsea, Hammersmith, Chiswick, Barnes, Kew, Twickenham and Richmond; northward to Hampstead and Highgate, and north-eastward to Clerkenwell, Islington and Hackney.

Across the different building types, three styles of architecture were adopted in Early-Hanoverian London: the Baroque, the Palladian and the Neo-Classical.

In contrast to many cities of the Continent, the Baroque style of architecture in Britain's capital never really got a foothold during the early eighteenth century despite the efforts of Nicholas Hawksmoor and James Gibb to stamp their mark on ecclesiastical architecture. With Protestant-Whig ascendancy there was a degree of hostility towards the extravagant exuberance of Baroque, particularly since it had derived from Ceicento Rome, and therefore an alternative architectural style became far more acceptable to patrons in high places, that of Palladianism rooted in Cinquecento Veneto. Based on Andrea Palladio's *Le antichitá de Roman* (1554), Palladian architecture though also Italian in origin, was more acceptable as a rational and less frivolous style than the Baroque and one that, after all, had been applied with some flare by Inigo Jones in the early-seventeenth century and was revived by Colen Campbell, the 3rd Earl Burlington and William Kent in the early eighteenth century.

However, by the middle of the century, the Palladian style had run its course and was superseded by the Neo-classical style of architecture which had emerged as early as the 1720's. As part of the Grand Tour, visits to Rome became increasingly popular among British architects in the eighteenth century, and it became increasingly the vogue among practitioners to go back to first principles, to the architecture of the Eternal City rather than to rely on its interpretation by Palladio and his immediate successors. Neo-classicism was "bound up with a nascent primitivism – a belief that architecture, like society, had been at is purest and best in its simplest and most primitive form" (5). Neo-classical buildings are therefore rather severe with the use of decorative classical motifs kept to the minimum. They are also less solid since columns were now used to support entablatures rather than to be applied to walls (6).

Constitutional Monarchy and the Growth of Britain's Capital, 1714-60

George I (r.1714-27)

Because of unsuccessful attempts by James Edward Stuart in 1715-16 and Charles Edward Stuart in 1745 to resurrect the Stuarts as the reigning dynasty, Britain had two successive kings in the first half of the eighteenth century who were not only foreign by birth, but – in focussing their attention on matters abroad – showed comparatively little interest in stamping their mark on both Britain and its capital. George I, who acceded to the British throne in 1714 at the age of 54 after spending his earlier years in Hanover as Duke – and then Prince of Brunswick Lüneberg and later as Prince Elector of Hanover, never learnt to talk "more than a few words of broken English and his interests remained essentially German centring on the welfare of his beloved north German principality, where he went whenever he could and stayed as long as possible" (7).

The Early Years of the Hanoverian Monarch, 1714-1718

Following the accession of George I in August 1714, the Tory-dominated parliament continued to sit for a further six months and was then dissolved. At the general election that followed, the Tories – who had been in power since 1710 – were defeated and were superseded by a large Whig majority under the leadership of Lord Townshend, Lord Stanhope and the Earl of Sunderland. The new parliament – strongly Protestant – subsequently impeached the Tory leaders –

the Earl of Oxford, Viscount Bolingbroke and the Duke of Ormond – on a charge of sacrificing the British interests at the Treaty of Utrecht (1713) and also for having intrigued with the Jacobites with a view to restoring the Old Pretender (James Edward Stuart) to the throne despite or because of his Catholicism and friendship with Bourbon France. Though the Tories were discredited and remained out of office for two generations, there was an element of sympathy for the Jacobite cause, particularly in Scotland. Therefore with the aim of re-establishing a Stuart monarchy, the Earl of Mar led a Jacobite rising in 1715 against Hanoverian rule to install the 'Old Pretender' on the throne. Though Mar's irregulars took Perth, the subsequent battle of Sherrifmuir was indecisive. Mar then marched into England, but planned uprisings south of the border failed to materialise and he surrendered to British troops at Preston. Though James Edward Stuart arrived in Scotland from France he failed to inspire his followers and was forced to flee the country. But his patron, the Anglophobe Louis XIV, died on September 1, 1715, and therefore his return to France would have embarrassed the duc d'Orleans, Louis XV's regent, who wished to establish friendly relations with Britain.

Since he could no longer seek sanctuary in France, the Old Pretender settled in Rome, where – with Papal support – he lived for the rest of his life. It was in response to this background of political uncertainty that the Whig government introduced the Septennial Act of 1717 to extend the maximum length of a Parliament from three to seven years to strengthen the House of Commons against the House of Lords and to create greater political stability between elections. Little did the Whigs know that this would keep them in government until 1762 and that during this time they would have to preside over economic fluctuations, involve Britain in several wars and subject the national capital to alternating periods of property boom and slump.

As for the monarchy, the Early-Hanoverians – faced with constitutional change – had little desire to demonstrate their opulence by developing sumptuous new palaces in London, particularly as there was already a plentiful stock of royal residences in or near the capital. George I, when not on one of his many visits to Hanover, was content to reside at Hampton Court Palace in the summer and St. James's Palace in the winter, and so too was George II though from time to time when he was Prince of Wales he resided in Leicester House on the northern side of Leicester Square to avoid the company of his authoritarian father. Leicester House was demolished in 1791-92 as part of a redevelopment scheme.

In contrast to the French aristocracy in the early eighteenth century who demonstrated its preference for a Parisian way of life and vacated their *châteaux* in the countryside particularly during the winter, in contemporary England aristocrats and wealthy merchants were often more at home in their rural estates than in London. Thus, a plethora of country mansions were built in early-Georgian England and the most famous in easy reach of the capital was Wanstead House in suburban east London built in 1713-26. Designed by Colen Campbell for Earl Tylney, the large mansion was a fine example of Palladian architecture consisting of a three storey central block flanked by two lower wings of two storeys. Its central block was dominated by a giant hexastyle portico with Corinthian pillars and surmounted by a triangular pediment, the first example of such a configuration applied to an English country house. With a length of 260 ft (79 m) the façade of the building would doubtlessly have been impressive to visitors notwithstanding that it was a little austere (8).

Wanstead House (1720), by Colen Campbell

Economic growth was discontinuous, particularly in the west and north, during the early years of George I's reign. This was largely because the Stuart rebellion (1715-16) created political uncertainty to the detriment of investment generally and construction activity in the capital, and in 1718-1719 war with Spain delayed construction yet again. If that was not all, in 1720 the bursting of the South Sea Bubble further reduced business confidence across many sectors of the economy, including building work.

St Alphage Greenwich (1712-14), by Nicholas Hawksmoor

Christchurch Spittlefields (1714-19), by Nicholas
Hawksmoor

The construction of churches, however, was a major
exception. This was mainly funded by money set aside
under the provisions of the Fifty Churches Act of 1710,
a piece of earlier Tory legislation. The products of this
Act remain largely extant and include the Baroque
churches of Nicholas Hawksmoor, Thomas Archer and
James Gibbs. Hawksmoor designed six of the most
original churches in and near the capital, all vividly
described by James Stephen Curl: St Alphege
Greenwich (1712-1714), is "a temple with huge
'serliana' at the east end"; Christchurch Spittlefields
(1714-1719) "has a broach spire set above a gigantic
serliana port"; St. George in East Wapping (1714-1729)
has "four pepper-pot staircase-towers and a curious top

to the western tower formed of alter-like drums"; St. Anne Limehouse (1714-1730) "has a powerful tower with a crowning lantern like a medieval element in Classical clothes"; St. Mary Woolnoth (1714-27) exhibits its "powerful Baroque modelling", and St. George Bloomsbury (1714-31) boasts an "immense Roman temple portico and a tower with a stepped pyramid derived from descriptions of the mausoleum at Halicarnassus" (9), and topped by a statue of George I, the only statue of the Hanoverian king in London.

St George East Wapping (1714-29), by Nicholas Hawksmoor

StAnne Limehouse (1714-24), by Nicholas Hawksmoor

St Mary Woolnoth (1716-17), by Nicholas Hawksmoor

289

St George Bloomsbury (1716-31), by Nicholas Hawksmoor

However, while Hawksmoor never ventured abroad, "Archer travelled in Holland, Italy, and probably Germany and Austria, and evolved a style with more direct echoes of Bernini and Borromini than that of any other English architect. His two London churches, St. Paul, Deptford (1712-1730), and St. John, Smith Square (1713-1728), are in some ways close to Hawksmoor, though the Deptford church had a centralised plan, possibly inspired by S. Agnese in Piazza Navona in Rome (10). In the opinion of John Summerson, "these churches are worth studying because they represent the most advanced Baroque style ever attempted in England" (11). Hawksmoor, however, did not restrict his architectural style entirely to the Baroque. In 1715-22, and not commissioned under the terms of the 1710 Act, he erected a Gothic tower and spire above St. Michael Cornhill, the church having been gutted by the Great Fire and largely rebuilt by Wren in 1670-72.

St Paul Deptford (1712-30), by Thomas Archer

St John Smith Square (1713-28), by Thomas Archer

St Mary-le-Strand (1714-17), by James Gibbs

Burlington House, Piccadilly (1714-15 and 1717-18), by Richard
Boyle, 3rd Earl of Burlington and Colen Campbell

Burlington House, Piccadilly after it was enlarged (1872)

Possibly the most influential London church architect of the first quarter of the eighteenth century, was neither Hawksmoor nor Archer but James Gibbs – a Scot, a Catholic, a Tory and possibly a Jacobite sympathiser. As one of the first of his generation to visit Italy – in the first instance to train for the priesthood – he became overawed by Baroque architecture, and it is not surprising that his first church in London, St. Mary-le-Strand, (1714-17) – built under the 1710 Act – reflected his studies under Carlo Fontana in Rome. Standing conspicuously on an island site and looking very much like a Catholic church, St Mary-le-Strand was severely criticised by the Protestant hierarchy. Gibbs was duly dismissed as one of the two building commissioners. The only notable secular buildings in London to be constructed in the Baroque style were the first stages in the reconstruction of Burlington House in Piccadilly Arches, 42 King Street (Russell House) in Covent Garden and Vanbrugh's Royal Arsenal at Woolwich. Situated on the north side of Piccadilly, Burlington House (originally built in 1664-65) was reconstructed by the 3rd Earl Burlington in association with James Gibb who built a Baroque curved colonnade along the sides of the forecourt in 1714-15. Contemporaneously, the Royal Arsenal at Woolwich was designed by Sir John Vanbrugh, Comptroller of the Office of Works, who presided over its construction in 1715-17, and the outcome being an austere Baroque brick edifice with its frontage decorated with white stone. Another austere building developed at the same time, but far less Baroque, consists of a range of alms houses in Hackney built at the bequest of Sir Robert Geffrye, Lord Mayor of London and Master of the Ironmongers Company.

Roayl Arsenal, Woolwich (1715-17), by John Vanbrugh

43 King Street, Covent Garden (1716-17), by Thomas Archer

Cheyne Walk (1700)

Geffrey Museum – former alms houses (1715)

A very subdued form of the Baroque (`Early Georgian') typified the architectural style of houses built in Cheyne Walk, Chelsea, at the beginning of the eighteenth century. At the eastern-end of the walk, the redbrick irregular terraced houses – with decorated gateposts and iron railings - rise to five storeys (including an attic) and are pierced by regularly-spaced segmental-headed windows.

Very soon Baroque completely gave way to Palladianism or an early manifestation of Neo-classicism. In 1717-18 Colen Campbell remodelled the main body of Burlington House in the style reminiscent of Palladio's Palazzo Porto at Vicenza (12), and with economic recovery in the early 1720's, Gibbs surmised that his professional future lay in shaking-off some of the manifestations of his faith and political allegiance, and in pandering to Protestant and Whig taste producing, what many would say is his masterpiece, the church of St. Martin-in-the-Fields (1721-1726), a building more Neoclassical than Baroque. Funded by

297

parishioners rather than by the provisions of the 1710 Act, St. Martin's – with its superb hexastyle portico of free standing Corinthian columns, a huge pediment, and a steeple in the style of Wren – became a model for Anglican worship not just in England but throughout much of the English-speaking world, though its critics pointed to the incongruity of constructing a steeple inside of the west wall as though it was standing on the ridge of the roof. Gibbs also adopted a distinctly Neo-classical style when designing secular buildings such as Sudbrook Lodge (1726-28) in Richmond upon Thames, a resplendent residence built for John Campbell, 2nd Duke of Argyll and Greenwich.

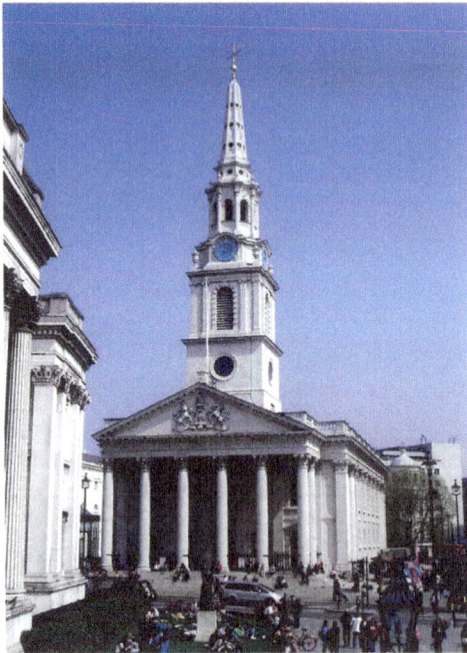

St Martin in the Fields (1721-26), by James Gibbs

Sudbrooke Lodge, Richmond (1726-28), by James Gibbs

War with Spain, 1718-1719

Despite the shortcomings of the Treaty of Utrecht, the new Whig administration recognised that it was preferable to accept its terms than to adopt a policy of non-compliance which could pave the way to a further continental war. In 1717, therefore, Britain, together with France and the Netherlands, formed an alliance to uphold the Treaty of Utrecht, and in 1718 a Quadruple Alliance of Britain, France, the Netherlands and Austria formed a coalition against Spain after it had captured Sicily. In the ensuing war, Britain played a major role in quelling Spanish ambitions. Admiral Byng destroyed the Spanish fleet off Cape Passaro, and in 1718 British forces defeated a Spanish and Jacobite alliance at the Battle of Glenshiel, the last close engagement of British and foreign troops in mainland Britain. Following Britain's military successes, the Quadruple Alliance made peace with Spain in 1720, but for two years previously little building work of any importance was undertaken in Britain, not least in London.

The South Sea Bubble 1720 and its aftermath

Though the Jacobite rebellion and foreign policy were centre stage during the early years of the Whig administration, the bursting of the South Sea Bubble in 1720 was of immediate concern to the government, particularly as many of its leading supporters faced financial ruin. Established in 1710 the South Sea Company was granted the monopoly of trade with the Spanish American colonies, including the *assiette*, the right to trade in slaves. In 1719, and inspired by the actions of the Mississippi Company in Paris, the South Sea Company took over £31 million (60 per cent) of Britain's national debt by exchanging stock in the company for government securities. The company bribed members of the government – including the Earl of Sutherland and Lord Stanhope – to support their plan and, with the prospect of substantial capital gains enticed bond holders to convert their high interest, irredeemable government bonds into low-interest easily tradable stocks. Company prices consequently rose rapidly from £128 on 1 January 1720 to £1050 on 24 June, and in their rush buy stock on the open market many landowners raised the necessary funds by selling-off their properties, not least in London. To prevent the speculative floatation of other companies, the government passed the 1720 Act that not only halted the rise in the market but, through a rush to sell, caused the value of the Company's stock to plummet to £150 by September 30. Many individuals, including aristocrat landowners, made substantial losses, putting a stop – in an already depressed market – to property development in London.

Largely as a result of the bubble, Sunderland

300

resigned. Lord Stanhope died of apoplexy, and Robert Walpole was appointed First Lord of the Treasury and Leader of the House of Commons in April 1721. It is from this date that his *de facto* tenure as Britain's first Prime Minister began though, in reality, he shared power with his brother-in-law Lord Townshend, controller of the nation's foreign affairs and Secretary of State for the Northern Department. Walpole's immediate task was to ameliorate the effects of the South Sea debacle. He ordered the Bank of England and Treasury to take over the last tranches of the National Debt that had been acquired by the South Sea Company, and activated the sinking find that he had set up as Chancellor of the Exchequer in 1717 to gradually pay-off the National Debt from the proceeds of taxation.

To ease the pressure on the nation's finances, Walpole and Townshend's long-term task was to keep Britain at peace. To this end, Britain was only too willing to join France and Prussia in signing the Treaty of Hanover (1725) to establish an alliance against a potentially hostile Spain and Empire, and so – for the time being – averted the outbreak of a European war.

A period peace, the 1720-1727

Although the South Sea Bubble, coming very shortly after a war with Spain, had an adverse effect on property development in London, this was fairly short-lived. Peace in the first-half of the 1720's brought about greater economic stability, and it was during this period that work began on a number of important buildings. Even before James Gibbs began work on St. Martin-in-the-Fields, a new generation of architects adopted Neoclassicism. John James, for example, who had succeeded Gibbs as one of the building

301

commissioners in 1715, designed the church of St. George Hanover Square, in St. George's Street. Erected under the Act of 1710, it was built in the newly fashionable West End in 1720-25, and pre-dating St. Martin-in-the-Fields, its portico was the first to be built for a London church in the eighteenth century (Inigo Jones, incidentally, had added a portico to the east end of St. Paul's church in Covent Garden in 1633). Also built before St.Martin-in-the-Fields, James Gibb's church of St. Peter (1721-24) similarly adopts the Neo-Classical style, though possesses only a modest portico. Located in Vere Street, on an island site north of Oxford Street, St. Peter's was built for the use of the residents of near-by Cavendish Square and its adjacent streets. Its small double cupola tower sits confidently above the simple rectangle of the brick church with its broad nave started by Wren.

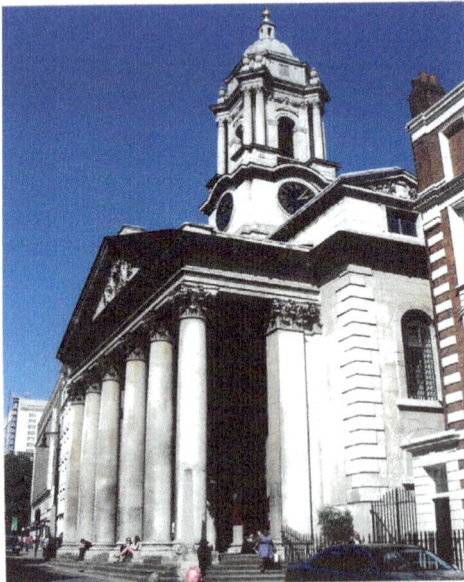

St George Hanover Square (1720-25), by John James

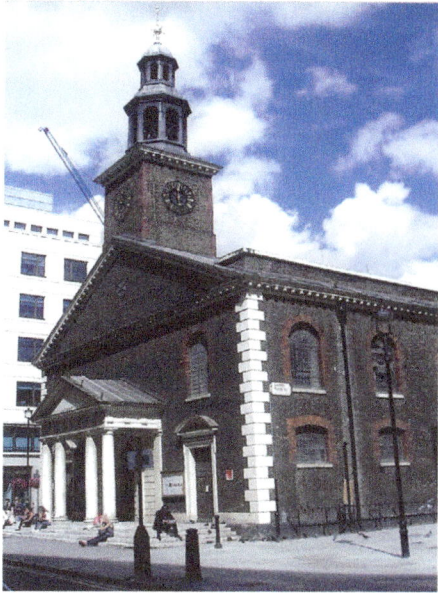

St Peter Vere Street (1721-24), by James Gibbs

Fournier Street (1722-8)

Meanwhile, Fournier Street in Spitalfields had become the centre of the silk industry introduced by Huguenot weavers fleeing Louis XIV's France in the late seventeenth century. The street – built in 1722-8 - consists of high density redbrick terraced housing, four storeys in height with the larger than normal windows in the loft to facilitate weaving.

St Botolph Bishopsgate, 1725-29, by George Dance the Elder

St Luke Old Street (1727-33), by Nicholas Hawksmoor and John James.

Later in 1725-29, Gibb's contemporaries , George Dance the Elder and James Gold built St Botoph in Bishopsgate, its relatively austere appearance mitigated by a tower in the style of Wren, and in the 1720s John James, worked with Hawksmoor on the church of St. Lukes, Old Street (1727-33), a striking though somewhat undecorated barn of a building supporting its only Baroque feature: a bizarre fluted obelisk steeple of considerable height (see above), and he added a steeple to Hawksmoor's church of St. Alphage at Greenwich in 1730, in imitation of Gibbs's edifice at St. Martin's.

College Residence, Westminster School (1722-30), by
Richard Boyle, 3rd Earl of Burlington

Since the Henrician Reformation in the sixteenth
century, a plethora of independent schools had
superseded the church in the provision of sub-
university education, and one of the earliest of such
schools in London was Westminster School that
expanded almost continuously up to the eighteenth
century and beyond. Designed by the 3rd Earl
Burlington and inspired by Inigo Jones, a new south-
facing dormitory block was constructed in the Little
Dean's Yard of the school in 1722-30, overlooking the
Palace of Westminster. With a 15-bay stone façade, the
dormitory has a ground floor decade (now glazed in),
first floor windows surmounted by alternating
triangular and segmental pediments, a top floor pierced
by smaller windows, and the whole edifice is capped
with a cornice.

George II, (r. 1727-1760)

Like his father George I, George II, was born in Hanover, and before he acceded to the throne of Britain in 1727 at the age of 44 had broadly followed in his father's footsteps as Duke of Brunswick and Lüneberg and Electoral Prince of Hanover. Though he was much more at home in Britain than his father, and could speak acceptable English, he was as much concerned with protecting the legitimate interests of Hanover as those of Britain, if not more so. With the war of the Austrian Succession – in which a coalition of Hanoverian, British, Dutch and Prussian forces took-on the might of France and her new ally Austria – "a sizeable group in Parliament did not think that Britain should be fighting in Europe for the sake of Hanover at all. Indeed, victory or no victory, it was a betrayal of Britain" (13). However, a similar coalition was formed at the outset of the Seven Years War to combat French ambitions, though this time, and under the influence of William Pitt, it was fought on a global rather than Continental state in which British interests were not only protected but – at the expense of France – greatly expanded, particularly in America, Canada and India.

Nevertheless, because of his Hanoverian roots remote from the Renaissance cities of Italy, George II, like his father before him, saw no reason to glorify London by funding the development of grandiose royal buildings or adopting triumphal planning schemes, in contrast to Bourbon attempts over the years to enhance the built environment of Paris.

Instead of ruling as absolute monarchs, the first two Hanoverian kings were willing to leave British domestic policy almost entirely to elected governments, and it is within this context and with the accumulation of funds derived from a maritime trade and the Agricultural and Industrial revolutions that the built environment of London was enhanced during the eighteenth century, in other words, not by royal patronage but as an outcome of aristocratic and middle-class activity.

Chiswick House (1727-29), by Richard Boyle, 3rd Earl of Burlington

During the first two years of George II's reign, Britain was at war with Spain and therefore resources were only available during the conflict for a limited amount of construction activity. This took place particularly in the environmentally attractive western environs of the capital where the demand for sumptuous mansions was high and where finance was forthcoming from private funds. Chiswick House in west London (1727-29), designed by Earl Burlington for his own use, is "a magnificent country villa modelled on Palladio's Villa Rotunda at Vincenza" (14). However, while it is suggested that "this tiny but completed symmetrical house may be regarded as the manifesto of the English Palladians" (15), Sir John Summerson argues that the "whole house is ….an architectural laboratory, a collection of expositions and experiments" (16), for example "the [octagonal] drum and dome emerging through the roof originate in Scamozzi while the stairs leading up to the single Corinthian portico have a Piedmontese source" (17). Nonetheless few would deny that, in the words of Sir Kenneth Clark, Chiswick House is a "masterpiece of domestic architecture" (18). Also in west London, George II, personally funded the villa of Marble Hill (1714-29) that was built for his former mistress, the Countess of Suffolk, and the building was designed by Henry Herbert, Earl of Pembroke, an architect in his own rite. In collaboration, with Robert Morris, he produced an elegant Palladian building in the Campbell rather than Burlington sense.

Marble Hill (1723-28), by Henry Herbert, 9th Earl of Pembroke and Roger Morris

However, by the 1730's demand picked-up. On the heels of John James, and in competition with Hawksmoor and Gibbs, Henry Flintcroft was commissioned under the Act of 1710 to design the church of St. Giles-in-the-Fields in St. Giles High Street. Completed in 1733, its unpretentious Neoclassical "exterior is faced with Portland stone, [its] tower rises above the west pediment and becomes octagonal at clock-face level [and its] stone spire is banded and topped by a golden ball and vane" (19). Following closely behind Flintcroft, George Dance the Elder built the church of St. Leonard (1736-1740) in Shoreditch High Street, not as a commissioner's church but as a replacement for one that had collapsed in 1713. Its prominent attributes are a 200 ft (60 m) tall multi-staged obelisk steeple and a Tuscan portico, built of Portland stone and reminiscent of St. Martins-in-the-Fields (20). Though not one of the fifty churches of the 1710 Act, the West Towers of Westminster Abbey was Hawksmoor's last project and it was unfinished when he died in 1736. The towers "show his extraordinary ability for imitation and innovation and are only one of two examples of his Gothic work in London, the other being the tower of St. Michael, Cornhill" (21).

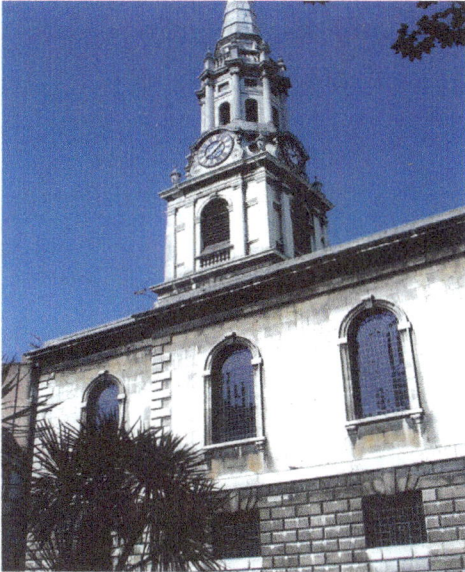
St Giles in the Field (1731-33), by Henry Flitcroft

St Leonard Shoredich, (1736-40), by George Dance the Elder

West Towers, Westminster Abbey (1736), by Nicholas
Hawksmoor

It was during the 1720's-30's that the Bank of
England occupied new purpose-built premises. It had
previously functioned from Mercers' Hall and Grocer's
Hall since its foundation in 1694. But because of an
increase in the volume of banking and the need for
more space the bank's governors appointed George
Simpson in 1724 to build the institution's new premises
in Threadneedle Street. Completed in 1734, its most
visible feature, the façade of its gatehouse, was entirely
Palladian in style comprising three storeys, its ground
floor being rusticated and pierced by three arched
entrances flanked either side by two bays, its first and
second storeys consisted of seven bays demarcated by
engaged columns and the whole width of the façade
was surmounted by a balustrade.

But it was housing development that accounted for
the greatest amount of construction activity in Georgian
London and its environs. In the 1720's-30's, as if to
balance the development of a proliferation of grand

country houses across England, a number of notable town houses or mansions were constructed in London, largely to satisfy the growing demand from rural aristocrats and their professional acolytes for residences in the capital. Generally larger in dimension than the Parisian *hôtel*, though not as numerous, standalone London mansions are best exemplified by Harcourt House, Pembroke House and Devonshire House, each of which were constructed in the Palladian style. Harcourt House (1722) was a very large edifice in Cavendish Square built for Baron Bingley from a design produced by Thomas Archer, Pembroke House (1723-24) in Whitehall was built for Henry Herbert, 9th Early of Pembroke (1723-1724) in accordance with his own design with the assistance of Colen Campbell, and after a short war with Spain in 1727, Devonshire House (1734-37) was built for William Cavendish, 3rd Duke of Devonshire and designed by William Kent. On the edge of London, the Hunting Lodge (known today as the White Lodge) was built for George II in Richmond Park by Roger Morris, the edifice being a fairly typical example of a medium sized Palladian country mansion, and other good examples of this genre include Moor Park (1720-8) in Rickmansworth and Danson House (1755) in Bexleyheath.

White Lodge, Richmond Park (1727-30), by Henry Herbert, 9th Earl of Pembroke and Roger Morris

Moor Park, Rickmondsworth (1720), James Thornhill

Danson House, Bexley (1751), by Sir Robert Taylor

However, it was not stand-alone town or country mansions that best epitomised Georgian residential development throughout much of the eighteenth century London and its environs, even though some town houses posed as terraced houses, for example 4 St James's Square (1726-8), with its five bay elevation, has an essentially horizontal rather than vertical elevation. But by the 1730's, a high proportion of construction work in the capital was geared to the development of multi-storey terraced housing. It was therefore necessary to achieve economy of site area and economy in road making. Thus, as explained by Sir John Summerson, "the size and shape of the London house [was] conditioned ….by the economic need to get as many houses as possible into one street. The typical site of a London house is therefore a long strip of ground running back from the street. The house covers the front part of the strip, the middle part is garden or courtyard, and the back is, in the larger type of house, a coach house and stable served from a subsidiary road" (22).

4, St James's Square (1726)

Most middle and upper class houses in Georgian London, normally with a total of four to five storeys in height, had a basement partly obscured by a raised street to facilitate access to the main front door of the dwelling. Whereas the road represented an artificial level, the rear garden and any ancillary rear building was the "natural" level. Such housing often had a number of aesthetic qualities, for example as exhibited at Colen Campbell's 31-34 Old Burlington Street (1718-23). Based on Inigo Jones's design for Lothbury in the City, almost one-hundred years earlier (see chapter 5), these Burlington Street houses with their austere elevations exhibit "a vista of an immaculately – proportioned façade with the vertical spacing of the window openings complimented by the embedded reminders of the conceptual temple front on crucial parts of the façade; a cornice marks the top of the temple entablature, a deep string course indicates the base of the columns and the start of the basement level" (23). Even more severe but equally imposing is the red-brick terrace of Great James Street (1720-30) in Holborn, the longest early-Georgian street in London.

31 Old Burlington Street (1718-30), by Colen Campbell

Great James Street (1720-30)

Even when renovating older terraces, there was a tendency to employ Georgian architecture. The late-seventeenth century terrace of Downing Street (see chapter 6) received a 'makeover' after number 10 had been acquired by the George II in 1730 (for the use of Sir Robert Walpole and all future Prime Ministers) and numbers 11 and 12 had been purchased by the Crown as the respective residences of all future Chancellors of the Exchequer and a miscellany of civil servants. All three houses were refaced in the Georgian style by Kenton Cuse. There were of course variations on the conventional Georgian terrace. Colen Campbell's houses in Grosvenor Square (1725) "were embellished with the full regalia of the Roman temple front; entablature, columns or pilasters, and a rusticated ground floor basement" (24). He ensured that like Palladian country houses but unlike Baroque homes, the occupants of his Grosvenor Square houses were not susceptible to the dirt and noise of the city street by designating the first floor as the *piano nobile* above a rusticated ground floor and basement. Non-conforming terraced housing was apparent in the western and northern suburbs. Stretching westwards on the north bank of the Thames, Chiswick Mall was developed in the 1730s and the Upper Mall throughout the eighteenth century, and both contained houses of a variety of shapes and sizes, and some lacked basements similar, to some extent, to those on the north side of Church Row in Hampstead, although there is a high degree of uniformity on its south side. In near-by Highgate village, large mansions – several of which are of seventeenth century origin – sit cheek by jowl with terraced housing that descends into the High Street. In contrast to housing in much of the Continent, where apartments tend to be arranged horizontally floor by floor, London housing - almost regardless of its value –

318

tends to be arranged vertically. Indeed, in the English capital, blocks of flats of high social standing were unknown until Henry Ashton built the flats in Victoria Street in the 1850s, and it was not until the following decade that Peabody housing becoming available for future generations of low-income flat-dwellers (see chapter 9).

Grosvenor Square, south side house (1725-30)

Chiswick Mall (mid-17th century – 18th century)

Upper Mall, Hammersmith (mid-17th century – 18th century)

Church Row, Hampstead (1720)

The Grove, Highgate (early 18th century)

It would, however, be a mistake to assume that the design of London terraced housing remained constant throughout the eighteenth century, it changed. The Palladian house of the 1730's-60's varied substantially from those constructed at the beginning of the century. Legislation of 1707 and 1709 (see chapter 6) had abolished the prominent wooden eaves and cornices characteristic of so many houses in late-Stuart London and the same building Acts resulted in roofs throughout the eighteenth century becoming "half hidden by a parapet wall, with a cornice of brick, stone, or in later years, stucco, a few feet below the summit" (25). Such attributes are not confined to terraced streets, they are also evident in a plethora of other housing developments of the period, for example at Devonshire Square, built c. 1740, and within the many new squares of the West End. Fashion also played a part in the evolving appearance of eighteenth century housing. Increasingly there was a great change-over from casement to sash windows, but throughout the century the Serliana window was popular, an attractive example of this embellishment being at 71 South Audley Street (1736). Together with the general adoption of parapet-roofs, the characteristic Georgian town house had arrived (26). A further change occurred early in the century when red bricks that had been widely used in construction fell out of fashion and were followed by grey bricks in most new housing projects. Except for large town houses, stone was rarely used in construction.

Devonshire Square, 1723-4

71 Audley Street (1736) by Edward Shepherd

The building of the London house was as much influenced by economic considerations as well as by legislation and changes in aesthetic appeal. Either a wealthy individual would find a site, commission an architect to produce a plan and an estimate, and then tradesmen would be employed to undertake the work, or less wealthy owners would eschew the assistance of an architect and deal directly with a master-builder but at much greater risk of getting a bad bargain (27). However, most house building took place in a speculative market where ground landlords would sign a building agreement with a master builder who would subsequently take a building-lease on the property of perhaps 60, perhaps 99 years with a peppercorn rent for the first year or two, and during this initial period he would erect a carcass of a house – simply a brick shell with floors and roof – and offer it for sale. With luck, he would find a purchaser before the peppercorn period expired, so that his outlay on ground rent was *nil*. The customer would buy the house, finished and decorated to his/her own taste for a lump sum, and the lease would be made out in the customer's name. Thus the builder could realise a speculative profit for little outlay (28). Taking the lead from major aristocratic landowners of the seventeenth century, such as the Earl of St. Albans or Earl of Southampton, some developers, often the landlords themselves acting as developers, realised that an attractive layout including shops and open space would be more commercial than one confined to housing.

While large scale house building catered for the needs of a rapidly growing population so too did the construction of a number of large hospitals. With the squalid living conditions of so many London households, diseases were rampant throughout much of the eighteenth century. The English capital thus witnessed a prolonged boom in the construction of hospitals extending over the first five decades of the century. Funded by private individuals and corporate bodies, hospitals were run as not-for-profit charitable institutions and therefore could be deemed to provide more of a public rather than private service. St. Thomas's Hospital, rebuilt several times since its foundation in 1106, was the first London hospital to receive a new building in the early eighteenth century (1709), and the almost as ancient St. Bartholomew's (founded in 1123) was rebuilt in stages between 1702-59 , with James Gibbs acting as its architect from 1730 to its completion. Some newly established hospitals were also constructed throughout the eighteenth century for example Westminster (finished 1719) and Guys (1721-25). Generally, all these new foundations were "symmetrical brick boxes, never quite without architectural features" (29), although Guys was more elaborately designed than the others giving it a distinctly Palladian appearance.

St Bartholomew's Hospital (1730-59), by James Gibbs

Guys Hospital (1721-5), by Richard Jupp

However, because of a low tax base and constraints on public expenditure there was a relative paucity of public sector development of all sorts throughout much of the first half of the eighteenth century. Though the demand for major public buildings may have been largely met during the preceding Restoration, the early 1700's witnessed the rise to power of the Whig oligarchy who were much more concerned with presiding over large scale private development and the creation of private fortunes that with the construction of public buildings. Even the requirements of the armed services were not adequately met. For example, at the age of 62 Sir John Vanbrugh as a high spending comptroller at the Office of Works was replaced in 1722-6 by Thomas Ripley nearly 20 years his junior. Ripley during the previous four years had demonstrated that he could keep expenditure under control when he had been responsible for the reconstruction of the Admiralty building in Whitehall, but this was at the cost of architectural quality, something that Vanbrugh would not have allowed to have happened. However, another more successfully-designed building was constructed south of the Admiralty building and at right angles to Whitehall on its western side. This was the Treasury Building constructed on the southern edge of a site that was to become Horse Guards Parade later in the century (see below). Palladian in style and built of Portland stone, the cube-shaped building was designed by William Kent and constructed in 1733-1736.

But before the parade needs of the Horse Guards could be met, the Honourable Artillery Company - the oldest military body in the United Kingdom dating back to 1537- expanded its headquarters in the City Road by commissioning the construction of a large five bay house facing the Artillery Grounds, a prelude to much greater expansion of its premises in the nineteenth century.

Treasury Building (1733-6), by William Kent

Honourable Artillery Company (1735)

Warfare and construction Activity, 1739-1763

From 1739 through to 1748, Britain's participation in warfare on the Continent had a debilitating effect on property development at home. The War of Jenkins Ear between Britain and Spain was, as far as Britain was concerned, a prelude to her involvement in the War of the Austrian Succession (1742-1748). During the short premiership of the 1st Earl of Wilmington (1742-1743), British forces led by George II (the last British monarch to command an army in battle) defeated France at the Battle of Dettingen in 1743, but under the Pelham government (1743-1747) the British army commanded by the Duke of Cumberland was defeated by the French at the Battle of Fontenoy. There was also a change of fortune in Scotland. Whereas the French-backed Jacobites under Charles, the Young Pretender, defeats George II's forces at the Battle of Falkirk in 1745, the following year Cumberland routs Charles's army at Culloden. Cumberland's reputation as an army commander, however, suffered a severe blow in 1747 when he led British forces to defeat by the French at the Battle of Lauffeld in the Netherlands. Only when outstanding dynastic and territorial matters across Europe were largely resolved did peace return to the continent, a situation confirmed by the Treaty of Aix-la-Chapelle in 1748.

After nine years of almost continual warfare, property developers and house builders had to compete with the armed forces for scarce resources with the inevitable result that much construction work in London was cancelled or postponed. However, a small number of commercial buildings were built in the City during the succession war. First, at the western end of Lomband Street opposite the Bank of England, Mansion House was built in 1739-42. Designed by George Dance the Elder as the official residence of the Lord Mayor, Dance was already well known in his capacity of 'Clerk of the City Works'. The edifice is Palladian in style and "has a nine-bay ashlar front with a giant six-column Corinthian portico standing on a rustic base" (30). But as Sir John Summerson points out its "tall pilastered face, with its ungenerously shallow portico, leaves an impression of uneasy restricted bulk; of the classical canon used without emotion, simply to harness a structure too large for its site" (31). Summerson goes on to comment disparagingly that "the building is a striking reminder that good taste was not a universal attribute of the eighteenth century, and that in the City in the 1730's there was a great deal more money than discrimination" (32). Second, in 1747 work began on the construction of the Corn Exchange in Mark Lane (that in a rebuilt form remained on its site until 1987). Like Mansion House it was designed by George Dance senior. It was serenely Neo-classical and had an open colonnade on

329

the ground floor that was roofed-over in the nineteenth century (33). Like Mansion House, but unlike the Corn exchange, several City Halls in the Palladian mould were built in the 1740's, possibly the most famous being Ironmongers' Hall in Fenchurch Street built in 1745. Designed by Thomas Holden, the hall was a three-storey building (excluding its basement), was rusticated on the ground floor and its face was graced with four Ionic pilasters. Its central bays contained a modest portal but a large Serliana window rose above it on the *piano nobile*. The whole was surmounted by a balustrade and a large centrally-positioned pediment. It was demolished in 1917.

Mansion House (1739-52), by George Dance the Elder

There was comparatively little church-building in London in the 1740s, but sufficient public/private resources were found to reconstruct St Botolph Aldgate (1741-4). Designed by George Dance the Elder, the church is modest in scale, built largely of brick and is adorned only by stone dressings on an obelisk tower.

330

Though public sector development during this period of war was at a low ebb, there were only two public buildings constructed during this period of war that are worthy of consideration. First: Westminster Bridge. Designed by Charles Labelye a Swiss engineer, it was the first structure to be built over the Thames in the capital since London Bridge had been constructed in the twelfth century. Erected between 1738 and 1750, it spanned 1,200 ft (390 m) of London's river and was an engineering triumph employing the latest technology such as the use of caissons (watertight chambers) instead of piling for building the peers, and using Portland stone voissoir courses to support a continuous arch of Purbeck stone. Second: Horse Guards Parade. It is situated between St. James's Park and Whitehall, and was developed as a monument to George II's interest in military display and order and as the headquarters of the general Staff and was built by William Kent and John Vardy in the Palladian style in 1750-1758. However, the development of the loosely-styled Palladian buildings on the eastern edge of the parade was almost certain to meet with approval and disapproval. Sir John Summerson, for example, suggests on the one hand that "with its complex projections and recessions and varied skyline [it] is irresistibly picturesque – especially in [its] spacious park setting and [its] linen sheen of …..Portland stone, but on the other hand "the plan is a collection of square or nearly square boxes … which on analysis are revealed as grotesquely out of harmony with the function of the elements which they form part" (34). He particularly drew attention to the five Venetian windows of the military building that overlook the park of which only one lights a room of any importance (the Commander in Chief's room), the other four are concealed in the corners of inconsequential rooms.

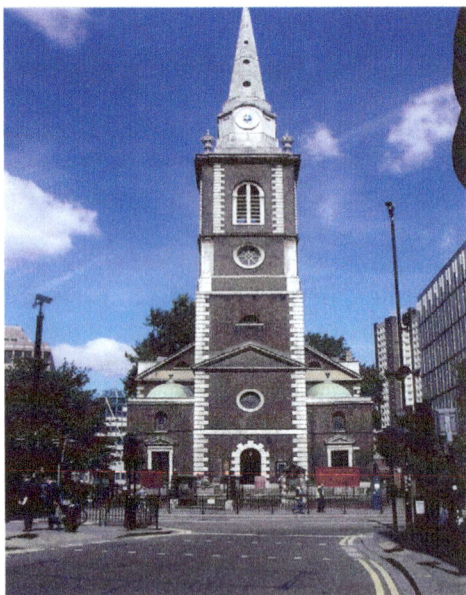

St Botaph-without-Aldgate (1741-44), by George Dance the Elder

Horses Guards (1751-3), by William Kent

Since hospitals were constructed and run as 'not-for-profit charitable institutions they could be deemed to provide more of a public – rather than a private service. In addition to the hospitals built or re-built in London earlier in the century – St. Thomas's, Bartholomew's, Westminster and Guys (see above) – three further hospitals were built in the capital in the 1740's-1750's. The Foundling Hospital in Guilford Street (1742-1752), the London in Whitechapel Road (1752-1757) and the Middlesex in Windmill Street (1755) but each was architecturally similar to those already built in the capital, essentially symmetrical brick boxes.

London Hospital (1752-7), by Boulton Mainwaring

Most developments of property in the mid-eighteenth century embraced the Neo-classical style of architecture, but in London there was one main exception to the norm, namely the large *villa suburbana* of Strawberry Hill in Twickenham. Designed by Horace

333

Walpole, the younger son of the Prime Minister William Walpole, and built between 1749-76, the remarkable edifice – with its Gothic tracery and Chinese fretwork - signalled the introduction of the Picturesque movement in English architecture. But in the capital the new style was not adopted again until well into the nineteenth century, but only on a limited scale.

Strawberry Hill (1749-76), by Horace Walpole

As soon as the six year War of the Austrian Succession was concluded by the Treaty of Aix-la-Chappelle in 1748, the construction of large Neo-classical town houses in London was resumed. The 4th Earl of Chesterfield (Lord Stanhope) built Chesterfield House in Great Stanhope Street. Designed by Isaac Ware, the house (demolished in 1938) was distinctly Palladian, and stylistically replicated in Spencer House (1756-67) in St. James's Place built for Earl Spencer from a design by John Vardy. Though Spencer House might be criticised for being a pretentious hybrid –

neither a villa nor a *palazzo* – it has received many plaudits over the years for being a truly beautiful piece of architecture (34). There were also a number of smaller houses of considerable merit built in the same period that is worthy of mention. Commenced just before the outbreak of war and completed early in the conflict, 44 Berkeley Square (1742-1744) was built for Lady Isabella Finch and was designed by William Kent, though today it is squeezed between two Georgian terrace blocks of a later date. In Roehampton, on the western fringe of London and set in a landscaped garden on the edge of Richmond Park, Besborough House (1750) was commissioned by Lord Besborough and designed by William Chambers (the house is currently called Manressa House and is part of the University of Roehampton).

Spencer House (1752-4), by John Vardy

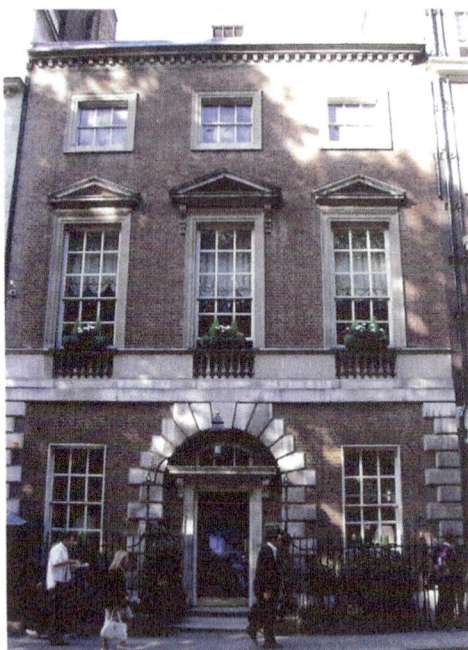

Berkeley Square, No 44 (1742-4), by William Kent

Besborough House (1750), by Sir William Chambers. Now known as Manressa House.

Notwithstanding a short period of recovery during the 1st Duke of Newcastle's government (1754-56), under the 4th Duke of Devonshire's administration (1756-57) and Newcastle's second government (1757-62) construction activity was again subdued during the Seven Years War (1756-63) with Britain and France engaged in armed conflict mainly in North America, the Caribbean and India. Only a small number of houses of merit were constructed in the capital in this period, possibly the most notable being Cambridge House in Piccadilly (1756-60) that was commissioned by Lord Egremont and built according to a design by Matthew Brettingham. However, during the peace that followed, property development in the capital increased substantially and reached a peak ten to fifteen years later. Demand now came increasingly from well-off families migrating from central London to the West End or from country gentlemen (rather than the aristocracy) anxious to get a foothold in a prestigious part of town. Neo-classicism was now in vogue and dominated architectural style during the remainder of the Georgian period. Possibly its finest earliest manifestation is the Neo-classical screen erected at the Admiralty by Robert Adam in 1759-61 to mask Thomas Ripley's Palladian edifice with its heavy portico, unloved from the time of its construction (1722-26).

Admiralty Screen (1759-63), by Robert Adam

Adam's early contribution to the development of London was not confined to the public sector. Between 1761-8 he attempted to update Syon House in Brentford for its current owner, the 1st Duke of Northumberland. However, in converting a sixteenth century convent into a contemporary *villa suburbana* , he lavishly refurbished the interior of the house in a very decorative Neoclassical style, but rebuilt the main facade in a very austere retro-style, omitting all decorative features except for crenellations and a small porch. Between 1763-7, Robert Adam was also involved in modernising another west London villa, Osterley Park in Isleworth, a large square-shaped Elizabethan pile, turreted in each corner. Commissioned by Sir Francis Child, a City banker, he not only introduced many fine Neoclassical features to the interior of the building but built a grand Ionic portico across one side of its courtyard, its Portland stone contrasting spectacularly with the redbrick of the original house.

Syon House (1761-8), by Robert Adam

Osterley Park, east facade (1763-7), by Robert Adam

The Agricultural and Industrial Revolutions and their effect on the development of London

Notwithstanding the impact of the South Sea Bubble and successive periods of war and peace on the construction cycle, the Agricultural and Industrial Revolutions underpinned property development throughout much of the eighteenth century, enhanced the wealth of Britain and raised the level of overall demand to unprecedented heights. Large country landowners enjoyed ever-increasing rental incomes as the outcome of land enclosure and the use of innovative farming tools such as the seed drill and mechanical hoe, the employment of new agricultural techniques such as the abandonment of rotational fallow through the use of new crops such as turnips and clover, and by the adoption of new methods of livestock breeding. Landowners, with their new-found prosperity, not only commissioned grandiose country houses but also invested heavily in London property, witness the development of, for example, the estates of the Burlington, Harley/Portland, Grosvenor and Bedford families.

The causes of Britain's Industrial Revolution are well-known. A proliferation of technical innovations predicated industrial development during the eighteenth century. Abraham Darby's coking process (1709) enabled coal to be used for smelting, the use of John Kay's flying shuttle (1733), Lewis Paul's roller spinner (1738), John Hargreave's spinning jenny (1764) and Richard Arkwright's frame (1768) brought about an expansion of the cotton textile industry facilitated by the introduction of the factory system; while Benjamin Huntsman invention of the crucible process (1740) heralded a marked increase in steel-making.

However, none of these developments would have

led to exponential economic growth had it not been for a ready supply of labour and capital, and the improvement of transport. Between 1700 and 1750 the population of England grew steady from 5 million to 6 million (largely because of an increase in birth rates), but more important a significant proportion of the rural population displaced from their homes and livelihood as a result of the enclosures migrated gradually to the new industrial towns and London, not only enhancing the supply of urban labour but, in due course, increasing the level of demand for urban-produced goods and services.

There was also an increase in the mobility of capital. Although joint-stock companies – a modern vehicle for raising capital – were prohibited by the Bubble Act of 1720, and from 1709 partnerships were limited to only seven members throughout the century, there were many other sources of finance. Maritime trade undertaken by a plethora of monopolistic companies set up in the sixteenth and seventeenth centuries and, even more importantly, overseas trade conducted by a multitude of small and medium-sized merchants assisted the growth of the London money market. Overseas borrowing, particularly from the Netherlands, was another source of capital, and so too were internal loans from one industry to another, while landowners provided mortgages to companies wishing to expand on their estates. However, it was often left to industrialists to plough their profits back into their businesses, industry more often than not being its own progenitor. In the words of the eminent historian, T. S. Ashton, "the currents of investment flowed in all directions as wealth increase here and opportunities there; it was from no single zone of thrift and enterprise that the trade winds blow" (35).

Improved transportation was required to link

together areas of supply with areas of demand. Until the eighteenth century the development of inland trade, including trade to and from London, was impeded by inefficient and costly means of transportation. However, between 1700 and 1750, 418 Acts of Parliament authorised the setting up of turnpike trusts as joint stock companies to build and improve roads across England, and from 1751 to 1770 a further 840 were added to the network. Not only were travel times substantially reduced, but the volume of commercial and economic transactions, including the Royal Mail, grew markedly especially after the introduction of stage coaches in the 1770's. The cheaper transportation of bulky goods, however, was largely dependent on the improvement of rivers and the development of canals. From the sixteenth century to the early eighteenth, the major rivers of England, the Thames, Severn, Trent, Tyne and the Tees – were straightened, widened and deepened, the Bridgwater Canal connected Worsley to Salford in 1769 (and later Manchester was linked to Runcorn), the River Trent was linked to the Mersey by the Grand Trunk Canal in the 1770's, and work began on the Staffordshire-Worcester Canal between the Trent and the Severn in 1772.

The effect of the Agricultural and Industrial Revolutions upon property development in London was immeasurable. Not only was the increased wealth of the nation derived from the expansion of overseas trade in the eighteenth century benefiting London above all other ports, it was also created in the industrial heartlands of the North and Midlands and was distributed in favour of the well-off in London with their accounts in the City banks even though many of the capital's more wealthy occupants emanated from the countryside or manufacturing towns of the provinces. Therefore, as the pace of industrialisation hastened throughout the eighteenth century, London attracted more and more property development particularly in her high-income residential sector, for example in the West End estates. In a micro-sense, house building in much of London utilised the products of the Industrial Revolution such as iron railings and drain pipes manufactured by companies in Coalbrookedale and Carron, earthenware pipes made in Stoke on Trent while coal was used throughout the capital to warm a rapidly growing number of homes.

Planned development

Town planning in London took two forms. First, the implementation of public works schemes, and second the planned development of private estates. Influenced by John Gwynn's publication of 1706, *London and Westminster Improved*, Parliament introduced innumerable Road Acts and lighting and Paving Acts in the 1750s-60s that affected mainly Westminster and adjacent parishes, and in 1760 an Act was obtained for improving and widening streets, while in the same year all the old City gates were demolished except for Newgate. The Corporation of the City of London also became a property developer since in 1767 it secured an Act for repairing the Royal Exchange, rebuilding Newgate prison and for completing the reconstruction of the old London Bridge under the plans of Sir Robert Taylor and George Dance the Younger.

But most planned development was undertaken by private speculators on what were largely open fields or market gardens. Subject to the Statute of 1707, but before the Road Acts and Lighting and Paving Acts of the 1750s-60 came into effect, extensive private development was undertaken between Piccadilly and Oxford Street. Streets were often laid out at 90 degrees to each other forming a grid-iron pattern. They were invariably interspersed with residential squares that were intended to form the centres of development to include high, medium and low income housing (the latter often being confined to side streets or mews) with a sprinkling of churches, often in the manner established by their seventeenth century counterparts such as Bloomsbury Square and St James's Square, and akin to the grid-iron pattern of streets and squares in many a Renaissance city in Italy. To the private developer, time was money and he could ill-afford to have his capital tied up in lengthy building projects, and a simple grid-iron plan could best ensure minimum construction times.

Extensive grid-iron development in London, in fact, took off towards the end of the seventeenth century and at the beginning of the eighteenth when the estate of the 3rd Duke of Albemarle situated on the northern side of Piccadilly was gradually developed in the general direction of Oxford Street to form Albemarle Street (1683), Dover Street (1684) and Bond Street (1684). Immediately to its east, the Burlington Estate was the next to be built-up: Burlington Gardens, Burlington Street, Savile Row and Clifford Street all from 1717. To the north, but still south of Oxford Street, the 13 acre (5.3 ha) Scarborough estate was built soon after the accession of the Elector of Hanover, George I in 1714 with its centrepiece Hanover Square with its large expensive houses being developed during the building boom of the early 1720's. Built to lead into the square, St. George's Street (with its German-style houses) and Hanover Square was constructed in 1720-25. To the west of the Scarborough estate lies the Grosvenor Estate. Within it Grosvenor Square, the largest square in London except for Lincoln's Inn Fields, was developed between 1725-31. However, despite the stately appearance of the square with its substantial houses "attempts to impose architectural uniformity were largely ineffective" (36), except on the east side of the square where an attempt to achieve symmetry was largely successful due to the development of "a large pedimented house in the centre with large houses at both ends, producing the effect of a single palatial building" (37).

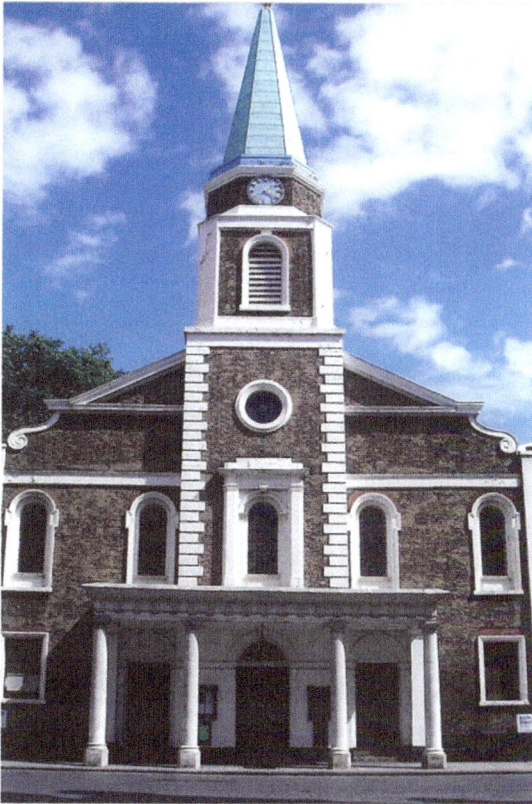

Grosvenor Chapel (1730), by Joseph Timbrell

25, Brook Street (1720-29)

Over the following twenty-two years a host of
terraced streets were built in the vicinity of the square:
Grosvenor Street, Brook Street (where George Frederic
Handel was a resident at number 25) , North and South
Audley Street, Duke Street and Carlos Street, together
with the Grosvenor Chapel built earlier in 1730. To the
south, and taking us back towards Piccadilly, the
Berkeley estate was laid out in the 1740's, with
Berkeley Square – with its long ranges of houses on its
east and west sides – dating from the beginning of the
decade, while Bruton Street, Hill Street, Charles Street
and Davies Street date from 1745. North of Oxford
Street lies the Cavendish-Harley Estate – dominated by
Cavendish Square (1717) with its two magnificent
stone houses (c1770) adorning its northern side. Other

highlights of the estate- all in the vicinity of the square - are Harley Street, Henrietta Place (formerly Street), Welbeck Street, Wimpole Street, Princes Street, and the Oxford Market, each developed from 1724. In complete contrast to Paris, town planning in eighteenth – century London was not so much an outcome of public policy, monarchical or municipal, but like most contemporary urban development in the English capital it was undertaken by private speculators from wealth generated by international trade, agricultural improvement and the early stages of the Industrial Revolution.

Cavendish Square (1717) showing north side houses (1770)

Harley Street (1753)

References

1. B. Weinreb and C. Hibbert, *The London Encyclopaedia*, Macmillan, 1993, pp 630-32.
2. S. Inwood, *The History of London*, Macmillan, 1998, p 283.
3. R. Tames, *A Traveller's History of London*, Castell & Co, 1992, p 86.
4. S. Jenkins, *Landlords to London. The Story of a Capital and its Growth*, Book Club Associates, 1975, p 43.
5. J. Fleming, H. Honour and Nikolaus Pevsner, *Penguin Dictionary of Architecture and Landscape Architecture*, Penguin Books, 5th Edit., 1999, p 117.
6. Ibid, p 117.
7. R. Starkey, *Monarchy. From the Middle Ages to Modernity*, Harper Press, 2006, p 232.
8. D. Watkin, *English Architecture*, Thames &

Hudson, 2001, p 124.

9. J.S. Curl, *Oxford Dictionary of Architecture*, Oxford University Press, 2000, p 9.

10. D. Watkin, *English Architecturer*, Thames & Hudson, 2001, p 119.

11. Sir John Summerson , *Georgian London*, Penguin, 1969, p 94.

12. Sir John Summerson, Ibid, p 101; B Weinreb and C. Hibbert, *The London Encyclopaedia*, Macmillan, 1993, p 111.

13. D..Starkey, *Monarchy. From the Middle Ages to Modernity*, Harper Press, 2006, p 246.

14. B. Weinreb and C. Hibbert, *The London Encyclopaedia*, Macmillan, 1993, p 158.

15. R. Furneux Jordan, *A Concise History of Western Architecture*, Thames & Hudson, p 265

16. Sir John Summerson , *Architecture in Britain, 1530-1830* 1993, p 313.

17. Ibid, p 313 and 315.

18. K. Clark, *Civilisation*, John Murray, 1971, p 15.

19. B.Weinreb and C.Hibbert, *The London Encyclopaedia*, Macmillan, 1993, p 732.

20. E.Jones & C.Woodward, *A Guide to the Architecture of London*, Weidenfeld & Nicolson, 2009, p 235

21. M. Butler, *London Architecture*, Metro Publications, 2006, p 82.

22. Sir John Summerson, *Georgian, London*, Penguin, 1969, p 68.

23. D.Avery, *Georgian and Regency Architecture*, Chaucer Press, 2003, p 17.

24, Sir John Summerson, *Georgian London*, Penguin, 1969, p 67.

25, Ibid, p.68.

26 Ibid, pp 77-8.

27. Ibid, p 78.

349

28. Ibid, p 119.
29. D.Avery, *Georgian and Regency Architecture,* Chaucer Press, 2003, p 27.
30. Sir John Summerson, *Georgian London,* Penguin, 1969, p 63.
31. Ibid, p 63.
32. Ibid, p 63.
33. Ibid, p 117.
34. B.Weinreb and C.Hibbert, *The London Encylopaedia,* Macmillan, 1993, p 830.
35. T. S. Ashton, *The Industrial Revolution*, Oxford University Press, 1948, p 95
36. B. Weinreb and C. Hibbert, *The London Encyclopaedia*, Macmillan, 1993, p 330.
35. D. Avery, *Georgian and Regency Architecture*, Chaucer Press, p 18.

Chapter 8

Late-Georgian London:
From the elegance of Robert Adam to
the exuberance of Regency

In 1700 London with an estimated population of 700,000 had become the largest city in Europe, and by 1801 the English capital had maintained its primacy with a population of 959,000 inhabitants. Its growth was mainly the result of inward migration attracted by a wide range of jobs particularly in trade, commerce and financial services. London – unique among other capitals – was also a major port, the largest in the world by the eighteenth century. It was also a capital of the first country in the world to experience the Industrial Revolution, and reaped many of the economic benefits derived from industrialisation elsewhere in Britain particularly in its coalfield regions.

During the last quarter of the eighteenth century, many new buildings of merit – public and private – were developed in the City and Westminster, normally on existing built-up sites, while the spatial extent of London also expanded substantially as large swathes of land on the western and northern fringes of the capital were rapidly developed, notably on the Portman, Bedford and Fitzroy estates, and in Finsbury. However, following the boom years of the 1780's, Britain found herself in a succession of Coalition Wars against France that lasted until 1815 except for a short respite between 1801-1803. It was broadly during this period that London expanded eastward with the construction of the first docks and associated development of low cost housing. Though Britain was not finally at peace until well into the second decade of the new century, some new development of distinction was undertaken between the wars, but it was not until the 1820's that new development on a substantial scale not only affected the fabric of much of the capital but substantially determined its spatial extent. For example, the newly constructed 'Royal Mile' from Regent's Park to the Mall separated throughout much of its length the older run-down district of Soho in the east from the resplendent early-Georgian estates in Mayfair in the west, while the resumed development of the Bedford and Foundling estates to the north west of the City, and the development of the Grosvenor estate in Belgravia to the west of Westminster pushed the boundaries of central London further outward into the suburbs.

Revolutionary Years and the Growth of London 1760-1825

George III (r. 1760-1820)

Since George II's eldest son, Frederick Prince of Wales, died in 1751, the king's second eldest son George William Frederick became heir apparent and acceded to the British throne in 1760 at the age of only 22. Though he was also King of Hanover and Imperial Elector, the new king, George III, "unlike his two predecessors was English through and through – by birth and inclination" (1). However, like his grandfather and great-grandfather, he too was reluctant to fund or promote development projects on any scale – perhaps wisely in view of revolutionary wars throughout much of his reign – preferring instead to leave matters mainly to the government and private entrepreneurs.

In 1760 Colonel Eyre Coote effectively ended French ambitions in India by taking Madras, and although Pondicherry became a French enclave Britain seized the French colonies of Belle Isle and Dominica in the Caribbean. Under Newcastle's leadership, there was now an increased appetite for extending hostilities, and in 1762 Britain declared war on Spain, captured her overseas possessions of Havana, Manila, Martinique, St. Lucia, St. Vincent and Granada and drove her out of Portugal.

Despite the competent prosecution of the war, George III was unable to trust neither Newcastle nor Pitt with the future of Britain. Solely because of personal animosity, the King removed Newcastle from office in May 1762 and replaced him with the Tory Earl of Bute, thereby ending the Whig monopoly of government that had lasted since the Hanoverian Succession in 1714. Soon there was peace, and Bute was able to gather the spoils of war. Signed by Britain, France and Spain, the Treaty of Paris of 1763 terminated the Seven Years War, and among its many provisions ceded Canada, Cape Breton, Nova Scotia, Minorca, Tobago, St. Vincent, Grenada and Florida to Britain. But though he was instrumental in ending the war, Bute – like his predecessors – fell out of favour with the King – largely for personal reasons – and was obliged to resign, and was succeeded by two Whig premiers, George Grenville (April 1763 to July 1765) and the Marquis of Rockingham (July 1765 to July 1766). During the former's administration, colonists were angered by the American Stamp Act which they saw as another attempt to raise revenue that would surely end up in the coffers of Westminster rather than being spent on their own administration or on their defence. In contrast, under Rockingham, British rule in Bengal and Bihar was consolidated. Thirty million people in the subcontinent were now governed through a puppet Mogul emperor, bringing in an annual revenue of £4 million. However, though Rockingham pacified the American colonists by repealing the Stamp Act in 1766 and consequently reduced their tax burden, he was faced with insurmountable divisions within his cabinet over other issues and was forced to resign.

Throughout the Seven Years War (1756-1763) – except for the on-going construction of the Middlesex Hospital (it was begun in 1755) – there was an absence of large scale development of public buildings in London, almost certainly because of financial constraints arising from the substantial increase in the national debt. Minor exceptions to this deficiency were, the completion of the Pagoda at Kew Gardens (1758-1763) and the completion of Admiralty Screen in Whitehall (1759-1761), designed by William Chambers and Robert Adams respectively.

Pagoda, Kew Gardens (1758-63), Sir William Chambers

In the private sector, there was less financial constraint, for example in 1764, ten years after William Murray (later the 1st Earl of Mansfield) had acquired a late-seventeenth century mansion – Kenwood House - as his principal mansion in Hampstead, he commissioned Robert Adam to completely redesign the building as he so desired. The north front of the building facing the Hampstead Road consequently "consists of a stucco block with a central portico rising to the height of the house and surmounted by a pediment" (2), and, on either side, George Sanders added projecting brick wings for the 2nd Earl in 1793-1796. The south front was also the work of Adam. Overlooking a sloping landscaped garden it mainly consists of a central stucco block with its upper two storeys adorned by slim pilasters, while its west flank is attached to the orangery of the previous building, and its east flank – extended by Adam – was designed as a library (3).

Kenwood House (1767-9), by Robert Adam

The Pitt Administration: 1766-6

In 1766, Rockingham was succeeded by a fellow Whig, William Pitt who, in choosing the office of Lord Privy Seal, became Earl Chatham and sat in the House of Lords rather than the Commons throughout his short premiership. From the outset, Chatham attempted to preside over a `government of all talents', Whig and Tory, an expedient and potentially effective way of dealing with the many problems facing Britain overseas, particularly the observance of the Treaty of Paris by France and Spain, the status of the East India Company, and the tension between the American colonists and the mother country. However, he remained in office for only two years. He was unable to coordinate his team of ministers, and in 1767 the Chancellor of the Exchequer, Charles Townsend, without even informing Pitt, imposed import taxes on tea, glass, paper and lead on colonists to pay for the defence and government of the colonies, stoking the fires of discontent smouldering across the Atlantic.

The North Government: 1770-1780

After a relatively uneventful premiership of the Duke of Grafton (1767-1768), Lord North was invited by the King in January 1770 to form a government, only the second Tory administration in 56 years. Almost immediately it was successful in preventing a Spanish attempt to occupy the uninhabited Falkland Islands and in ensuring that Spain ceded the islands to Britain. However, although this incident possibly drove a wedge between France and Spain and enhanced the reputation of the Royal Navy, Britain's policy towards North America was at best fragile because the colonists were increasingly vociferous in objecting to taxation without political representation. Thus within a year of taking office, North attempted to quell discontent among the colonists by abolishing all import duties apart from the one on tea. But even this was not enough. In 1773, a group of radical colonists disguised themselves as Native Americans, boarded British ships and poured their cargoes of tea into the sea. In response, the British government closed the port of Boston, withdrew the colony's charter of limited self-rule and planned to impose direct rule from Westminster. The following year, angry American colonists convened a congress at Philadelphia and, as an outcome, prohibited the import of goods from Britain. The following year the American War of Independence broke out.

Since events in North America (1771-1774) made it increasingly probable that Britain would either have to fund most of the cost of defending her overseas possessions or impose taxation on her colonists and risk war, it was certain that there would be an increased financial burden on Britain domestically, either in the form of increased taxation or an increase in the national debt or both. Because of the cost of the American war, public sector development virtually ground to a halt. The government limited itself to funding the construction of Blackfriars Bridge (1767-1768), the third stone-built bridge to be constructed in the capital after London Bridge (1176), but was unwilling to undertake any more major projects. However, in the private sector, funds were apparently available for a substantial amount of 'up-market' house building.

20, Portman Square (1775-7), by Robert Adam

Albany (1770-4), by Sir William Chambers

Robert Adam was commissioned to design a number of magnificent houses in the West End squares, notably 20 St. James's Square for Sir Watkin William Wynn in 1771-75, 23 and 26 Grosvenor Square for the Earl of Derby in 1773-74, and 20 Portman Square for Elizabeth, the Countess of Home, in 1773-77. Around the same time, a plethora of other magnificent town mansions were constructed or completed in London and its environs such as: Melbourne House (later Albany) in Piccadilly designed by William Chambers for the 1st Viscount Melbourne and built in 1770-1774, Montagu House in Portman Square designed by James Stuart for Mrs Elizabeth Montagu and built in 1773-1777, Uxbridge House in Burlington Gardens in 1785, and Dover House in Whitehall, which although being built initially in 1754-1758 by James Paine for Sir Matthew Featherstonehaugh was completed through the addition of a circular entrance hall and portico by Henry Holland for its new owner, Frederick Duke of York, soon after 1787. Off Oxford Street, on its northern side, a superlative Neo-Classical residence, Derby House, was built c 1770 across the end of a short cul-de-sac, Strafford Place, while around the same time in Ealing, west London, Thomas Gurnell's Pitzhanger Manor was substantially reconstructed by George Dance the Younger, creating a central block with projecting redbrick wings. In 1800 the property was bought from Gurnell's executors by John Soane who demolished it except for its south wing, and built a new central block adorned idiosyncratically with four astonishing columns supporting an entablature for statuary, together with a new north wing (4).

Uxbridge House, Burlington Gardens (1795), by John Vardy the Younger

Dover House (1787-8), by Henry Holland

Pitzhanger Manor (1770), by George Dance the Younger

Derby House, Stratford Place (c 1770)

The construction of middle class housing in late-eighteenth century London was, as in the earlier part of the century, conditioned by legislation rather than solely by the endeavours of individual developers. One major exception was the development of the Adelphi. Designed in the Neo-classical style by John, Robert, James and William Adam, 24 terrace houses were built on a riverside site occupied by Durham House until the Restoration but currently a slum. The brothers (*Adelphi* in Greek) bought a 99 year lease for £1,200 from its freeholder, the Duke of St. Albans in 1768 and immediately began work on the site building a substructure of vaults and tunnels to convert the slope from the Strand to the Thames into a raised base, level with the Strand. Four years later, house-building began, but because of the high costs of construction, lack of demand and – contrary to expectations – the failure of the Ordinance Department to rent its vaults for storage, the Adam brothers soon faced insolvency, but this did not stop Robert Adam from incorporating into the Adelphi project the majestic headquarters of the Royal Society of Arts in 1772-74, with its portico, attached pediment and fluted Corinthian columns designed to provide a fashionable venue for the appreciation of the arts and sciences. Because of the governmental concern in 1773 about the finances of the Adam brothers, an Act was passed to set up a lottery to raise funds to complete the project (5). By 1780, the Adelphi development was finished. The centrepiece of the rectangular block – overlooking the river – was the Royal Terrace comprising 11 houses with 41 bays, with central and flanking pilasters, but on its two sides similar houses were built in Adam Street in the east and Robert Street in the east. However, after the demolition of the Royal Terrace in 1936-1938, the streets on the rear side of the Adelphi – James Street, John Street and William Street were together renamed John Adam Street.

The Adelphi (1768-74), by James, John, Robert and William Adam

Royal Society of Arts (1772-4), by the Adam brothers as part
of the Adelphi development

Adam Street (1768), by the Adam brothers as part of the
Adelphi development

However impressive the Adelphi may have been, its
provision of middle class housing was dwarfed in the
late-eighteenth century by large scale speculative
development throughout much of west and north
London. The form in which this took place was
conditioned by the provision of the Building Act of
1774. Drafted by the architects Sir Robert Taylor and
George Dance, the Act aimed to consolidate earlier
building legislation, stop slipshod construction of party
walls, make the exterior ordinary houses as fireproof as
possible, and to establish – for the purposes of rating –
four categories of housing ranging from a "First Rate"
house with a value of over £850 and a floor area of
more than 900 square feet (83 m²) to a "fourth Rate"

house valued at less than £150 and occupying less than 350 square feet (32m²) (6). Though the Act imposed a code of structural requirements relating to foundations and party walls, its main effects were to produce a standardised form of speculative housing with the minimal amount of adornment and external woodwork and – as a consequence – to increase both the supply of housing and affordability, to the benefit of at least middle-income households.

Bedford Square (1775-83), by Thomas Leverton

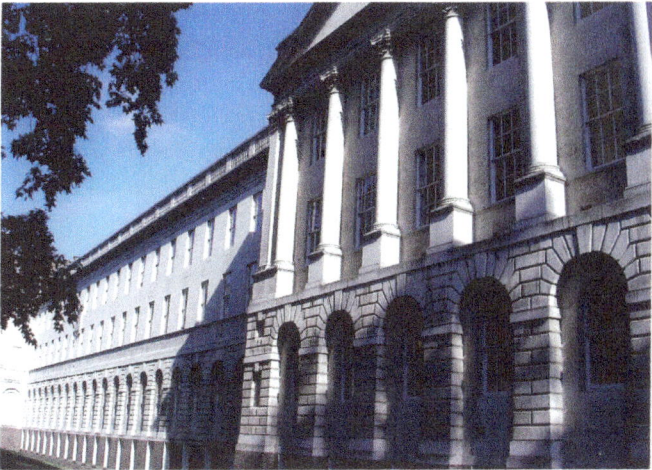

Stone Buildings (1774-80), by Sir Robert Taylor

In addition to the Adelphi, a small number of residential properties of considerable merit were developed in the 1770's – early 1780's. Among these the following stand out: Apsley House, Hyde Park Corner (1771-1774), 37 Dover Street once a residence of the Bishop of Ely (1772), the Stone Buildings in Lincoln's Inn (1774-1780) and all those in Bedford Square (1775-1783).

Of these buildings, Apsley House possibly ranks as the finest residential property built in London towards the end of the eighteenth century. Situated at the southern end of Park Lane and the south-east corner of Hyde Park it was commissioned by its future owner, Lord Apsley, the Lord Chancellor. Built by Robert Adam between 1771-1778, Apsley House was a redbrick mansion with a pedimented four-columned portico, and because it was so greatly valued by its new owner in the early nineteenth century it was restored and expanded to meet contemporary needs and fashion.

367

Of equal merit, but a town planning scheme rather than an individual house, Bedford Square was developed on the eponymous Duke's estate in Bloomsbury in 1775-1783 as an upper-middle class residential area that has been preserved in its entirety as a set piece of Georgian architecture.

Britain's Colonial and Post-Colonial Wars

In the thirty five years from the mid-1770's to 1830 Britain was at war for longer periods of time than she was at peace, though unlike France she did not have to suffer the trauma of a political revolution. Wars were *either* colonial or post-colonial conflicts and mainly took place in North America or India, *or* were fought on the continent of Europe during the French Revolution and later against Napoleon. Though the Industrial Revolution gathered pace throughout most of these years, adding substantially to the wealth of the nation, the cost of warfare also escalated, adding enormously to the National Debt, and severely constrained both the ability of governments to incur expenditure on the construction of new public buildings, and – from time to time – because the shortage of resources reduced the willingness of the private sector to undertake property development on any scale. The population of London nevertheless continued to soar to over 1 million inhabitants by 1801, the year of its first census, making the capital the largest urban area in Europe. However, although inward migration and poor living and working conditions reduced the quality of the urban environment, many new buildings of some merit were constructed to ameliorate much of the doom and gloom, though the timing of such development was much dependent on the cycle of war and peace.

368

Somerset House, northern facade looking on to the court
(1776-1801), by Sir William Chambers

London, as the national capital, required an adequate
supply of government offices from which to run the
country, but throughout most of the eighteenth century
the national capital had few public buildings in its
midst, except for the Banqueting House and the Horse
Guards in Whitehall and, of course, a plethora of
churches funded from the public purse. With the
construction of Somerset House the situation changed
dramatically and London soon surpassed Paris in the
provision of public buildings and the construction of
public works. Like the Adelphi, Somerset House was
constructed on the site of an historic building
overlooking the Thames – in its case the `Old Somerset
House' – but instead of being a speculative residential
development it was built with public funds under an
Act of Parliament of 1775 to accommodate government
offices and governmentally supported learned societies
in an environment not dissimilar to that of the Louvre.

Designed by William Chambers in a fairly austere neoclassical style and completed in 1802, the building consists of an enormous central courtyard and is entered from the Strand through a narrow but technically perfect Doric loggia (7). The Strand block with its columns and arches are reminiscent of Inigo Jones's original edifice, though the other three blocks around the courtyard and the river façade exhibit French and Italian influences while the lower level of the river frontage consists of arcades and Watergates blocked-off from the Thames by the Victoria Embankment in the late nineteenth century.

Somerset House, southern facade looking on to river(1776-1801), by Sir William Chambers

To provide a more grandiose building for the government of London, George Dance the Younger, Clerk to the City Works added a new façade to the Guildhall in 1788-1789 screening much of the Late Medieval building. Though his façade embedded the old Gothic porch, it was Indian in style with its ornamentation based on the Corporation's regalia, a recognition of the increasing importance of Indian trade to the city's economy (8).

Guildhall frontage (1788-9), by George Dance, the Younger

In the private sector, estate development continued to be the principal medium for satisfying the residential demands of the burgeoning middle and professional classes. The first two estates to be developed for this purpose in the late eighteenth-early nineteenth century were the Portland and Bedford estates, with their largely first-rate terraced houses that extend respectively from St Giles to Marylebone Road and from New Oxford Street to Euston Road. In the former estate, Portman Square was developed between 1775-

80; Manchester Square including Manchester House (now the Wallace Collection) was built in 1776-88, while in the latter estate Bedford Square was developed around the same time.

Manchester House (1776-88). Since 1890 it has housed the Wallace Collection

Midway through the Tory administration of Lord North, the American Congress drew up and passed the Declaration of Independence in 1776. In the following year the British General, John Burgoyne, surrendered at Saratoga and Washington defeated a British force at Princeton. In 1778 France and the Netherlands formed an alliance with the Americans against Britain, and in consequence Britain declared war on France, and in the process lost Dominica. In India, Warren Hastings captured Chandernagore from the French, while in 1779 Spain not only declared war on Britain but with France began the siege of Gibraltar. In the same year, Anglo-French colonial rivalry continued unabated when Britain captured Senegal from the French, and the French in turn took St. Vincent and Grenada. In 1780 petitions were organised across Britain against the high taxes required to fund the war effort, but this did not deter the North administration from declaring war on the Netherlands because of its support for the American colonists. Also in 1781 Admiral Rodney destroyed the Spanish fleet off Cape St. Vincent and lifted the siege of Gibraltar, while the French fleet in support of the American colonists won the battle of Chesapeake Bay. Later in the year, and realising that all was lost, Lord Cornwallis and an army of 7,000 troops surrendered at Yorktown, Virginia, thereby ending the American War of Independence. Throughout these colonial adventures there was a significant reduction in the amount of notable construction activity in London. Although work began in 1776 on the construction of Somerset House, Portland Place and Brooks Club, each in the Neoclassical style, in the late-1770's and during the wars that immediately followed, the construction of further buildings of prominence ceased.

Following the demise of Lord North's discredited government, the 2nd Marquess of Rockingham, a Whig, became Prime Minister (1782) but died very soon after. He was succeeded as Prime Minister by another Whig, the 2nd Earl of Shelburne (1782-83) and, through the offices of Thomas Grenville, a peace settlement was negotiated in Paris with Benjamin Franklin and the Comte de Vergennes in which Britain, France, Spain and the Netherlands agreed to recognise the 13 United States. However, at home Shelburne was censured over the peace negotiations with America and consequently resigned in 1783. He was succeeded as Prime Minister by yet another Whig, the 3rd Duke of Portland who – through the Treaty of Versailles of 1783 – reluctantly recognised American independence, but was willing to cede Tobago, St. Lucia, Senegal, Pondicherry and Chandernagore to France in exchange for Granada, Dominica, St. Vincent, Nevis, Monserrat, St. Kitts and Gambia. Britain also gave Florida and Minorca to Spain in exchange for Providence, the Bahamas and Gibraltar. In December 1783, and because of the unpopularity of Whig policy particularly in respect of the loss of the American colonies, Portland was replaced by the Tory, William Pitt the Younger who retained his role as Prime Minister until 1801.

William Pitt the Younger: His First Ministry 1783-96

Taking office at the age of only 24, Pitt became Britain's youngest Prime Minister and he subsequently dominated colonial and foreign policy for nearly two turbulent decades. Within a year Warren Hastings had made peace with the Marathas in India and the East India Company was put under a Board of Control. However, in 1785 Warren Hastings resigned in protest at the control imposed by Pitt on the East India Company and was replaced by Charles Cornwallis, the newly appointed Governor General of India.

Carlton House (started 1783), by Henry Holland

During the period of peace between England and France from 1783 to 1793, palace building in London was driven by the extravagant needs of the Prince of Wales for a sumptuous London residence. George III bequeathed Carlton House, an early-eighteenth century royal residence in Pall Mall, to the heir to the throne on condition that he renovated the run-down property. The prince duly commissioned Henry Holland to rebuild and enlarge the property, converting it – in effect – into a palace, "the most perfect in Europe" according to Horace Walpole in 1785 (9). However, in the same year, the enormous amount of building work that was being undertaken on behalf of the Crown came to a halt because of the prince's mounting debts, and construction activity remained on hold while a Parliamentary commission investigated large cost over-runs. Only with a contribution of £60,000 from George III could work resume in 1787. In due course, new wings were attached to the existing two-storey façade, a fine centrally-positioned Corinthian portico was added, and the house was extended southward to look on to the Mall and St. James's Park. But that was not all: "Screening the Palace from the street was a colonnade of coupled Ionic columns, with arched entries at either end; a Parisian idea, which Londoners found slightly ridiculous" (10). Taking nearly 30 years to complete, the high cost of development was partly attributable to the building's resplendent furnishing and interior decoration created by French craftsmen under the expert direction of Dominique Daguerre, who previously had been in the employ of Marie Antoinette.

Many of the Prince Regent's close acquaintances were members of gentlemen's clubs. Whereas Paris in the Enlightenment had its salons for intellectual debate, London in the late-eighteenth and early-nineteenth centuries had its elite clubs for political, economic and social networking and for recreation, and each one occupied a grandiose town house of Neoclassical design. The first club of any note was Brooks's Club which, for its social and non-political members, was initially located in Pall Mall but from 1778 situated at 60 St. James's Street in a building designed by Henry Holland. Also originating in Pall Mall, Boodles club – likewise established for social and non-political members – moved to 53 St. James's Street in 1783, and its façade – designed by John Crundon – sported an attractive fan window on its second floor.

Boodles Club, 53 St James's Street (1783), by John Crundon

However although the Prince Regent in the 1780's was a patron of architectural endeavour *par excellence* , and the club culture was booming, his capital as a whole did not immediately benefit architecturally from the Industrial Revolution that was now well under way. Therefore, apart from Carlton House, the only other buildings of merit that were built in London in the 1780's were Dover House in Whitehall (1787-1788) and Great Russell Street (completed 1788) , both developments employing the Neo-classical style of architecture. While the London Hospital in Whitechapel was established as a general hospital earlier in the century, St. Lukes, in Old Street Road, Moorfields, was built in 1782-1784 as a hospital for the mentally ill. Designed by George Dance the Younger to relieve the overcrowded Bethlehem Hospital, its imposing four-storey façade of 500 ft (152m) in length exhibited a central portico with a pediment, and was flanked by pavilions at either end.

At the same time as Somerset House was being constructed, the Gordon Riots shook the foundations of power in London when, in 1780, nine years before the storming of the Bastille in Paris, an angry mob opposed to Catholic emancipation went on the rampage and destroyed far more properties than those later destroyed in Paris at the height of the French Revolution. During the course of the riots, on 2 June 1780, Newgate Prison was severely devastated and, having been built initially by George Dance the Younger in 1770-1778, the prison authorities commissioned him to rebuild the prison after the riots. As before, it was constructed in a particularly awesome Neoclassical style concealing dark and dank conditions within. The monotony of its massive rusticated walls with blind windows was relieved only by a centrally situated governor's house, three main storeys in height, and flanked by study porticos.

Newgate Prison (1770-8), by George Dance the Younger

There was a wide variety of commercial projects undertaken in late eighteenth – early nineteenth century London reflecting the English capital's pre-eminence in both domestic and international trade. Possibly the most important commercial building to emerge in London in this period was the reconstructed Bank of England. Though the bank had been founded in 1694 to finance the War of the Spanish Succession, its role was substantially greater during the French wars of 1793-1815 when the National Debt had increased from £230 million to over £500 million. The first bank built on the Bank of England's present site in Threadneedle Street dated from 1734, but because of an increase in business it was expanded by Sir Robert Taylor in 1765 and, following his death in 1788, John Soane was commissioned to extend the bank further to cover the whole of its present 3.5 acre (1.4 ha) site. Though Soane designed the Bank Stock Office, Lothbury Court, the Consols Transfer Office, the Governor's Court and the Five Pound Note Office, all internal additions, he is

378

probably better known for his screen wall which eventually surrounded the whole site (11).

Bank of England screen wall (1788), John Soane

Commercial activity was also promoted by the age-old practice of people of similar trades meeting to discuss matters of common concern. To accommodate such discourse, the leading members of the various trades of the City, when necessary, commissioned the reconstruction of their livery halls across the city. Remodelled in the Neoclassical style, the Apothecaries hall in Blackfriars Lane was partly reconstructed in 1779; the Skinners' hall in Dowgate Hill was re-fronted by R. Mylne in 1790; and the Stationer's Hall at its eponymous address was re-fronted by the same architect in 1800.

Britain's response to the French Revolution

In 1789 the French Revolution sent Britain into a state of shock particularly as there was a possibility that the French might attempt to export changes of regime throughout the monarchies of Europe. Therefore in the belief that Pitt among all politicians would be the best qualified to ensure the security of the realm, the British electorate gave him an increased majority at the general election of 1790. At first it seemed that the French threat would emanate from Ireland since, in response to an invitation from the newly formed Society of United Irishmen in 1791 French troops might have invaded Ireland, driven out the English and formed a republic, but this was not to be. Instead in 1793 the French republic declared war on Britain, widening the War of the First Coalition that already saw Austria and Prussia in conflict with France. The war went well with Britain, Lord Howe defeated the French fleet at Brest, and in 1795 in an attempt to stabilize events in the Low Countries, Britain declared war on the Netherlands, an ally of France. In the same year, Britain took Ceylon (Sri Lanka) and the Cape of Good Hope from the Dutch, and in 1796 a French invasion of Ireland was aborted when the French fleet was scattered by a storm, while in 1797 1,400 French troops landed at Dyfed but soon surrendered to British troops. In 1798 Britain, Austria and Russia formed the Second Coalition against France, in which – among the many conflicts in Europe – a British fleet under Horatio Nelson defeated a French fleet at the Battle of the Nile, leaving a French army stranded in the Middle East. In 1799, the

Coalition rejected a French peace offer and prolonged the war to 1802 but at a price to Britain since, under the Duke of York, her forces in the Netherlands were forced to surrender to the French at Alkmaar. Britain, however, was more successful in her imperial role than on the Continent, seizing southern India after the last ruler of Mysore, Tipu Sahib, died in battle.

Despite the high cost of the French wars and following the completion of the Bank of England another building of considerable importance was built, the London Stock Exchange. Situated in Capel Court it was designed by James Peacock and built in 1801-1802. However, the Bank alone was no longer capable of funding the nation's wars, while the Stock Exchange was mainly concerned with private ventures. Therefore because of the need to meet the soaring cost of contemporary warfare, Pitt found it necessary to introduce income tax of two shillings in the pound (10%) on earnings of more than £200, a measure that in view of continuing hostilities was undoubtedly necessary. Though Britain captured Malta in 1800, Pitt recognised that British interests could be put at risk by the formation of the Armed Neutrality of the North, an alliance of Russia, Denmark, Sweden and Prussia formed to combat British naval power in the North Sea and Baltic.

However, at home political stability was enhanced by the creation of the United Kingdom of Great Britain and Ireland by the Act of Union of 1801. Under the Act, Ireland would send 100 MP's and 32 peers to Westminster, and in February, 1802 the United Kingdom as distinct from the British parliament met for the first time at Westminster, but since William Pitt the Younger was not allowed to make concessions to Catholics in the plan for the Union he therefore resigned. Pitt was succeeded by another Tory Prime

381

Minister, Henry Addington (1801-1804), who unlike his predecessor governed in a period of largely successful military action. In March 1801, Britain was victorious over the French at the second Battle of Abukir and at the battle of Alexandria, and, in April, Nelson defeated a Norwegian-Danish fleet at Copenhagen. In June, Britain took Cairo, but in July a French fleet defeated the British at Algeciras. On 27 March 1802, the War of the Second Coalition – in so far as it affected Britain and France – was ended at the Treaty of Amiens. With Britain appearing to be the eventual loser, she returned most of the gains she made in the Coalition Wars.

But peace was short-lived. In May 1803, France refused to withdraw from Dutch territory prompting the United Kingdom once again to declare war. In response, Napoleon, now commander-in-chief of the French armies, assembled a huge fleet and army for an invasion of Britain, but in spite of the threat of an imminent war on the shores of Britain, Addington's policy of imperial expansion led to further military engagement in India with the outbreak of Second Anglo-Maratha War in August 1802, albeit a short-lived conflict with British-led forces victorious at the Battle of Assaye in September.

Royal Artillery Barracks, Woolwich (1775-1805)

Royal Military Asylum, Chelsea (1802), by John Sanders

To enhance the ability of Britain to be effectively engaged in Continental or colonial wars, governments for over a quarter of a century perceived that it was necessary to commission a series of military establishments designed to improve the professionalism of her army. The first such building was the Royal Artillery barracks at Woolwich, built between 1775-1805. Its imposing façade 1,000 ft (305 m) in length, consisting of a triumphal arch at its centre flanked by an eastern wing was built between 1776-1786, but its western wing was not completed until 1802 except for its chapel that was finished in 1808 (12). Second, around the same time as the Woolwich barracks were nearing completion, James Wyatt was commissioned to design the Royal Military Academy on Woolwich Common. Built between 1800-1806, the building was more Gothic than Neo-classical in design, the brown and yellow brick edifice being surmounted by corner turrets reminiscent of the Tower of London. Third, in 1802, work began on the Royal Military Asylum in

Chelsea. Designed by John Sanders, the asylum was built as a school for the children of soldiers' widows. The building is an imposing brown-brick mass with a stone portico of four Roman Doric columns and, with its Soane-like chapel within its grounds, it is a fit companion of the Royal Hospital only a quarter of a mile (400 m) away. In 1892, the Asylum was renamed the Duke of York's Headquarters.

Trinity House (1793-96), by Samuel Wyatt

Military adventures overseas at the end of the eighteenth century did not seem to jeopardise the development of maritime trade nor the need for new dock facilities. To improve safety at sea and thereby facilitate trade, Trinity House was built in 1783-96 close to the Tower of London and the Thames to administer the construction and operation of lighthouses around the coasts of Britain. With the Pool of London – from the Tower to London Bridge – becoming more and more crowded as an outcome of an increasing amount of trade particularly with the eastern hemisphere, it was deemed necessary to construct a number of dock basins downstream from the Tower to beyond Deptford. Thus, under the West India Dock Act of 1799, the West India Dock Company built an Import Dock of 30 acres (12 ha) traversing the northern edge of the Isle of Dogs, and an Export Dock of 24 acres (9.7 ha) immediately to its south. Designed by William Jessop and Ralph Walker and opened in 1802, the docks were immediately successful since they were not only connected to the Thames by means of modern locks, but accommodated extensive and secure warehouse space, the Import Dock alone being served "by continuous line of three-quarters of a mile of warehouses, five storeys high" (13). Authorised by an Act of 1800, the London Docks were constructed over the following five years by the London Dock Company to provide import and export facilities in Wapping and thus as close as possible to the City. Designed by Daniel Alexander and John Rennie, the docks were built in two parts, a Western Dock of 20 acres (8.1 ha) and an Eastern Dock of 7 acres (2.8 ha) and both were served by locks and "splendid warehouses of brick with stone plinths and rustications [and each were] mostly four storeys high" (14). Based on an Act of 1801, the Surrey Docks and eight others in its vicinity were built by a succession of companies on a peninsula in Rotherhithe, two miles east of London Bridge. Dating back to 1697, the system – as developed in the early nineteenth century – consisted of dock basins, the Grand Surrey Canal 3.5 miles (5.6 km) long, and multistorey warehouses covering 300 acres (121.5 ha). Since the East India Company employed the largest ships on their voyages to and from the Orient, it required dock facilities no higher up the river than Deptford some distance from the city's boundaries, and therefore – under an Act of 1803 – it was permitted to construct its own dock at Blackwall, where John Rennie and Ralph Walker built an import dock of 18 acres (7.4 ha) in area, and a slightly smaller export dock, both

Highbury Terrace (1789)

Inevitably, military uncertainty abroad and financial constraints at home, resulted in very little residential development of merit taking place in London during the Coalition and Indian wars, the only notable exceptions being Highbury Terrace (1789), Fitzroy Square (1790-94), Sir John Soane's House in Lincoln's Inn Fields (1792), Sundridge Park (begun in 1801) and the extension of Albany of Piccadilly in 1804, all of which were Neoclassical in design. Baker Street, three quarters of a mile (1.2 km) in length, was also developed before the turn of the century, and so was the equally lengthy Gloucester Place, though adjacent to these thoroughfares Dorset Square was built in the early nineteenth century.

Dorset Square (c.1815)

Apart from a modest number of residential developments, a handful of purpose-built theatres were constructed or redeveloped across the West End towards the turn of the century, all with Neo-classical facades. The most prominent were: the King's Theatre Haymarket, designed by Polish architect Michael Novosielsky and completed in 1791; and the Theatre Royal Drury Lane, rebuilt by Henry Holland between 1791-1794.

The second administration of William Pitt, the Younger: 1804-1806

To counter the threat of a French invasion, William Pitt

the Younger returned to office as Prime Minister in March 1804. To add strength to Napoleon's Iberian mission, Spain declared war on Britain in September 1805 but in October, at the outset of the War of the Third Coalition, Nelson defeated a combined French and Spanish fleet at the Battle of Trafalgar and established Britain's ascendancy at sea but, in December, Napoleon – showing mastery of land warfare – defeated the Austrians and Prussians at the Battle of Austerlitz, France's most decisive victory. Determined to expand her Empire, Britain seized Cape Colony – a former Dutch possession – in January 1806, and in February the Royal Navy defeated a French fleet off Santa Domingo enabling her to control the sea lanes of the Caribbean. Meanwhile William Pitt the Younger died at the age of only 47, a Whig coalition was hurriedly formed by Lord Grenville to enable Britain – as a member of the Fourth Coalition – to continue war with France without interruption.

However, although Britain defeated France at Maida in Calabria in July, in November Napoleon declared a blockade of Britain forcing food prices to rise and the textile industry to decline. In March 1807, Grenville's coalition collapsed when he rejected Catholic Emancipation, and a Tory, the 3rd Duke of Portland is asked again to form a government. In foreign policy, his task was no less difficult. In July, Napoleon formed an alliance with Russia against Britain, and in September the British navy was ordered to bombard Copenhagen to prevent Denmark surrendering its fleet to Napoleon. In February 1808, the French occupied Spain and the Peninsular War begins. In August British troops under Sir Arthur Wellesley defeated the French at Vimiero, near Lisbon and in January 1809 the British beat the French at the Battle of Corunna.

On France's north-eastern flank in the following July, a British force under Lord Chatham invaded Walcheren in the Netherlands, but if failed to take Antwerp, its principal objective. Wellesley, meanwhile, defeated the French at the Battle of Talavera in Catalonia, but in October 1809 – because of ill health – the Duke of Portland was replaced as Prime Minister by Spencer Percival, also a Tory and a strong supporter of the Peninsular War. However, although Percival encouraged Sir Arthur Wellesley in 1810 to build a line of forts – "the Lines of Torres Vedras" – to defend Lisbon against enemy incursion, the Prime Minister – for a while – would have been at least equally occupied with King George III's insanity and the establishment of the Regency in February 1811 under George Prince of Wales, and, in March, with the defeat of the French fleet by the Royal Navy at the Battle of Lissa in the Adriatic. During these traumatic years, very little development of merit takes place in London, the Royal Mint (started in 1809) and the Dulwich Picture Gallery (1811) were notable exceptions.

Royal Mint (1807-9), by Robert Smirke

Dulwich Picture Gallery (1811-14), by Sir John Soane

Parish Church of St Marylebone (1811-14), by Thomas Hardwick

During the French Wars there was a hiatus in church-building in London, with one notable exception, the construction of the parish church of St. Marylebone. Situated on the Marylebone Road, on a site previously occupied by successive churches since 1400, the new church was built between 1811-1817. As many as six plans had been produced by Sir William Chambers between 1770-1774, but all had been rejected by the vestry. The same body (though with later members) also turned down John Nash's proposal to locate the church on a site at the southern end of Portland Place. Eventually, a design by Thomas Hardwick – a former pupil of Chambers was accepted, even though it was based on one of his masters earlier Neoclassical submissions. The church's six-columned portico and pediment faced St. Marylebone to the north while its altar faced south, and its nave was surmounted by a square shaped tower on which stood a lantern and small cupola.

The Regency: 1811-1820

A year after the Prince of Wales was appointed Regent, his Prime Minister, Spencer Percival was assassinated in the House of Commons in May 1812. The premier's replacement was another Tory, Lord Liverpool, who with a month of taking office took Britain to war with the United States, while in Europe British forces led by Sir Arthur Wellesley defeated the French at Salamanca in July. In August the British entered Madrid, and in the War of 1812, the American General William Hull surrendered Fort Detroit without a fight, though in October the Royal Navy suffered losses on the Atlantic seaboard and in the Great Lakes. In June 1813 British troops defeated a larger American force in the Battle of Stony Creek, and in the Peninsular War, an allied force defeated the French under Joseph Bonaparte at the Battle of Victoria. However, in October British forces under Sir Arthur Wellesley, together with other members of the Sixth Coalition, are defeated by the French army at the Battle of the Nations at Leipzig and, in the American state of Connecticut, British forces are defeated at the Battle of the Thames in December and, as if in revenge, the British burnt Buffalo in New York state. From then on, until the demise of Napoleon, Britain achieved ascendancy in Europe. In January 1814 Britain made peace with Denmark, and in March allied forces defeated Napoleon at the Battle of Laon, and Wellesley took Bordeaux. The allies then entered Paris and easily persuaded the French senate to depose

Napoleon as Emperor. In April, Napoleon consequently surrendered, but Wellesley went onto defeat a French army at the Battle of Toulouse since news of Napoleon's surrender had not yet spread throughout France.

For his military successes against Napoleon, Wellesley was created Duke of Wellington, and he undoubtedly played a major part in creating the circumstances in which the First Peace of Paris of May 1814 stipulated that France must return to her 1792 borders. But across the Atlantic, Britain was still at war. In July 1814, an American force defeated the British in the Battle of Chippewa, Ontario, but in August British troops burnt Washington DC and torched the White House – the Anglo-American War being concluded by the Treaty of Ghent on 24 December. Back in Europe, and stemming from the Peace of Paris, the Congress of Vienna in September 1814 aimed to negotiate the Resettlement of Europe, but this was far from an easy task since the problems of boundary change and sovereignty seemed intractable. To further their national aims, Austria, Britain and France formed a secret alliance in January 1815 against Prussia and Russia, but before these could be realised Napoleon escaped from Elba in February 1815 where he was exiled, not only by the Allies, but by the new French regime under Louis XVIII. In June, Napoleon regrouped his troops in France but was defeated at the Battle of Waterloo by the British and Prussians under Wellington and Blücher. Napoleon abdicated for a second time and was banished to St. Helena by the British in October. In November, the Second Peace of Paris restricted France to her 1790 borders.

93-99 Park Lane (1823-7)

Dudley House, Park Lane (1824-7), by William Atkinson

The Tory administration of Lord Liverpool attempted to ameliorate the consequences of the post-war economic depression by abolishing income tax in 1816 in order to raise the overall level of demand and thus create employment (the tax was not reintroduced until 1842). After the upheaval of the Revolutionary and Napoleonic Wars and the post-war depression, high-class residential development resumed in the West End particularly in Park Lane where numbers 93-99 and 100 (Dudley House) were built between 1823-27. At the southern end of Park Lane, Apsley House (built of redbrick in 1771-78) was bought by Richard Wellesley in 1807, but because of his financial difficulties he sold it to his brother Sir Arthur Wellesley (the future Duke of Wellington) in 1817. The new owner henceforth commissioned Benjamin Dean Wyatt to completely renew and extend the house by adding an extra bay to each side of the original five bay façade, and facing the whole exterior with Bath stone. Because of its prominent location, and the reverence shown to the Duke after Waterloo, Apsley House received the accolade of being called "Number One, London".

13, Lincoln Inn Fields (1809), by Sir John Soane

The most innovative houses of the period were those owned by John Soane in Lincoln's Inn Fields. His first house in the Fields was number 12, and since it had been built in 1652 and was in a poor state of repair, he reconstructed it in 1795 soon after purchase as a somewhat plain Neo-classical residence. However, in 1809 and 1824 he respectively bought and rebuilt 13 and 14 Lincoln's Inn Fields, and superimposed an incised three-storey loggia to the façade of number 13 and topped it with statuary, illustrative of his abstract Neo-classical style, and after his death in 1837, at his bequest, the three houses were left to the nation as a museum for the study of architecture and allied arts.

St John's Wood Chapel (1813), by Thomas Hardwick

During the Napoleonic Wars church-building was negligible in London due to a shortage of funds, but one church stands out: St John's in St John's Wood. Close to the north-west corner of Regent's Park, and designed by Thomas Hardwick, the elegant Neo-Grecian edifice with its Ionic portico and turret was begun in 1813. The building of hospitals at this time was also constrained, though a main exception was the construction of the Bethlem Royal Hospital for the care of the insane ('Bedlam'), a project intended to transfer its facilities from Moorgate to a new site in Lambeth. Initially designed by J.Lewis in an austere style in 1812, it soon became dominated by a giant Ionic portico and large dome (added by Sydney Smirke in 1839), and since 1920 the building has been the Imperial War Museum in 1920

Bethlem Royal Hospital (1812-15 & 1839), by J.Lewis and
Sidney Smirke.
(Became the Imperial War Museum in 1920)

After Waterloo, the development of retail shops gathered pace, and taking a lead from Paris shopping arcades became the vogue in parts of London's West End. Of those that survive, Burlington Arcade in Piccadilly – designed by Samuel Ware – is the most famous, and was built from 1815-1819, and John Nash's Royal Opera Arcade from Pall Mall to Charles II Street dates from 1816-1818. The post-Waterloo years also saw the development of conventional shopping streets particularly in the West End where, for example, the Quadrant of John Nash's Regent Street attracted high class retailing form c.1820; while small shopping centres were developed across the capital such as Woburn Walk in St. Pancras, designed by Thomas Cubitt in 1822.

Burlington Arcade (1815-19) by Samuel Ware

Royal Opera Arcade (1816-18), by John Nash

Woburn Walk (1822), by Thomas Cubitt

Post-War Recovery and Architectural Exuberance

George IV (r. 1820-1830)

Following the Prince Regent being crowned George IV in 1820, Lord Liverpool continued to hold office as prime minister for a further seven years, and was succeeded in turn by George Canning in 1827, Viscount Goderich in 1827-1828, and the Duke of Wellington in 1828-1830, all Tories. Apart from military action in 1827, where British, French and Russian ships defeated a Turkish-Egyptian fleet at the Battle of Navarino, the United Kingdom enjoyed a period of relative peace overseas. Colonial and European wars had come to an end at least for the time-being, and the economy was beginning to recover from depression, though a significant proportion of the population were excluded from the benefits of economic growth, and in the worse-case scenario resorted to crime.

As a consequence, the prison population of London dramatically increased resulting in Newgate, Marshalsea and other prisons in the capital bursting at the seams with dire effects on the welfare of inmates. Thus, in response to calls from prison reformers for more humane conditions in London's gaols, the government granted the great Utilitarian philosopher and activist, Jeremy Bentham, a contract to build a prison based on his politician ideas, but his personal funds were soon depleted and the government therefore took over financial responsibility and built a modified version of his plans, completing the prison – the

Millbank Penitentiary – in 1821. Intended at first to mainly accommodate prisoners sentenced to transportation, the building was in the shape of a six-pointed star and occupied 7 acres (2.8 ha), making it the largest prison in London, but it too offered very cramped and unhealthy conditions and was consequently closed in 1890 and since then its site has been occupied by the Tate Gallery, now called Tate Britain.

Custom House (1825), by Robert Smirke

Elsewhere in the public sector, much more attention was paid to producing buildings of architectural merit, although to this end progress was sometimes tenuous, for example, when David Laing, surveyor to the Board of Customs, began to design a new Custom House in Lower Thames Street in 1813 (to replace Thomas

Ripley's custom house of 1717-1725), he approached the task with greater urgency after Ripley's building burnt down in 1814 so that by 1817 the new Custom House was completed. However, because of imperfections in its construction Robert Smirke redesigned its river façade of 1,190 ft (363 m) in 1825-27 in a distinctly Grecian style that enabled the new building to efficiently facilitate the taxing of imports and the regulation of trade.

In the private sector, the post-war economic depression and a depressed property market made most developers hesitant about embarking on building projects in central London. Therefore, it took until 1819 before a massive surge in property development took off, particularly in Bloomsbury and Belgravia.

During the early years of the nineteenth century, the west end of London witnessed the development of a number of theatres to profitably satisfy the growing demand for public entertainment. Having been rebuilt by Henry Holland between 1791-1794, the Theatre Royal Drury Lane was enhanced in 1810 when a new façade and a rotunda were added to the building by B.D. Wyatt , and its portico and colonnade were built by Samuel Beazley in 1831; the Royal Opera House, Covent Garden was reconstructed by Robert Smirke in 1808-1809; the Theatre Royal Haymarket, was built by John Nash in 1820-1821; and the Lyceum in Wellington Street, rebuilt by Samuel Beazley in 1831-1834.

Theatre Royal, Drury Lane (1810), by Benjamin DeanWyatt;
and by Samuel Beazeley (1831)

Theatre Royal, Haymarket   (now the Haymarket Theatre)
(1820-31), by John Nash

Private benefactors were, however, far less affected by market conditions than most other developers in the private sector, for example William Brooks directed the construction of the London Institution in Finsbury Circus which, following its completion in 1819, provided – for the benefit of the general public – the venue 'for the Advancement of Literature and the Diffusion of Useful Knowledge' (15); Dissenters and other non-conformist bodies funded the construction of University College in Gower Street in 1826-27 and – being designed in the Grecian style by William Wilkins – it is notable for its array of steps leading up to a central portico, a somewhat petty dome and wings that are unsympathetically joined to the centrepiece; and, on the Strand in an attempt to provide the Church of England's answer to University College, Robert Smirke concluded work in 1829-31 on King's College in a more restrained Grecian style than its Gower Street counterpart, notwithstanding that it was attached to the east block of Somerset House. By the third decade of the nineteenth century, Somerset House was at last completed when, in 1835, the offices of the Inland Revenue – designed by Sir James Pennethorne – were added to its west block, both edifices being Grecian in style.

University College (1826-7), by William Wilkins

King's College (1829), by Robert Smirke

Offices of Inland Revenue, Somerset House (1835), by Sir
James Pennethorne

As in the late-eighteenth century, increased
commercial activity in the City of London was
facilitated by the reconstruction of Medieval livery
halls normally in the Neoclassical style. Among several
examples, Goldsmiths' Hall in Foster Lane was rebuilt
on its original site by P. Hardwick between 1829-1835;
and the Fishmongers' Hall in King William Street was
rebuilt *in situ* by H. Roberts in 1831-1833. Commodity
and food markets also became important commercially.
Designed by George Smith and A. B. Clayton, the
London Corn Exchange was constructed in St. Mary
Axe in 1827, while modernised food markets appeared
such as the Covent Garden fruit and vegetable market,
designed by Charles Fowler and built in 1828-1829;
two years later the same architect designed the
Hungerford Market on the site of the future Charing
Cross Station to facilitate the sale of meat and fish as
well as fruit and vegetables .

Fishmongers' Hall (1831-3), by H.Roberts

Covent Garden food markets (1828-29) by Charles
Fowler

But it was the growth of maritime trade and the development of turnpike roads in the eighteenth–and early nineteenth centuries that were the principal engines of commercial development in the early-nineteenth century. Both increased the volume of mail very substantially, and therefore to harness the economic potential of vastly enhanced communication there was a very great need for the development of a new General Post Office in central London. A massive new edifice was consequently built by Robert Smirke between 1823-29 on the site of St. Martin-le-Grand. It was a lengthy two-storey building built in the Grecian style with two porticos at either end, both with four fluted Ionic columns supporting entablatures, and a central portico six fluted Ionic columns supporting its pediment.

General Post Office (1823-9), by Sir Robert Smirke

By the mid-1820's, the economic growth of London and the nation as a whole was dependent on maritime trade more than ever before. Thus to help the handling of a greater volume of exports and imports, further docks were required. Consequently St. Katharine's Dock was constructed in 1825-1828, very close to the eastern boundary of the City on a cleared site between London Docks and the Tower of London. Designed by Thomas Telford and Philip Hardwick, the docks consisted of a "large basin of 1.5 acres (0.6 ha) leading to two docks of irregular shape of 4 acres (1.62 ha) each. These were surrounded by warehouses of yellow brickwork, six floors high, supported by heavy Tuscan columns of iron and providing 1.15 million sq. feet (110,000 m2) of storage area" (16).

St Katharine's Dock (1825-8), by Thomas Telford and Sir Philip Hardwick. Closed in 1968, now a marina

By the mid-1820's the economic growth of London was such that transport across the capital was increasingly problematic as congestion got worse. Therefore, with government funding, work began in 1823 on a new London Bridge upstream of the old bridge, and in the following year a start was made on the construction of a bridge over the Thames at Hammersmith. Designed by Sir John Rennie, London

Bridge with its five stone arches was opened in 1831 by William IV and Queen Adelaide, and to ease the flow of traffic, Moorgate and King William Street were built as approaches. Hammersmith Bridge, in contrast, was not only a completely new bridge on its stretch of the Thames, but was also the first suspension bridge in London. Designed by William Tierney Clarke, the construction of the central span – 422 ft (129 m) in length – was quite an engineering achievement of its day and it is surprising that the bridge took only three years to build. It was replaced in 1883-1887 by the present suspension bridge (17).

Buckingham Palace (1825), by John Nash

In addition to the demand of private developers for new buildings in the nation's capital, royal patronage played a major part in the development of London in the 1820s. Soon after the prince ascended the throne as George IV, he decided to demolish and rebuild his parent's London home. He was no longer enchanted by Carlton House even though the resplendent building had sumptuously served as his residence, albeit for a relatively short time. Even in 1819, a year before he

411

became king, the prince had estimated that the cost of reconstructing Buckingham House would amount to £500,000 (dwarfing the sum spent on Carlton House), whereas the government, according to the Prime Minister, the Earl of Liverpool, would only be willing to allocate £150,000 to the project in the prevailing post-war depression. The project was consequently dropped, but in the early 1820's when the economy was gradually recovering it was resurrected though its proposed location was contentious. Whereas Sir John Soane produced plans for a new royal palace to be located in Green Park, the king had a sentimental preference for replacing Buckingham House *in situ*. The government now agreed to help fund the project to the extent of 'not less than £200,000', but only on condition that building work be confined to repairs and maintenance. The king duly commissioned John Nash to undertake the design work, but while he kept and improved the original shell of the house, what emerged bit-by-bit was a substantial edifice, Buckingham Palace, consisting of a "three-sided court opened at the east [facing the Mall], in front of which to stand the Marble Arch as the main entrance to the forecourt" (18). No expense was spared particularly in the employment of Bath stone and massive blocks of Carrara marble, and although the cost of construction had soared from an original estimate of £252,690 to £700,000 by 1828 building work was often of a poor standard, and after the king's death, Nash was dismissed from his commission in 1830. Almost simultaneously George IV commissioned Jeffry Wyatville to undertake the development of a long low south wing on the southern edge of Windsor Castle, overlooking the Great Park, with construction work spread over the years 1824-28 (19).

412

Lancaster House (York House until 1912), (1825), by
Benjamin Dean Wyatt

But back in London, within close proximity of Buckingham Palace, two further royal residences – each on the scale of a palace – were constructed in the 1820's. The first, York House (renamed Lancaster House in 1920), was begun in 1825 for Frederick Duke of York, the second son of George III. Built mainly by Benjamin Dean Wyatt on the north side of the Mall west of St. James's Palace, the building was initially a two storey rectangular town mansion of Bath stone with a two storey eight-columned portico on the front. In 1841, the building gained an extra storey designed by Sir Robert Smirke. The second, the eponymous Clarence House was commissioned by William, Duke of Clarence in 1825, designed by John Nash, and completed in 1828. Built on the eastern side of St. James's Palace, and sharing the same garden, Clarence House is a stuccoed four story rectangular edifice. Though the Duke ascended the throne as William IV in

1830, he continued to live in Clarence House until his death in 1837 since Buckingham Palace was not yet ready for occupation. Very close to the palace, in Birdcage Walk, Wellington Barracks was built in the 1830's to accommodate the five regiments of foot guards whose duties were to protect the monarch when in residence at the palace and to be engaged in front-line activity during times of military conflict. Designed by Philip Hardwick, the three-storey Neo-classical building looks on to an extensive parade ground and has a façade of 394 ft (120 m) in length featuring Greek Doric ornamentation.

Wellington Barracks (1830s), by Philip Hardwick

Not connected to the needs of the monarch other substantial buildings were also erected in the 1820s. Though not superlative in design, the College of Physicians – situated on the western side of Trafalgar Square - was nevertheless part of an awesome edifice whose members were dedicated to medical treatment. Designed by Sir Robert Smirke in his inimitable Greek style between 1824-27, the College was the northern part of a substantial building whose southern part accommodated the Union Club (since 1935 the whole building has housed the Canadian High Commission). In 1827, the first major hospital of the nineteenth century, St. George's, was constructed on the western side of Hyde Park Corner. Designed by William Wilkins it too was a very imposing building. In the Grecian style, it was constructed on a high plinth its large central portico is surmounted by a pediment supported by four square columns, and its flanks are marked by projecting pavilions, the whole ensemble reminiscent of St Luke's and the London Hospital (In the late 1980's St. George's Hospital was refurbished as the Lanesborough Hotel that opened in 1991, and the hospital was relocated to a site in Tooting, in south west London).

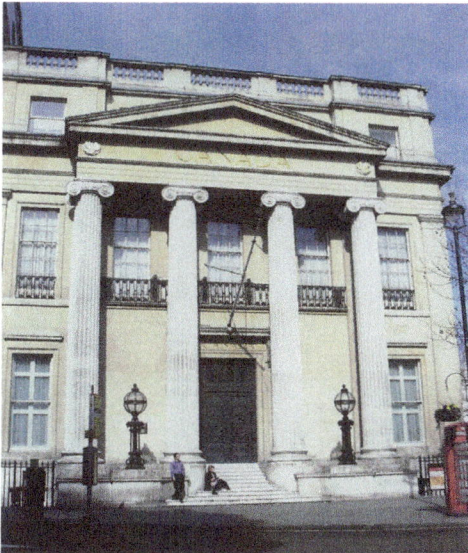

College of Physicians (now Canada High Commission) (1824-7), by Sir Robert Smirke

Within society as a whole there was a staggering unevenness in the distribution of wealth and incomes and nowhere was unbridled affluence more apparent than in the plethora of gentlemen's' clubs that were established in the 1820's-30's, most of which were of notable architectural merit exhibiting the best of Neo-classical or Grecian design. The Union Club, set up to accommodate supporters of the union of Britain and Ireland, initially occupied premises in Pall Mall but moved in turn to St. James's Square, Lower Regent Street and finally to Carlton House Terrace; Arthur's Club, founded in 1811 for the use of officers of the East India Company, occupied a house at 69 St. James's Street, designed by Thomas Hopper and built in 1826-1827; and in 1828 Crockfords, a private club and gambling house for the aristocracy, occupied a house at 50 St. James's Street designed by Benjamin Dean Wyatt. In the same year, John Nash's United Services Club in Pall Mall opened its doors to senior naval and army officers, and – intended for gentlemen who had travelled abroad – the Travellers' Club at number 106 Pall Mall was designed by Charles Barry in an Early Italian Renaissance style and was built in 1829-1832. Away from the club district of Pall Mall, St James's Street and Lower Regent Street, the Oriental Club in Hanover Square was founded in 1824 – intended for officers of the East India Company, and built to the design of Benjamin Dean Wyatt and Philip Wyatt in 1827-1828. Back in Pall Mall, and established for the intellectual elite, the Athenium Club, founded in 1824, moved into new premises designed by Decimus Burton at 107 Pall Mall in 1830, while at 104-105 Pall Mall, and adjoining the Travellers Club, the Reform Club – designed by Charles Barry in 1837 for Whig politicians and their wealthier supporters – similarly exhibits an Italian Renaissance façade of the Quattrocento.

United Services Club, Pall Mall (1828), by John Nash

Travellers' Club, Pall Mall (1829-32), by Sir Charles Barry

Atheneum Club, Pall Mall (1824), by Decimus Burton

Reform Club (1841), by Sir Charles Barry

Church building was another activity that recovered rapidly in the aftermath of Waterloo. In 1819, work began on St Pancras New Church in Upper Woburn Place. Designed by William Inwood and his son Henry William Inwood, it was remarkably Grecian in style. Henry had recently visited Athens and had returned with measured drawings. Completed in 1822, the church has a spacious Ionic portico surmounted by a pediment running the length of the wet façade, and above it is an octagonal tower based on the Tower of the Winds' in Athens. However, the most Grecian aspect of the church is its "two pavilions at the east end whose roofs are supported by caryatids of terracotta" (20), features derived from the Erechtheum. In complete contrast, St. Luke's Church in Sydney Street, Chelsea, is Neo-Gothic in style. Designed by James Savage and built between 1820-1824, the tall stone church is notable for having, in the words of the eminent Victorian architect, Philip Hardwick, the 'earliest groin church in the modern revival' (21).

St Pancras New Church, west front (begun 1819), by William and Henry William Inwood

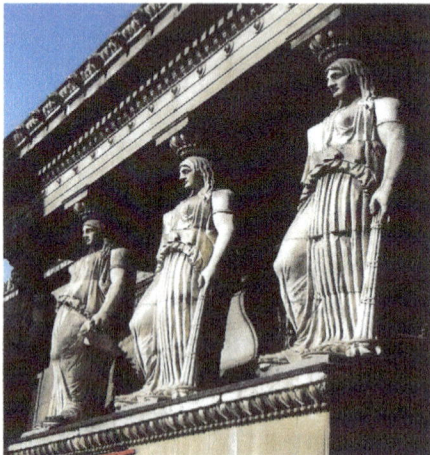

South side of St Pancras New Church, showing a replica of the Caryatids of the Erechtheum, (begun 1819), by William and Henry William Inwood

The Grecian style of church architecture, however, remained in vogue for another few years, as is exemplified by six more London churches dating from the 1820's. The first is St. Mary's in Wyndam Place. Designed by Robert Smirke and built at the end of a newly created vista in 1821-23, its principal features include a convex portico with Ionic columns, and – somewhat incongruously – a tall and narrow tower with a cupola. The second is All Souls in Langham Place. Built under the direction of John Nash between 1822-1824, it is situated at the northern end of Regent Street but at 45 degrees to it on its eastern side; faced with Bath stone, the church displays an unusual combination of a Greek peristyle with a spire above. The third is All Saints, Camden Town, designed by William Inwood and Henry William Inwood and built under their direction between 1822-1827, after they had completed their work on their St. Pancras church. As one might expect, All Saints exhibits many Grecian design features, notably its semi-circular portico, its Ionic columns and style and much of its decoration (22). The fourth is the church of St. John, Waterloo Road. Designed by Francis Bedford and built in the Grecian style between 1823-1824, it characteristically exhibits a portico and a steeple, and is possible the finest church of its kind south of the river. The fifth example is the church of St. Peter Walworth, one of the "Waterloo churches" funded by the government in 1818 to celebrate deliverance from invasion. Built in 1823-25, it is perhaps the best of Soane's churches in the capital. Its wide flat main façade is dominated by a portico of four engaged Ionic columns, with its flanks pierced by arched windows that continue along the sides of the church. The façade is surmounted by a frieze displaying Greek decoration along its whole width, above which there is a plinth – the same width as the portico – that supports a tall two stage lantern steeple. The final example was also designed by Soane, the church of the Holy Trinity, Marylebone. It is unlike its close neighbour, the parish church of St. Marylebone since it faces south rather than north and – like St. Peter Walworth – it features four large Ionic columns on its portico and a lantern steeple.

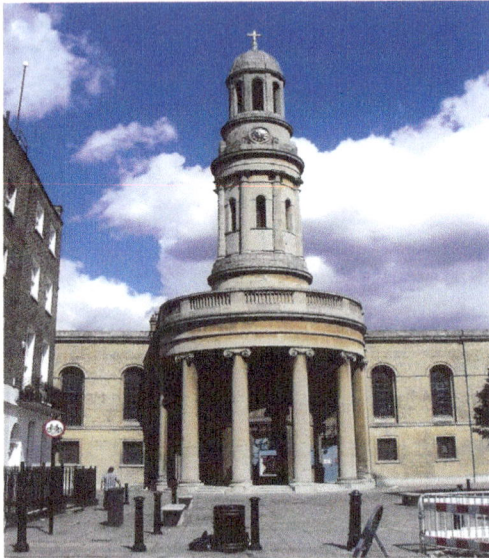

St Mary's Wyndam Place (1821-3), Sir Robert Smirke

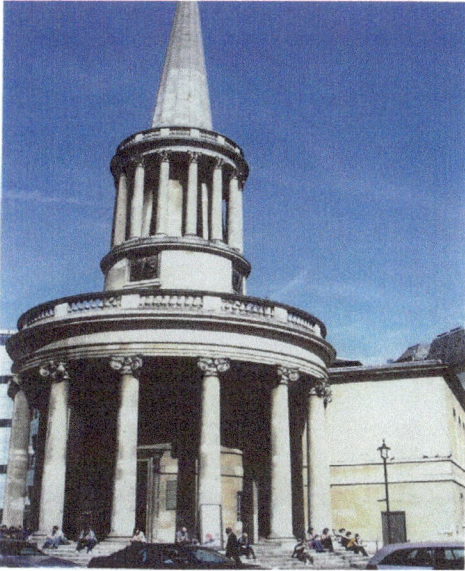

All Souls' Langham Place (1822-4), by John Nash

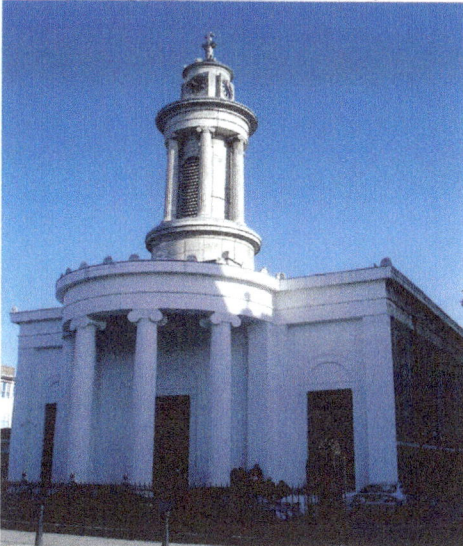

All Saints, Camden Town (1822-7), by William & Henry Inwood

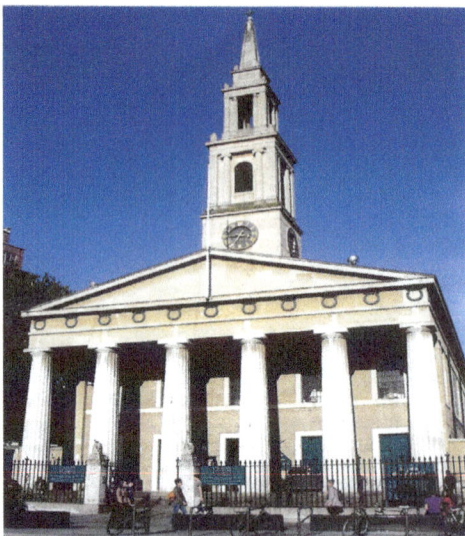

St John, Waterloo (1823-4), by Francis Bedford

Holy Trinity, Marylebone (1824-8), Sir John Soane

Town Planning

It was an outcome of George IV's ambition to emulate the grandeur of Napoleon's Paris that an enormous development was undertaken under the king's patronage in the 1820's designed to link Regent's Park with a new Buckingham Palace. In contrast to hesitant urban development in the private sector during the war years and their immediate aftermath, the Prince Regent, later George IV, made use of Crown resources to fund a massive programme of planned development. Utilising a series of reports produced between 1793 and 1809 by John Fordyce, Surveyor General for His Majesty's Land Revenue, the Prince Regent, broadly adopted Fordyce's proposal to create a north-south royal route way from Regent's Park – a former hunting ground of 166 acres (41 ha) – to Carlton House, a distance of around 2 miles (3000 m) from the park's southern boundary. It was deemed necessary to enable the nobility and professional classes to live north of the New Road (later known as Marylebone Road) while continuing to enjoy adequate access to the Mall, Whitehall and Westminster Palace. As soon as Marylebone Park reverted to the Crown in 1811, a development plan of John Nash and James Morgan was accepted by the Treasury, and building work commenced with the construction of Park Crescent in 1812-22. Within eight years a series of palatial terraces were built, Greco-Roman in design, and with stucco facades and the generous use of Corinthian, Doric or Ionic columns.

Park Crescent (1812-22), John Nash

Sussex Place (1822), by John Nash

After the completion of Park Crescent, Nash went on to design and develop Park Square (1823-5) on the south-east periphery of Regent's Park, and four buildings to its west: Ulster Terrace (1824) and York Terrace East, York Gate, and York Terrace West (all between 1821-2). Then to the north on the western side of the park, Cornwall Terrace (1821) and Clarence Terrace (1823) were both designed by Decimus Burton under the direction of Nash, and further to the north work began on Nash's Sussex Place (1822) which with its bay windows, "pointed roofs and curved wings [was regarded as] one of Nash's major outrages on the taste of his time" (23). Even further north, Nash reverted to copybook Roman style in designing Hanover Terrace (1822-23), but at its rear he built Kent Terrace in a Neo-Grecian style, not unlike that adopted by Soane (24). It is the only terrace that faces outwards from the park and onto Baker Street .

Development on the eastern side took place later. Progressing northward from the east side of Park Square, Cambridge Terrace is a fairly conventional Greco-Roman block, Chester Terrace with its "two gimcrack `triumphal' arches superscribed with the names of the terrace, is [relatively] moderate in its pretensions" (25), Cumberland Terrace "with its seven porticos, its courtyard and arches, is the crowning glory [of the park] and easily the most breath-taking architectural panorama in London" (26), and Gloucester Terrace – like Cambridge Terrace – is conventionally Neo-Classical. The West and East Park Villages, to the north-east of the park, were also designed by Nash in a variety of styles, including Neo-Gothic and Italianate and were begun in 1824, while Decimus Burton, John Raffield and others designed eight Picturesque villas spread across the park to adorn the artificially created landscape.

Cumberland Terrace (1825-7), by John Nash

West Park Village (started 1824), by John Nash and

J.Pennethorne

East Park Village (started 1824), by John Nash and
J.Pennethorne

St John's Lodge (1817-18), by John Raffield

From Park Crescent southward, the already-built
Portland Place linked Regent's Park with the newly

developed Regent Street (also Neo-Classical in style) that commenced at All Souls' Church (see above) and travelled longitudinally to Oxford Circus and the curved Quadrant at Piccadilly Circus. Then, from Lower Regent Street, the `Royal Mile' turned westward along the Mall flanked on much of its northern side by Carlton House Terrace (1827-33), and via the Duke of York Column it ultimately reached Buckingham Palace in the process of construction with its Marble Arch frontispeace (1828) which was relocated to its present location at the western end of Oxford Street in 1851. To the east of Lower Regent Street, Trafalgar Square was being laid-out and led to the West Strand Improvement (started 1827) marking the last stage in the construction of the planned north-south routeway across London, which hitherto was the largest planning project in the history of the capital.

Portland Place (1778), by Robert and James Adam

The Quadrant,Piccadilly Circus (1910), based on the smaller
and more Classical original by John Nash (1819) that had an
arcade with six openings, was only three storeys in height
and was surmounted by a frieze and balustrade.

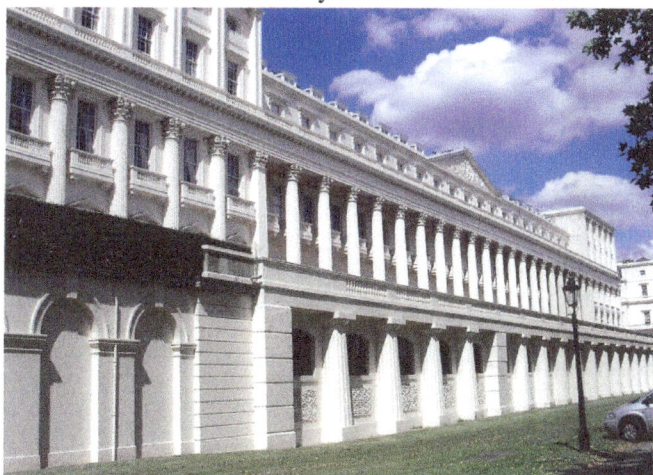

Carlton House Terrace (1827-33), by John Nash

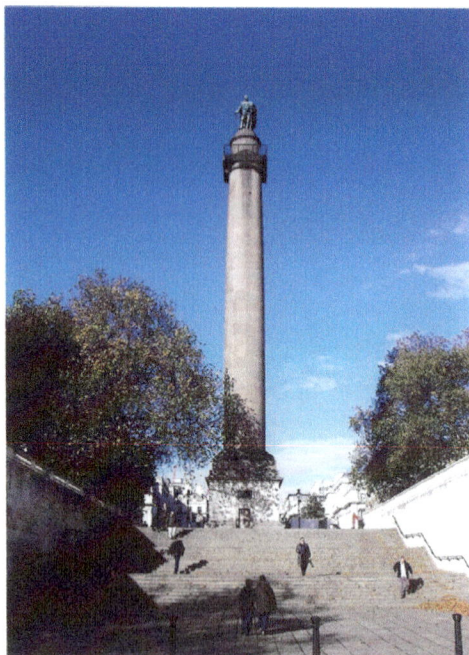

Duke of York Column (1830s)

Marble Arch (1828). Re-located to its present site in the

north-east corner of Hyde Park (1851)

West Strand Improvement (started 1827)

West Strand Improvement (started 1827)

Although the patronage of George IV was responsible for the spectacular development of Regent's Park and the `Royal Mile', most planned development in London was attributable to the private sector. Despite the French wars, there was an enormous quantity of development in the great estates on the fringes of the City and Westminster beyond the densely-packed areas of late-seventeenth and early-eighteenth century expansion. As before, in their desire to produce residential squares set within grid-iron street patterns (possibly the quickest, most profitable and aesthetically-pleasing approach), estate-owners commissioned the architects and dictated the street plans, and then leased the land to private speculators and builders.

Canonbury Square, north-west corner (1800)

Richmond Avenue, Barnsbury (1820s), by Thomas Cubitt

Montagu Square (1810-15), by David Porter

Bryanston Square (1810-15), by David Porter

One of the first such developments was around four miles to the north-east of the Royal Mile in the manor of Canonbury. It was here that Henry Leroux secured a building lease of 19 acres (7.7 ha) in 1800 and built Canonbury Square, the imposing Compton Terrace and a host of other streets in the area. Close by, on the Tuffnell estate in Barnsbury, Thomas Cubitt's entry into property speculation was marked by his development of an extensive area of new middle-class terraced housing c. 1820 in the form of squares, crescents and streets. Located between Liverpool Road and Caledonian Road, examples of his work include Barnsbury Street, Barnsbury Square, Richmond Avenue and Belitha Villas. In the Portman estate to the west of the Royal Mile, Montagu Square and the neighbouring Bryanston Square were built by David Porter in 1810-15, while to the east, and from its seventeenth and eighteenth century beginnings, the Bedford estate was further developed , with Humphrey Repton building middle class housing in Russell Square in 1800-14 , Cubitt developing Tavistock and Gordon Squares and adjacent streets (such as Endsleigh Place) in the 1820s, and James Sim building Torrington Square in 1821-25 (demolished in the 1980s) and the somewhat diminutive Woburn Square in 1828. Although there was a building boom in Bloomsbury in the 1820s, few people at the beginning of the nineteenth century predicted that it would happen. It was therefore ironic that one of the first buildings on the estate, and possibly its grandest, the late seventeenth-century Bedford House on the north side of Bloomsbury Square, was demolished in 1800 because its owner, the 5th Duke of Bedford , believed that the area was no longer fashionable and decided to relocate in `up and coming' Belgravia.

Russell Square (1800-14), by James Burton and Humphrey
Repton

Gordon Square (1820s), by Thomas Cubitt

Endsleigh Place (1820s)

Immediately to the east of the Bedford estate, the relatively small Foundling estate – largely coinciding with the grounds of the Foundling Hospital – was gradually built-up by the construction of Cartwright Gardens c. 1790, Brunswick Square in 1795-1802 and Mecklenburg Square after 1812. While to the west of Bedford Square, the relatively small Fitzroy Estate was developed from c.1790 to c.1820. Its most prominent feature is Fitzroy Square, "one of London's finest squares" (24). Its east and south sides accommodate full length terraces designed by Robert Adam in the early 1790's , but although the western side of the square "provides one of the best examples of Adam's work"(27), the southern terrace was seriously damaged in the second world war and has replaced as authentically as possible. The western and northern terraces of the square were added in 1825-1829.

Fitzroy Square (1790-1820) by the brothers Adam

Around the same time, Hyde Park Corner was being extensively developed with the construction of William Wilkins's St George's Hospital (1827-9) in the west, Decimus Burton's Ionic Screen (1825-30) and Philip and Lewis Wyatt's Apsley House (1828-9) in the north, and Burton's Wellington Arch (1827-30) in the south - in all an impressive exercise in urban design. However, because of the increased traffic congestion that ensued, Wellington Arch was re-sited a short distance to the south-east   at the top of Constitutional Hill in 1883.

St George's Hospital (1827), by William Wilkins

Apsley House (1828-9), by Philip & Lewis Wyatt

Screen at Hyde Park Corner (1825), Decimus Burton

Wellington Arch (1827-30), by Decimus Burton

Separated from its eighteenth-century Mayfair property by Hyde Park, the Grosvenor estate was extended into Belgravia after the French Wars, particularly to accommodate the upper classes. The first major Grosvenor developments in the area were Wilton Crescent (1825) and Belgrave Square (1826-1840s), the former being constructed by W.H. Seth-Smith and Thomas Cubitt and the latter being built by Cubitt and George Basevi. The elegance of the crescent is surpassed only by the grandeur of the square - the largest in nineteenth-century London and a favourite location for a host of foreign embassies. It consists of four substantial Graeco-Roman terraces with Corinthian centres and ends, and each contain up to 12 first rate houses, each one with three bays, four storeys, a basement and access to a mews, while substantial mansions are situated in three of the four corners. To the south – and divided by the main thoroughfare that connect Victoria with Chelsea – Eaton Square was also developed by Cubitt to provide first-rate housing for upper class households. Built by Cubitt the large mainly stuccoed houses were similar to those in Belgrave square but some have five main storeys and are grouped into six terraces, three on either side of the main thoroughfare, a routeway adorned at its eastern end by the Neo-Greek church of St Peter, elegantly designed by John Hakewill in 1824 with its giant portico and six Ionic columns. Still further to the south, there is a smaller but equally high status residential development, Chester Square. Built as late as the 1840's, it virtually duplicates the design of Eaton Square, though its houses are slightly smaller in scale.

Belgrave Square (1826), by Thomas Cubitt and George
Basevi

Eaton Square (1826-53), by Thomas Cubitt

St Peter's Church, Eaton Square (1824-7), by John Henry
Hakewill

The final manifestation of private-sector town planning in the early nineteenth-century London was to be found in the Bishop of London's Paddington Estate located in a triangular area between Bayswater Road and Edgware Road. Designed initially by S. P. Cockerell and later by George Gutch, several planned developments were undertaken between 1830-1836 including the stuccoed Southwick Crescent, Gloucester Square and Sussex Square, but these and others of the same period were unworthy examples of contemporary architecture and were demolished after the second world war to make way for new development.

William IV (r. 1830-1837)

With William IV on the throne for seven years, and with a succession of five Whig, Tory and Conservative governments in power throughout this relatively short period Britain enjoyed peace on the Continent of Europe, faced difficulties in Ireland and exploited trading opportunities in India, particularly through the East India Company. In Britain, the Industrial Revolution gathered pace with the development of the railways, though squalid conditions in the towns, and not least in London, led to serious outbreaks of cholera. Though the Reform Act of 1832 enfranchised a segment of male middle-income homeowners, a high proportion of the population felt aggrieved, the price of food remained high under the Corn Laws (that restricted imports), trade unionism was constrained and the able-bodied poor were confined to workhouses under the Pool Law Amendment Act of 1834. With varying degrees of success and failure in foreign and domestic policy, governments presided over a period when the built environment of London remained remarkably unchanged save for the completion of a handful of planning schemes and some minor projects mainly begun before William IV's accession. We must look to Queen Victoria's reign that followed before we can examine some positive effects of foreign and domestic policy upon the future shape of London.

References

1. D. Starkey, Monarchy, *From the Middle Ages to Modernity*, Harper Press, 2006, p 252.
2. B. Weinreb and C. Hibbert, *The London Encyclopaedia*, Macmillan, 1993, p 441.
3. Ibid, p 441.
4. Ibid, p 617.
5. Ibid, p 7.
6. Sir John Summerson , *Georgian London*, Penguin, 1969, pp 126-128
7. Ibid, p 141.
8. Sir John Summerson, *The Architecture of Britain 1530-1830*, Yale, 1991, p 418.
9. D.Watkin, *English* Architecture, Thames & Hudson, 2001, p 141.
10. Sir John Summerson, *Georgian London*, Penguin, 1969, p 151.
10. Ibid, pp 157-8.
11. B. Weinreb and C. Hibbert, *The London Encyclopaedia*, Macmillan, 1993, p 683.
12. Ibid, p 965.
13. Ibid, p 486.
14. Ibid, p 489.
15. Ibid, p 477.

16. Ibid, pp 747-8.
17. Ibid, p 489
18. Ibid, p 105.
19. Ibid, p 105.
20. .Ibid, p 774.
21. Ibid, p 752.
22. Ibid, p18.
23. Sir John Summerson, *Georgian London*, Penguin, 1969, p 183. 26.
24. Ibid, pp 183-4 27.
25. Ibid, p 184.
26. Ibid, p 184.
27. B. Weinreb and C. Hibbert, *The London Encyclopaedia*, Macmillan, 1993, p 290.

Chapter 9

Early and Mid-Victorian London: the formation of a megalopolis and the agglomeration of styles

From having a population of 959,000 in 1801 and 1,660,000 in 1831, the number of London's inhabitants soared to 3,261,000 in 1871 making the British capital the largest city in the world. But these numbers relate entirely to Inner London and if the outer boroughs were included the population of the metropolis rose from 1.1 million in 1801, to 1.9 million in 1831 and to an enormous 3.8 million in 1871. As in previous centuries, immigration was a major cause of the population growth of London, the largest single immigrant group being the Irish particularly in the wake of the Great Famine (1846-1849), followed by immigrants from the rest of Europe and elsewhere in the world. In total, London absorbed 328,000 immigrants in 1841-1851, 286,000 in 1851-1861 and 331,000 in 1861-1871 (1).

There were sizeable French, German, Italian and Spanish communities in London in the 1840's-50's, refugees fleeing from economic and political disorder in their countries after their revolutions of 1830 and 1848. There were also smaller communities of Chinese, Indian and African sailors living and working along the riverside, and a thriving and substantial Jewish community, replenished decade by decade by further European migration. But the greatest proportion of migrants into London were from the counties of South East England. As a result the working population of

London tended to be younger and contained a higher proportion of females than the inhabitants of other British regions. However, in contrast to the past, the birth rate in the capital remained relatively constant at around 35 births per 1000 of the population (1840-1847), but the death rate declined to 24 per thousand in the same period (2), largely because of better building standards, food supplies and sanitation, and London was no longer a sink of mortality for rural immigrants, as their death rate in London came into line with that of the surrounding counties (3). As a result of population growth, the spatial extent of the capital increased from 4 miles from east to west in 1720 to 10 miles across in 1900 covering nearly 70 square miles (4).

The growth of the British economy

The development of the British economy was not solely the outcome of free market forces. The supply of public services – operating alone or in some sort of relationship with private sector – was an important component in the growth of London. With a mixed economy Britain had entered what W. W. Rostow called the 'Drive towards the Age of Economic Maturity' (5). Its main attributes were the rapid development of transport infrastructure; the diversification of the industrial base with the expansion of multiple industries expanding and new ones taking root; manufacturing shifts from investment driven capital goods towards consumer-durables and domestic consumption; and large scale investment in social infrastructure. Rostow claimed that whereas the United States reached the stage of maturity around 1900, Germany in 1910 and the Soviet Russia in 1950, Great Britain reached economic maturity as early as 1850, and evidence showed that London was very much in the forefront of this drive for growth.

In the case of Britain, in particular, the drive to economic maturity was driven by the abandonment of mercantilism and the adoption of free trade with few barriers or tariffs. This was most evident in the repeal of the Corn Laws in 1846 which opened the British market to unfettered imports of grain with a consequential reduction in food prices. This, in large part, enabled Britain to become the 'workshop of the world' since, with a world-wide breakdown of mercantilism, Britain was able to dramatically increase her exports of manufactured goods, supplying half the needs of such nations as Germany, France,. Belgium and the United States.

Between 1831-1871 the British gross domestic product (GDP) grew at a steady rate – averaging 2.21 per cent per annum between 1831-1871 – "reflecting the growing pace of industrialisation and technological progress" (6). However, in Britain's 'drive to maturity', the economy was subject to a succession of relatively minor booms and slumps, each economic cycle lasting on average eight years. Booms were evident in 1836, 1843, 1850-51, 1858-59 and 1863, whereas slumps occurred in 1840-41, 1847, 1855-57 and 1867. According to Hills and Thomas the cycle was the outcome of three factors: "fluctuations in investment and durable consumption expenditure that are the result of shifts in expectations; the impact of government purchases resulting from changes in fiscal policy; and movements in exports dependent on the world economy"(7).

Because the booms and slumps were only minor in scale, Whig administration under the 2nd Viscount Melbourne (1835-1841), the Conservative government of Sir Robert Peel (1841-1846), the Whigs under Lord John Russell (1846-1852), the Conservatives under the 14th Earl of Derby (1852) and the Peelites under the 4th

Earl of Aberdeen (1852-1857), were able to pursue policies that were conducive to economic growth, and thereby prepared the ground for a sustained drive towards economic maturity in the second half of the century. Economic policies were based on the notion that *laisser-faire* would stimulate growth, and it is ironic that although Peel re-introduced Income Tax in his 1842 budget (it had been removed at the end of the Napoleonic War) to eliminate an on-going trade deficit, the revenue collected was more than expected and he was able to remove or reduce over 1,200 tariffs on imports, freeing-up trade. Later, in 1846, Peel was able to extend free trade further by gaining sufficient parliamentary support to repeal the Corn Laws. Further intervention was required to expand the free market, particularly with regard to the development of a rail network for the movement of people and freight. As an outcome of 272 Acts of Parliament, new railway companies were permitted to build 5,000 miles of track by 1846, but in response to the Irish potato famine of 1845-1849 legislation was not necessary to encourage a large influx of refugees from Ireland into Britain increasing both the size of Britain's labour force and its GDP during the second-half of the century.

Britain's interests overseas

Compared to the end of the eighteenth century and first fifteen years of the nineteenth when Britain was heavily involved in the revolutionary and Napoleonic Wars with France, the first half of Victoria's reign was remarkably peaceful. However, to ensure that free trade fully benefited the domestic economy, British governments deemed it necessary to further the development of free trade overseas, and this often brought Britain into conflict with the interests of other countries. At the beginning of Victoria's reign it was therefore considered vitally important to safeguard her country's maritime trade from Russia's territorial ambitions in India and the Near East. Initially this resulted in the First Afghan War of 1838-1842 since the Afghans opposed Britain's attempt to install a puppet ruler who had pro-British and anti-Russian sympathies. Following a major rebellion in the capital, Kabul, British forces suffered an ignominious defeat and the massacre of around 20,000 soldiers on the road from the capital to Jalalabad. Russia also had territorial ambitions in south-east Europe and also wished to secure direct access to the Mediterranean, aims that inevitably brought her into war with the Ottoman Empire in 1853. Britain and France were consequently fearful of Russian expansion and therefore declared war on Russia in March 1854. The ensuing Crimean War lasted almost two years during which time the armies of the Franco-British alliance won the battles of Alma, Balaclava, Inkerman and Sebastopol before Russia agreed to preliminary peace conditions at Vienna in February 1856 prior to the Treaty of Paris in March of that year finally terminated the war. Britain henceforth enjoyed a long interlude free from major wars in which her transport system, industries and built environment expanded to hitherto unprecedented levels.

London's industries

Within an increasingly world economy, manufacturing goods were by far the largest British exports by volume and value, and London was the leading manufacturing city in Britain during the mature stage of economic development, but manufacturing in the capital – as elsewhere in Britain – was rarely associated with the production of goods in large work places until the late nineteenth century. Though as many as 86 per cent of the capital's manufacturers employed ten workers or less in 1851, only 17 had a labour force of 250 or more (8), for example breweries, iron founding and ship-building, the latter industry producing Isambard Kingdom Brunel's *Great Eastern*, the largest ship of its time launched from John Scott Russell's yard in Millwall in 1859. While the larger manufacturers in Victorian London normally chose a riverside location, there were major exceptions, for example Bryant and May's huge match factory was located aside a railway line in Bow, while a major metal-working complex sprung up in Stratford around the locomotive and rolling stock works built for the Eastern Counties Railway in 1847. Smaller-scale industries were widely dispersed across much of north, south and east London (the West End cultivating its high-status residential and retail image). The leather trades were concentrated in the Bermondsey area, quality furniture-making was located north of Oxford Street while cheaper furniture was manufactured in Shoreditch, piano-making took place mainly in Camden and Lambeth – the latter district also producing sanitary-ware and glazed pipes, and well to the east the Lee Valley was the favoured location for a cluster of plants processing the fruits of colonial trade, such as sugar, rubber and guano (9).

However, above all, technical advance in the manufacture of garments and footwear provided the driving force of change. With the introduction of the sewing machine in the 1860's, productivity soared as unskilled operators could now sew 30 times faster than the most accomplished and diligent hand-worker (10). This made possible both the development of a more complex division of labour and the creation of a larger market not least to the benefit of the working classes of London. There was, however, a 'downside'. Located increasingly in the slums of Tower Hamlets, the industry relied on much exploited labour. It employed mainly women or male youths who – in order to earn enough on which to live – were obliged to work for very long hours as out-workers' either at home or in crowded sweat shops, on derisory piece-rates.

With the substantial increase in overseas trade in the decades following the Napoleonic wars, there was a need in London for new port facilities. Three miles downstream from the existing docks, the Royal Victoria dock was opened in 1855 – the first built to handle increasingly large iron steamships. Located in the former Plaistow Marshes, the Royal was provided with hydraulic cranes and was linked by rail to traditional port facilities upstream, while earth excavated from the new basins was shipped to facilitate the laying-out of Battersea Park in south-west London. On the Isle of Dogs, Millwall Dock was opened in 1868, and in 1880 the Royal Victoria Dock was extended to form the even larger Royal Albert Dock – then "the most advanced port facility in the world" (11). By this time, rapidly-growing trade with Argentina and New Zealand required the use of refrigerated ships and cold storage equipment at ports of entry. The new London quays provided such facilities and, with electricity being increasingly used to light the docks at night, 24 hour handling became feasible.

Notwithstanding the very great contribution of manufacturing and port activity to the economy of London, capital, finance and commerce became more important as generators of wealth. In the vicinity of the Bank of England and Royal Exchange, bankers and brokers built impressive new offices, while the number of Lloyd's underwriters – specialising particularly in maritime and life insurance – expanded respectively in-line with the growth of world trade and the ascendance of the middle class and skilled working class.

To provide outlets for the wide range of consumer goods produced by manufacturers in London, elsewhere in Britain and from abroad, there were major developments of retailing in the capital, including the introduction of department stores and multiples. Oxford Street was chosen by Peter Robinson in 1833 as a location for its store from where it would sell linen drapery and similar merchandise, the large-scale furniture retailers of Maples and Heals were established in Tottenham Court Road in the 1840's, and Harrods (originally tea dealers in Eastcheap) took over retail premises in Knightsbridge in 1849 and diversified into stationery, perfumes and patent medicines (12). After being founded in 1846, and establishing a bookstall at Euston station in 1848, W. H. Smith's rapidly expanded its chain of bookstalls throughout the country, while Sainsbury opened its first grocery store in Drury Lane in 1869.

The improvement in transportation

Ahead of all other countries, and regardless of the booms and slumps that occurred in the economy and the vagaries of conditions abroad, the development of railways in Britain performed an immeasurable role in the drive towards economic maturity. Railways were not only a technological triumph greatly enhancing both the mechanical and civil engineering industries but were also a commercial bonanza. With the first fare-paying passenger service opening in 1830 from Liverpool to Manchester, an increasingly dense railway network was constructed across Britain throughout the nineteenth century. It consolidated the national economy by improving access to and from London and other major cities – the location of Britain's largest productive resources and markets – and also decreased inter-city travel times dramatically, for example in 1820 stage coaches took at least 18 or more hours to travel from London to Birmingham and 30 hours to Manchester, whereas in 1845 rail journeys from London to the two cities took respectively only 4 and 6 hours. Apart from enabling a greater number of passengers to travel longer distances more quickly and at lower fares, commercial and industrial activity was substantially increased not only because transport costs were reduced but because communications were improved through the gradual extension of the telegraph from 1837, the introduction of pre-paid 'penny post' in 1840, and the increase in the overnight distribution of London-based national newspapers. Economic growth across the country was also accelerated since, for any given consignment of freight, the amount of capital tied up in goods and services in transit was greatly reduced freeing funds for investment in ventures with a quicker return.

The boom years for railway development were 1836 and 1845-1847 when the construction of 8,000 miles of railways was authorised by parliament at a projected capital cost of £200 million, a sum equal to Britain's gross domestic product for one year in the mid-1840's. The spatial expansion of London was driven by improved transportation and not, as in Paris and many other cities on the Continent, by the development of high-income housing close to the centre of the city pushing out low-income housing to the suburbs. Whereas, for example, middle-and high-income Parisians favoured living in apartments close to the centre of their city, the equivalent social-economic class in London had a preference for terraces, houses and villas in the leafy suburbs or later in the Home

Counties of Middlesex, Hertfordshire, Essex, Kent and Surrey. Unlike mid-nineteenth century Paris, where most urban development was government-planned under the direction of Napoleon III and Baron Haussmann, the growth of mid-Victorian London occurred under *laisser-faire* conditions tempered only by a succession of railway Acts. This resulted in wave upon wave of suburban development, led normally by the middle- and upper-classes who had a much greater predilection for a suburban way of life than their French counterparts.

Though the first passenger line out of London provided only a suburban rail service between London Bridge station and Greenwich, its completion in 1836 just preceded the development of inter-city services from London termini to more distant destinations. To fuel the ensuing 'Railway Mania' of the 1840's, 272 private Acts of Parliament authorised new rail companies to lay 5,000 miles of track by 1846. From Euston Station the London – Birmingham Railway was completed in 1837 to be superseded by the London North Western Railway to Manchester in 1846; from Paddington the Great Western Railway operated trains to the West Country and most of Wales from 1838; from Waterloo, the London and South Western Railway began operating services to much of Southern England in 1848; in 1852 King's Cross became the London terminus of the Great Northern Railway to York; Fenchurch Street Station opened in 1854 and subsequently provided the terminus for the London, Tilbury and Southend Railway; Victoria Station was the terminus for the London Brighton and South Coast Railway from 1860, and was widened to accommodate the London-end of the London, Chatham and Dover Railway in 1862; Cannon Street Station was the terminus of the London and South East Railways from

457

1865; and St. Pancras Station was completed in 1868 to enable the Midland Railway to provide services to Derby and Leeds .

While London enjoyed most of the economic benefits of railway development, it also incurred a very major diseconomy arising from the construction of railway termini around and within the West End and City, namely the substantial increase in the number of horse drawn wagons that were required to carry goods to and from each station adding greatly to the congestion of London's streets and the amount of horse excrement that needed to be cleared daily from their surfaces. The ease to which goods and people could use the streets of Early Victorian London clearly needed to be improved. The capital thus witnessed the construction of new roads, the introduction of omnibuses and the digging of an underground rail system (13). In the late 1830's, parliamentary select committees agreed that four new streets should be built in the City, specifically Cranbourne Street linking Piccadilly to Long Acre, Endell Street connecting Bloomsbury to Waterloo Bridge, New Oxford Street eliminating a bottleneck at the eastern end of Oxford Street, and Commercial Street that would join Shoreditch High Street with Whitechapel Road and Commercial Road. Following their completion in 1844-1845, it was soon recognised that contrary to expectation the new roads failed to destroy some of London's most notorious slum districts along their routes by providing them with the benefits of daylight, fresh air and lower-density occupancy. Instead their inhabitants resettled in neighbouring slums making conditions even worse. Following the construction of a realigned Victoria Street in 1851 there was a similar impact on slum housing in Tothill Street, Orchard Street and nearby alleys, all within close proximity of

458

Westminster Abbey.

To ease the lot of the travelling public, George Shillibeer – imitating a successful Parisian innovation - introduced the omnibus into London in 1829. It was an elongated coach pulled by three horses and seating up to 20 passengers on a single enclosed deck. By 1845 they had replaced short-stage coaches and were competing effectively with hackney cabs and providing services from Islington, Paddington, Belgravia, Holborn, Finsbury, Shoreditch, Southwark and Lambeth into central London and adding to the congestion of City and West End streets (14).

But to overcome horse-drawn congestion and to minimise the volume of associated excrement polluting the streets, the City of London funded much of the development of the Metropolitan Railway, the world's first underground railway. It was built by the 'cut and cover' method, completed in 1863 and linked Paddington, Euston, King's Cross and Farringdon, the latter station being but a short walk for commuters to their newly-built city offices. In 1868 the same company built a section from Paddington to South Kensington, and although the newly-formed Metropolitan and District Railway completed a track from South Kensington to Mansion House in 1871 it was not until 1884 that further tunnelling finally converted a horseshoe shaped route into the Circle Line skirting the whole of central London. Earlier, from 1825 to 1843, tunnelling work was undertaken below the Thames to link Rotherhithe on the south bank with Wapping on the north. Designed by Marc Brunel and his son Isambard Kingdom Brunel, and assisted by Thomas Cochrane's tunnelling shield, the resulting transport facility, Thames tunnel, was intended for pedestrians and horse-drawn wagons, but from 1865-1869 it was converted to carry trains operated by the new East London Railway, and is still used today by London Overground trains.

Railway termini and hotels

London Bridge Station was the very first railway terminus to be built in the capital. Although an early version of the station, with wooden platforms and no substantial buildings, was completed in 1836, the first 'fully-fledged' station was constructed in the Italianate style in 1840-1844, but it was reconstructed in 1849 to a design by Samuel Beazley. From this moment on, London Bridge Station in effect has operated as two stations. On the one side a line runs to Greenwich and to destinations in northern Kent (the route of the original South Eastern Railway), and on the other to Brighton and other destinations in Surrey and Kent (the route of the Brighton and South Coast Railway). The station was rebuilt again in 1864 when its western end was opened-up to allow track to be built to the Charing Cross and Canon Street stations nearing completion. Earlier, in 1861 the Terminus Hotel was built for the benefit of passengers, but since this was situated on the south bank of the Thames it was inconvenient for their needs and demolished in 1892. Today, after many years of reconstruction, Beazley's station of 1849 is unrecognisable except for its arched iron and glass train shed and the "simple elegance of the fine and slender cast-iron trusses over the platforms" (15).

1837 saw the opening of arguably the grandest railway terminus of the nineteenth century, Euston Station. Designed by Philip Hardwick, its majestic portico consisted of an arch supported by four giant Doric columns flanked by two lodges. Behind this frontispiece, Philip Hardwick jnr. provided a monumental booking hall and waiting room, and these

460

in turn led to two 420ft (128m) platforms with 40ft (12.2m) spans by Charles Fox. The whole complex was demolished in 1963 against much opposition to make way for the station that was completed in 1968.

Euston Arch (1838), by Philip Hardwick.

Timed to accommodate tourists travelling to and from the Great Exhibition, King's Cross Station was opened as the terminus of the Great Northern Railway in 1850. Lewis and Gilbert Cubitt, its architects, gave the station a substantial brick façade, with its two enormous arched windows "indicating the roofs of the train sheds, each spanning 71 ft (26 m), and separated by the central clock tower 129 ft (37 m) high" (16). As part of the project, the Great Northern Hotel was added in 1854 for the benefit of rail travellers, but in contrast to several later railway hotels in London it was completely detached from the main body of the station and is situated on a curved site to the west of the train sheds so as not to mask the splendour of the station's façade.

Kings Cross Station (1850), by Lewis and Gilbert Cubitt

Great Northern Hotel (1854), by Lewis Cubitt

Also, in 1854, work started on the construction of Paddington Station, the new terminus of the Great Western Railway. It replaced a smaller wooden terminus built in 1838 that was situated slightly to the west of the new building. Designed by Isambard Brunel, Paddington Station had three parallel sheds with roofs of wrought iron and glass supported by cast iron columns. A fourth shed was constructed in 1909-1916. The south front of the station is marked by a gracious hotel with twin towers rising above the white façade and with a pediment by the sculptor John Thomas illustrating peace, plenty, industry and science (17). Designed mainly by Philip Hardwick and built in 1851-1853, the hotel (currently called the Hilton London Metropole) established the tradition of situating hotels at the *front* of large railway sheds in an attempt to enhance the appeal of rail travel.

Paddington Station Hotel (1851-53), by Philip Hardwick

Victoria Station was the next large railway station to be developed in the capital. It was developed in two stages. First, its western section – opened in 1860 – provided a terminus for the London, Brighton and South-East Railway, and second its eastern section completed two years later was used by the London, Chatham and Dover Railway. Since the station is on the north bank of the Thames and was built to provide services with destinations south of the river, the Grosvenor Bridge, designed by J Fowler and opened in 1860, became the first railway bridge over the Thames. But Victoria Station is essentially two railway sheds and a northern façade with few architectural merits. It is the Grosvenor Hotel, situated on the western edge of the station that exhibits some interesting attributes. Built of Bath stone in 1861, and designed by J. T. Knowles, the edifice consists of seven storeys, the top two being dormers. The hotel is surmounted by French pavilion roofs on each of its four corners, each of which is adorned with carved foliage, while on the façade looking on to Buckingham Palace Road, there are – in Portland stone – medallion portraits of Queen Victoria, Prince Albert, Lord Palmerston and others, encased in spandrels between arches.

Victoria Station (1860), by J.Fowler

Grosvenor Hotel (1861), by J.T.Knowles

Inspired by the Grosvenor Hotel, the Langham Hotel was constructed in 1864 at 90 degrees across the southern end of Portland Place on a site previously occupied by a house built by Lord Foley in 1767. The noble lord had previously bought the house from the Duke of Portland on condition that the width of Portland Place would be retained to preserve the view from the house northward to Hampstead and Highgate. This proviso has been honoured to this day and explains why Portland Place with a width of 125 feet is one of the widest streets in London. After being sold to John Nash c. 1814, it was subsequently sold to Sir James Langham who commissioned John Giles and James Murray to redevelop the site as a hotel – the eponymous Langham Hotel. It soon attracted a succession of distinguished guests, such as statesmen, artists, writers and exiled royalty, most famously the exiled Napoleon III. Built in the Italianate style (modelled on astylar Renaissance buildings in Florence or Rome), the seven storey hotel originally had 600 rooms, but today has only 410 for greater comfort.

Charing Cross Station Hotel (1864), by E.M.Barry

Charing Cross Station was also opened in 1864 on the site of the old Hungerford Market (that had only been rebuilt in 1833 but had burned down in 1854). The tracks of the station were roofed over by a single arch spanning 164 ft (50m), and rising to a height of almost 100 ft (30.5m) above its six platforms. As at Paddington and Victoria stations it is the accompanying hotel that has the more interesting attributes. Designed by E. M Barry and completed in 1864, the hotel faced with artificial stone was initially four main storeys in height surmounted by two additional storeys with dormer windows, but early in the twentieth century the original roof line has been re-built to give the edifice a straight horizontal double storey. Like Victoria Station, Charing Cross Station is located on the north-side of the Thames, and as the terminus of the South Eastern Railway needed a river crossing to connect with its rail network. This was provided by Sir John Hawkshaw's newly-built Hungerford Bridge, a nine span wrought-iron lattice girder bridge that in 1864 replaced Brunel's Hungerford Suspension bridge of 1841-45.

Midland Grand Hotel , St Pancras Station (1864), by Sir George Gilbert Scott

In 1863, one year before the completion of Charing Cross Station, work started on the construction of St. Pancras Station, a 689 ft (210 m) long iron and glass train shed situated on the northern side of Euston Road immediately to the west of King's Cross Station. Designed by W. H. Barlow for the Great Northern Railway, the station's roof spans 240 ft (73 m) and is 100 ft (31 m) above the rails at its apex (18). In 1864, the GNR next commissioned Sir George Gilbert Scott to design the Midland Grand Hotel that would enclose the southern end of the train shed and provide a façade looking onto the Euston Road. Built between 1868-72, the Neo-Gothic hotel with its towers, gables and pinnacles was visible from afar, particularly from the slopes of Pentonville Road. Its dimensions are awesome. It has a total frontage of 565 ft (31 m) and is flanked at both ends by 270 ft (82 m) high towers, the eastern one of which carries a clock just below its summit.

In contrast to the growth of London in earlier centuries, political factors played a relatively small part in the development of London during the reign of Queen Victoria. Economic factors were dominant – a consequence of the preceding Industrial Revolution and the expansion of international trade. But even the economic cycle – in contrast to the booms and slumps of the eighteenth century, did not seem to have had much of an impact on construction activity in London: First, in the mid-nineteenth century there were often lengthy time-lags in the construction process in the capital due to the scale of many building projects; second, because London – unlike the industrial areas of the north – had a very diversified manufacturing base and was largely insulated from the vagaries of the economic cycle; and third because the increased scale of a number of important building projects and the use of more sophisticated materials shielded the industry from occasional and relatively minor downturns in the economic cycle. In consequence a number of notable

468

commercial buildings of different uses were constructed across the capital, as well as the development of extensive areas of housing. There was also the employment of a range of architectural styles in the development of notable Victorian buildings: Neo-Gothic or Neo-Tudor, and Neoclassical being the most prevalent.

Public buildings

Possibly the most important building project of Victoria's reign was the reconstruction and enlargement of the Houses of Parliament, most of the old buildings having been destroyed by fire in 1834. Begun in 1835 before her accession to the Crown, the new Westminster Palace was not completed until 1860. Built on the same site as the earlier structure, the new edifice was Neo-Gothic or Neo-Tudor in style, the exuberant interior was designed by Augustus Welby Pugin and the grandiose exterior is attributable to Charles Barry. The palace has an axial plan aligned to a north-south spine parallel to the Thames that marks its eastern boundary. The principal rooms of the building – from north to south – comprise the House of Commons, the Commons Lobby, the Central Lobby, the Lords Lobby, the House of Lords, the Princes Chamber and the Royal Gallery, and while the northern end of the building is marked by the 320 ft (98 m) high clock tower, now renamed the Elizabeth Tower (housing Big Ben), the southern end features the even taller Victoria Tower that rises to 336 ft (103 m) in height.

Houses of Parliament (1835-60), by Sir Charles Barry

Other giant bastions of government were developed in Whitehall, most notably Charles Barry's somewhat subdued Neo-classical Treasury building (1844) and George Gilbert Scott's awesome Italianate Foreign Office (1868-73), while to a mile to the east in Chancery Lane, the Public Record Office – designed in a fun ctional Neo-Gothic style by James Pennethorne - was built in 1851-66.

Treasury Building (1844), by Sir Charles Barry

Foreign Office, Whitehall (1868-73), by Sir George Gilbert Scott

Public Record Office (1851-61), by James Pennethorne

But the construction of public buildings was not just confined to the functioning of government. Art galleries and museums were important too, if not politically at least culturally and educationally. Thus, at the northern end of Whitehall, the National Gallery was constructed across the northern edge of Trafalgar Square   peering down on the Palace of Westminster in the far distance. Designed by William Wilkins and built in 1832-8, the gallery's facade, however,   is aesthetically far from adequate since it is divided into as many as thirteen separate sections, six of which are on either side of a central portico crowned by a dome, the portico itself having been relocated stone by stone from Carlton House. The completion of the gallery was soon followed by the construction of the Nelson Column in 1839-42 designed by William Railton . As much as 145ft (44m) high, the fluted Corinthian column is constructed of Devonshire granite, while the statue of Nelson – another 17ft (5 m) high - was sculptured – from Craglieth stone by E.H,Baily. Some might suggest that it is the column rather than the National Gallery that makes Trafalgar Square important as a centre point.

National Gallery (1832-6), by William Wilkins

Nelson Column (1839-42), by William Railton and
E.H.Baily

Throughout much of the time that the National
Gallery and Nelson Column were being built, the first
stages in the reconstruction of the British Museum were
taking place on a site immediately to the north of its
original premises - Montagu House in Bloomsbury.
Designed largely by Sir Robert Smirke, the new
museum was constructed around a quadrangle in a
number of stages beginning in 1823: first the east wing,
then the north and west wings, and finally from 1842
Montagu House was demolished and in its place the
south wing of the new museum was constructed and
completed in 1847. It is dominated by a magnificent
Neo-Greek façade whose attributes include a lengthy
Ionic colonnade and a gigantic pedimented portico. But

work on the museum was far from finished. A great circular and domed reading room, designed by Smirke's brother, Sydney, was constructed within the museum's quadrangle and was not completed until 1857.

British Museum (1823-57), by Sir Robert Smirke

Innovatively using cast-iron and glass, Decimus Burton in 1845-1848 built a giant curved conservatory, the Palm House in the Royal Botanical Gardens, Kew. In so doing, he not only designed "one of the world's finest ....nineteenth century glasshouses" (19), but the building almost certainly inspired Joseph Paxton to apply the same design principles to the Crystal Palace in 1850. Even as early as 1851, a successful attempt was made to celebrate the Britain's new role as 'Workshop of the World'. Although London hosted 'The Great Exhibition of the Works of Industry of All Nations', the exhibition particularly emphasised Britain's achievements in advancing the progress of civilisation within the context of peace rather than war. Conceived by Prince Albert and organised mainly by Henry Cole, the Great Exhibition was accommodated in a purpose-built edifice known as the Crystal Palace. Situated in Hyde Park and designed by Joseph Paxton, the enormous building covering 19 acres (7.69 ha) was 1848 feet (563.64 metre) in length and 108 feet (32.94 metre) tall and was constructed largely of specially manufactured iron frames and glass and housed 100,000 exhibits. However, after six months the exhibition closed and the building was subsequently demolished and re-built in Sydenham, south London in 1854, but in 1936 it was burn to the ground and never again reassembled.

Palm House, Kew (1845-8), by Decimus Burton

Crystal Palace (1851), by Sir Joseph Paxton

With an increasingly populated London during the first-half of Victoria's reign, the government considered it necessary to build a number of new prison buildings. Marshalsea Prison in Southwark had been closed in 1842, and Millbank and Newgate – not demolished until 1890 and 1902 respectfully – were decreasingly fit for purpose. Based on the design of the Eastern Penitentiary in Philadelphia, Pentonville Prison in Caledonian Road was established in 1842 and comprised a central hall with five radiating wings and became a model for 54 other British prisons built over the next six years and hundreds throughout the Empire; Holloway Prison with its turreted gateway was built in a castellated Neo-Gothic style in 1852; and Wandsworth Prison was completed in 1851 and contained five wings for male prisoners and three for female, each wing radiating from a central control point. Wandsworth was possibly the best designed prison in London, and being situated on the top of a hill, its inmates were more likely to benefit from fresh air rather than be debilitated by dank conditions. Though Brixton Prison was established in 1820, it was expanded in 1853 when its cell-blocks were rebuilt in the form of a rough crescent incorporating the governor's house in the centre, but conditions remained bleak.

Pentonville Prison (1840-2), by Major Jebb

Commercial buildings

Whereas the new Houses of Parliament dominated the skyline of Westminster, the new Royal Exchange – opened by Queen Victoria in 1844 – became an iconic landmark within the City. Replacing the mid-seventeenth century exchange burnt down in 1838, the new edifice designed by William Tite was an attempt to symbolise London's importance as the trading centre of the world. Situated between the Bank of England and the Mansion House, the exchange – facing west – is dominated by its giant Corinthian portico behind which is a large arcaded courtyard, initially open to the sky but glazed over in 1880, and until recently containing offices but now replaced by shops, bars and restaurants. Its eastern façade is marked by a baroque spire similar to that of its predecessor.

Royal Exchange (1841-4), by Sir William Tite

During the mid-Victorian years a vast number of new offices were built in the City. All by present day standards were small, normally no more than four or five storeys in height and many were built in the Italianate style. Of those that survive, four are of particular interest. At 20 King Street, EC2, an office block initially of four storeys was built on a corner site

478

in 1850 to the designs of Sanction Wood. Though a skimpy attic was added in the 1980's, the building retains the appearance of a palazzo; Tuscan columns are employed on the ground floor to support segmental arches, regularly spaced windows give a sense of unity to all floors, and a Classical cornice connects the two facades. Now very much an oddity, a branch of the National Provincial Bank was constructed at 15 Bishopgate, EC2 in 1865. It was designed by John Gibson at a time when architects were looking for an appropriate style for the new institution of the branch bank. Ward innovatively produced a one storey pavilion, richly decorated with Classical motifs particularly the use of engaged Corinthian columns, and surmounted by a cornice supporting 'sky-puncturing' statuary (20). The building is now a branch of the National Westminster Bank, Most offices built subsequently in mid-Victorian London were, of course, conventional multi-storey buildings, for example at 103 Cannon Street, EC4, a four-storey office designed by Frederick Jameson and built in 1866 is notable particularly for its four bays containing arched Venetian windows that diminish to the top, whilst the four-storey Albert Buildings on a corner site in Queen Victoria Street, EC4, - built to the designs of Frederick J Ward in 1869 – is more French Gothic than Italianate.

20. King Street, EC1 (1850), by Santon Wood

National Provincial Bank, EC2 (1865), by John Gibson

103 Canon Street, EC4 (1866), by Frederick Jameson

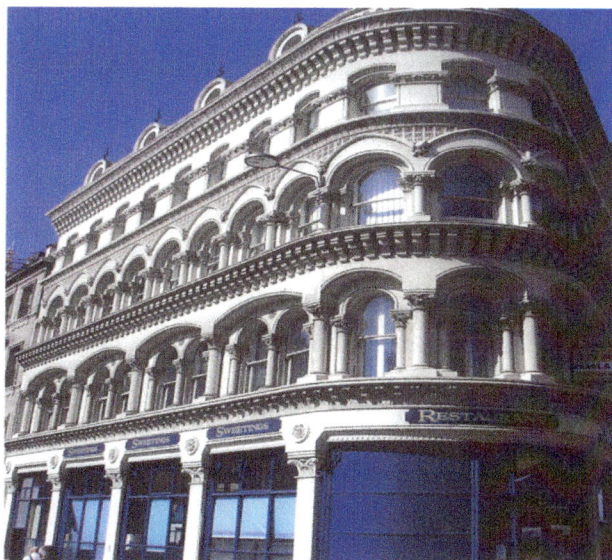

Albert Buildings, EC4 (1869), by Frederick J Ward

Food markets can also be classified as commercial buildings. At Smithfield, north of Newgate, work began in 1851 on constructing a large enclosed market for the wholesale distribution of meat. It occupied much of the site that for centuries had accommodated a large open livestock market but this had been closed down on environmental health grounds and relocated to the newly built Metropolitan Cattle Market in Islington. Smithfield Market, as it has been known colloquially since its completion in 1866, is a massive building extending east to west from Lindsay Street to West Poultry and consists of four enormous trading halls illuminated from above by linear glazed lanterns, and encased within a redbrick building with stone dressings and domed turrets in each of its four corner turrets (21). Some distance away on the north bank of the Thames, Billingsgate wholesale fish market – dating from Medieval times – was rebuilt to the designs of J. B. Bunning around 1850, but since it was not predicted that in future years the demand for fish would increase substantially Bunning's building was soon unfit for purpose and a new building designed by Sir Horace Jones was built in 1874-1877. Facing the river, its façade is somewhat French Renaissance in style, but behind it a large iron framed market hall extends northward to Lower Thames Street. No longer suitable for modern wholesaling needs, the fish market closed in 1982 and it has since been used as offices by an investment trust.

Smithfield Market (1851-66), Horace Jones

Billingsgate Market (1875)

The Royal Opera House and Royal Albert Hall

Located incongruously in Bow Street, unceremoniously beyond the eastern end of Covent Garden, the present Royal Opera House, dating from 1857-1858, is the third theatre to be developed on its site, the first two – opening in 1732 and 1809 – were burnt down respectively in 1808 and 1856. Far less grandiose than its near-contemporary, Jean-Louis-Charles Garnier's Paris Opera, E. M. Barry's Royal Opera House – built at 90 degrees to the street – is nevertheless architecturally renowned for: its "giant Corinthian six-column portico above the rusticated ground floor [presenting] an image of great size" (22); its long frieze behind the portico depicting Comedy and Tragedy and statues in niches either side of the front (relics of Robert Smirke's building of 1809); and its magnificent auditorium which is both enormous (it can accommodate an audience of 2,256) and, for is size, intimate. Next to the Opera House, and on the site of Smirke's auditorium (which ran parallel to Bow Street) Berry built the Floral Hall in which flowers would be sold to opera-goers (21).

Royal Opera House (1857-8), by E.M.Barry

484

Royal Albert Hall (1867-70), by Captain Francis Fouke and
General H.Y.D.Scott

Albert Memorial (1863-75), by Sir George Gilbert Scott

Funded largely from the profits of the Royal Exhibition of 1851 and built between 1867-70, the Royal Albert Hall in Kensington was designed by Captain Francis Fouke and its construction was supervised by General H. Y. D. Scott, both of the Royal Engineers. With its distinctly dour elevations in the mid-Victorian manner and its elliptical plan 735 ft (225 m) in circumference, the building can house an audience of up to 8,000. The edifice is, in effect, a domed cylinder with terracotta decorations, further ornamented by a frieze around the full circumference (22). Situated around 328 ft (100 m) to the north the Albert Memorial faces the entrance façade of the Royal Albert Hall. It was designed by Sir George Gilbert Scott and erected at the same time as the hall. The memorial has a Neo-Gothic spire 175 ft (53 m) in height, a bronze statue of Prince Albert seated on a plinth at the base of the edifice, and groups of marble figures symbolising Britain's colonies in the four projecting corners of the monument.

Residential development

In the early part of Victoria's reign, Pelham Place and Pelham Crescent in South Kensington were two of the first residential developments to be developed in the capital for higher-income households of the period. Built around 1840, the three storey houses (together with their basements and attics) are of uniform late-Georgian design, and in Pelham Place look on to individual gardens, while in Pelham Crescent – 491 ft (149 m) in diameter – front gardens are absent but each house has a projecting porch. Elsewhere in west and south-west London, there are numerous other examples of early-Victorian upper-class housing. Much larger than the Pelham's, St. George's Square in Pimlico is also a fine example of early-Victorian high-income housing. Developed on the Grosvenor estate by Thomas Cubitt and George Basevi, the wide rectangular square – begun in 1844 – stretches back from the Thames and is lined on its east and west sides with five-six storey terraced housing whose bay windows look diagonally toward the river as well as on to the landscaped square itself.

Pelham Crescent (1840) by George Basevi

St George's Square (1844), by Thomas Cubitt

In North Kensington, there was broadly comparable development in Kensington Park Gardens, Ladbroke Grove and Ladbroke Square in North Kensington, together with Lansdowne Crescent, Elgin Crescent and Clarendon Road to the north of the square. All comprised the Ladbroke Estate, were designed by Thomas Allom and were developed around 1850, but although the estate exhibited few architectural innovations it was a model of mid-Victorian planning. The Boltons in South Kensington – with its facing crescents and palatial mansions designed by George Godwin and built in 1850-1860 – also stood out as one of the finest London developments of its time, and so too did Onslow Square and Grosvenor Crescent in South Kensington and Belgravia respectively, both being completed around 1860.

Kensington Park Gardens (c.1850), by Thomas Allom

The Boltons (1850-60), by George Godwin

Onslow Square (1846-60), by C.J.Freake

Following the opening of the London Bridge to Greenwich railway in 1836, middle-class housing was developed on the edge of London's built-up area sparking the construction of middle-class villas and respectable terraces (23) in such areas as New Cross, Brockley, Forest Hill and Lewisham in south-east London; and Kentish Town, Kilburn, Crouch End, Stroud Green, Hornsey and Wood Green in north London. However, whereas horse-drawn omnibus services had previously been 'environmentally friendly' and had been associated with the development of idyllic housing in areas such as Belgravia, Pimlico and Bayswater, the earlier suburbs that grew-up with the railways soon deteriorated and degenerated into slums. By the 1860's-1870's middle- and higher-income households began to move out, leaving their properties to be converted into multi-occupied housing for the relatively poor. A further phase of outward migration occurred, as richer families "moved out from Camberwell to Streatham or Sydenham, Norwood or Beckenham ...Balham was abandoned for Wimbledon and Surbiton, Battersea for Barnes. All such places between five and ten miles [eight and sixteen kilometres] from the centre – enjoyed a brief summer when the opening of a station brought superior villa housing, followed in due course by smaller, cheaper properties for petty clerks and shop assistants" (24). With the introduction of workmen's' fares in east London in the 1860's, and soon elsewhere in the metropolis, clerks, shop workers and skilled craftsmen were able ' to follow their 'betters' out of the inner city, creating what were in effect working-class suburbs in areas such as Deptford, Walthamstow and West Ham (25).

However, regardless of location, the level of rents that the poor could afford within a largely free-market economy were insufficiently high to have enabled landlords to provide acceptable accommodation. Dwellings were consequently very cramped with many families often confined to only one room, shared washing and toilet facilities were minimal and the fabric of the housing stock was generally in a poor state of repair. The disequilibrium of housing need and housing supply was often exacerbated by slum clearance and redevelopment since the only type of housing that replaced the cleared stock was only financially viable if it was let to the regularly employed on 'living wages'. In several parts of the capital the housing problem was particularly severe since an undesirable outcome of the so-called 'railway mania' was that large scale slum clearance - necessary to make way for the construction of large termini and associated track, sidings, sheds and bridges - inevitably led to the creation of even worse slums. Since most, if not all, of the dispossessed were already poverty-stricken they had little choice but to seek alternative low-cost accommodation in housing that was already overcrowded, in neighbourhoods where the degree of squalor was barely endurable, and where the incidence of disease and criminality frequently soared.

Peabody Housing, Chequer Street (1870), by H.A.Darbishire

Because of their attachment to a *laisser-faire* economy, governments were reluctant to tackle the housing problems of the poor, leaving improvement instead to private benefactors, the most famous of which was the American ex-banker George Peabody. Coming to Britain following a major financial crisis in the 1830's, Peabody became a respected figure in the City and performed a useful role representing United States interests at the Great Exhibition. On his retirement he established the Peabody Donation Trust in 1862 whose trustees devoted a £500,000 endowment for the construction of 'cheap, cleanly, well-drained and healthy dwellings for the poor' (26). While Peabody's housing takes the form of barrack-like blocks (some would say prison-blocks), they were well-managed and 19,000 properties still stand. Established initially in Commercial Street, Spittlefields, other estates soon followed, for example in Islington, Poplar, Shadwell, Bermondsey, Westminster and Chelsea.

Schools

Since public schools often consist of a number of substantial buildings of architectural merit, they have a visual impact on their immediate neighbourhood and play a part in shaping their local built environment. In mid-Victorian London, two such schools were either developed further or built anew. First, Harrow School – founded by John Lyon under a royal charter granted by Elizabeth I in 1572 – was expanded by the addition of a school chapel in 1855 and by the new Vaughan library in 1863, both buildings being Neo-Gothic in style and designed by the same architect, George Gilbert Scott. But while the chapel was built mainly of flint and stone, the library was built of redbrick conforming to the principal material used in the construction of the

492

Old School of the late-sixteenth century. Second, Dulwich College is almost as ancient as Harrow dating from 1619. But while the original college buildings are situated on either side of Gallery Road facing the southern end of Dulwich Villager, the Victorian buildings of 1866-1870 lie to the south in College Road, are large, symmetrical and ornate and were designed in the Renaissance rather than Neo-Gothic style by Charles Barry Junior. However, while the central block of the college rightly contains the hall, the symmetry of the building is impaired since the tower erected on the southern block is not matched by a similar tower on its northern counterpart (27).

Dulwich College (1866-70), by Charles Barry Junior

Churches and cemeteries

Though church-architecture in Victorian England is often dismissed as being homogenous in appearance and in the use of building materials this is far from the

493

truth when examining the principle design features of mid-nineteenth century churches in London. Taking just a small sample of London's churches will demonstrate the great variation in design, albeit within the Neo-Gothic paradigm – Neo-Classical design no longer being in vogue after about 1840.

Located in the Grosvenor Estate, St. Paul in Wilton Place was designed by Thomas Cundy III and constructed in 1840-1843. Its main feature, a Neo-Gothic castellated tower is notable for its grand porch, while inside the church fine cast-iron columns support its three galleries, an innovative structural feature in the first half of the nineteenth century. But St. Paul Wilton Place did not quite fit the design requirements of the Anglican church,. It was the church of St. Giles, Camberwell 1844, that set the pattern for a very large number of Victorian churches that were built in most English towns throughout the rest of the nineteenth century. In designing the church, George Gilbert Scott ensured that it conformed with the basic tenets of Anglican church architecture as favoured by the Camden Society; it is of considerable length 153 ft (47 m), it is Neo-gothic in style, it has a tall spire and it is well built in stone (Kentish ragstone in the case of St. Giles).

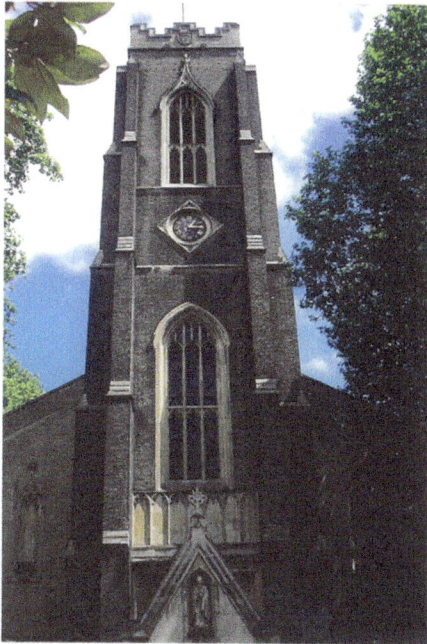

St Paul's Wilton Place (1840-43), by Thomas Cundy III

All Saints Margaret Street, close to Oxford Circus, is completely different stylistically from St. Giles. Commissioned by the High Church of the Anglican faith (the Oxford Movement), it was designed by William Butterfield and built between 1850 -1859, replete with spire. It was considered by the eminent Victorian architect, G. E. Street, to be "not only the most beautiful but the most vigorous, thoughtful and original of the Neo-Gothic churches, it was the first important building in London where brick was used decoratively (28). Unfortunately All Saints is compressed between two large twentieth century buildings in commercial use, and its novel design is not easily visible from the street. On a much more open site, the church of St. Mary Magdalene is situated in

Woodchester Square, west London and was designed by George Edmund Street. Built in 1868-1878, it is regarded to be "one of the finest Gothic Revival churches in London" (29) with its banded stone and dark brown brick exterior and its imposing but slender spire situated asymmetrically to the main body of the church.

All Saints Margaret Street (1850-59), by William Butterfield

St Mary Abbot Kensington (1869-72),
by Sir George Gilbert Scott

St. Mary's Abbott in Kensington, like All Saints
Margaret Street, is partly obscured from view.
Designed in the Neo-Gothic style by Sir George Gilbert
Scott and built in 1869-1872, the brick-built church is
mainly distinguished by its disproportionately high
spire which somewhat belies the length of its nave.
Located in Rosslyn Hill, Belsize Park, the church of St.
Stephen was designed by Samuel Teulon and built in
1869-1876. Its massive tower with its capped roof, its
square headed aisle windows and its extensive use of
different tones of Luton brick and granite dressings
collectively suggest the application of a mixture of
thirteenth-century Gothic and idiosyncratic Victorian
architecture.

Previously noted for the decorative appearance of All Saint's Margaret Street, William Butterfield remained obsessed with his use of colour in church architecture, as he demonstrated in designing the Neo-Gothic church of St. Augustine Queen's Gate, built between 1870-1877. In addition to its brightly patterned and decorated interior, the exterior of the church is strikingly multi-coloured and makes extravagant use of diaper-patterned brickwork.

As a result of a campaign in the 1820's for the formation of public cemeteries on the edge of London to relieve the grossly overcrowded and insanitary parish cemeteries across the capital, Parliament authorised the establishment of seven commercial cemeteries in a ring around the residential suburbs. Thus, Kensal Green came into being in 1832, West Norwood in 1837, Highgate in 1838, Abbey Park, Brompton and Nunhead in 1840 and Tower Hamlets in 1841. The 'Magnificent Seven', as they were called, varied in size from 30 acres (12 ha) at Nunhead to 54 acres (22 ha) at Kensal Green, all were landscaped and some contained buildings of some merit.

In Highgate Cemetery, for example, its owner and architect Stephen Geary used a mixture of Gothic and Egyptian styles to construct two ingeniously designed chapels in 1838-1840 at the entrance to the western end of the cemetery, while his successor J B Bunning built the Gothic Catacombs at the northern end in 1842. Also to the north, the Lebanon Catacombs was subsequently built by J Oldred Scott who also designed the two storey mausoleum to Julius Beer "the most ambitious architectural work in the cemetery [with its] magnificent stepped pyramidal derived from the tomb of the Greek King Mausolus at Halicarnassus" (30), though it was also reminiscent of a similar pyramid (also inspired by King Mausolus's tomb) on top of the tower of St. George Bloomsbury (see chapter 7). Whereas Highgate cemetery was built on the slopes of the north London ridge, Brompton Cemetery was laid out on flat land between Old Brompton Road to the north and Fulham Road to the south. Founded in 1831, the cemetery's principal architectural feature – designed by Benjamin Baud and completed in 1839 – is its domed octagonal Anglican chapel and its extensive arcading close to the southern entrance to the site (31).

Anglican Chapel, Brompton Cemetery (1840)

Environmental health and planning

Many of Queen Victoria's subjects in London lived in appallingly squalor and unhygienic conditions similar to that endured by many of the capital's inhabitants in centuries past. There were two principal problems: first, most of London's quarter of a million dwellings had cesspits rather than water-closets, with human waste often seeping into water courses. The remainder were connected to centuries-old sewers that discharged untreated effluent into the Thames; and second, the majority of the capitals inhabitants relied upon street pumps for their water rather than supplies connected to their houses, but in either case the water was normally contaminated since its source was the Thames and its tributaries were greatly polluted by the sewage of over two million people (32).

Greatly concerned with the state of public health, barrister and Poor Law Commissioner Edwin Chadwick published a government report entitled the *Sanitary Condition of the Labouring Poor* (1842), followed by a *Report on Interment in Towns* (1843) and a *Report on the Supply of Water to the (*1850). He also encouraged Parliament to produce the Public Health Act of 1848 that set up a Central Board of Health and in the same year was the driving force in amalgamating a number of separate boards into the Metropolitan Commission of Sewers. However, in 1849 cholera, a waterborne disease, broke out across much of the capital. Though there were earlier outbreaks, for example in 1832, there was little understanding of the cause of the disease, it being wrongly thought that it was caused by foul vapours – 'miasma' – emanating from rotting garbage and effluent. Remedial measures, such as watering of streets and flushing sewers, spread the epidemic more widely and made it twice as deadly. It was only when Dr John Snow painstakingly mapped and analysed the distribution of deaths resulting from the outbreaks of cholera in 1848-49 and 1853-54 that a link was found between the quality of drinking water and the incidence of cholera. One particular case-study conclusively found that within the immediate vicinity of a single water pump in Broad Street (now Broadwick Street), Soho, the degree of infection was particularly high. But although Snow published his research findings in *On the communication of cholera* in 1855, it was not until the late 1880's that his hypothesis was accepted by the medical profession.

Existing public health legislation was shown to be inadequate during the long hot summer of 1858 when the Thames sunk to such a low level that the sewage that it carried was barely diluted, an obnoxious stench – the 'Great Stink' – threatening to close down both Parliament and the Law Courts. Three years earlier the Metropolitan Board of Works had been established, superseding the public health functions of a miscellany of parish vestries and commissions. In response to the 'Great Stink', its engineer Joseph Bazalgette narrowed the Thames and speeded its flow by building the Victoria, Albert and Chelsea Embankments between 1864 and 1874. Of very great relevance to public health, Bazalgette also installed five new main sewers running west-east across London, three north of the river and two to the south, and connected these to processing plants far down-steam where the sewage was treated before being discharged or shipped to the North Sea. As by-products of Bazalgette's sewage system, 37 acres (15 ha) of reclaimed land were converted into gardens and a roadway on the Victoria embankment, while – using the 'cut-and-cover' method of construction – the Metropolitan District Railways encased the Circle line aside new sewers along part of the route from South Kensington to Mansion house that was completed in 1871.

Victoria Embankment (1864-74), by Sir Joseph Bazalgette

Holborn Viaduct (1863-9), by William Heywood

The City Corporation also played a role in urban improvement, albeit on a small scale. In 1855, five years after work started on Smithfield wholesale meat market (see above), the Corporation closed Smithfield Cattle Market to eradicate the appalling squalor and health-risk that it caused in the vicinity of St. Paul's. But in mid-Victorian London town planning schemes were a rarity. Apart from the Victoria, Albert and Chelsea embankments, planning schemes were mainly confined to two major projects funded by the City Corporation. First, Queen Victoria Street was constructed through an area of high density buildings in 1867-1871 to link Bank Junction with Blackfriars Bridge, and second the Holborn Viaduct was built in over the valley of the Fleet River in 1869 to form a major east-west route through the capital from Cheapside to Oxford Street. But in contrast to many cities abroad, and particularly Paris, town planning in London was virtually non-existent and the development of the built environment was determined by market forces within the framework of public sector development not that different from London after the Great Fire when Wren's imaginative plan for a rebuilt-capital was rejected because of pressure from existing property and commercial interests (see chapter 6).

References

1. R. Inwood, *London. A Social History*, Penguin, 2000, p 412.
2. Ibid, p 416
3. C Emsley, T Hitchcock and R Shoemaker, *A Population History of London, Old Bailey Proceedings on 14 January 2014*
4. R. Inwood,_*London. A Social History*, Penguin, 2000. p 411.
5. W W Rostow, *The Stages of Economic Growth: A*

Non-Communist Manifesto, Cambridge University Press, 1960,

6. S. Hills and R Thomas, 'The UK Recession in context – What do three centuries of data tell us', Bank of England , vol. 50, issue 4, 2010, *Quarterly Bulletin.*
7. Ibid, p 212
8. R. Tames, *A Travellers History of London*, Cassel & Co, 2002, p 140
9. Ibid, p 141.
10. Ibid, p 141.
11. Ibid, p 169
12. Ibid, p 142.
13. R.Inwood,_*London. A Social History*, Penguin, 2000, pp 545-50
14. Ibid, pp 346-7
15. E Jones and C Woodward, *A Guide to the Architecture of London*, Weidenfeld and Nicolson, 2009, p 317.
16. Ibid, p 128.
17. S. Reynolds and G Davies, *One Thousand Buildings of London*, Black Dog & Levanthal Publishers, 2006, p 540.
18. B. Weinreb and C Hibbert, *The London Encyclopaedia*, Macmillan, 1995, p 775.
19. S.Reynolds and GH.Davies, *One Thousand Buildings of London*, Black Dog & Levanthal Publishers, p 629.
20. E Jones and C Woodward, *A Guide to the Architecture of London*, Weidenfeld and Nicolson, 2009, p 318
21. Ibid, p 257.
22. Ibid, p 203.
23. R. Porter, *London. A Social History*, Penguin, 2000, p 280.
24. Ibid, p 281.

25. R.Tames , *A Travellers History of London*, Cassel & Co, 2002, p 137.
26. Ibid, p 155.
27. E.Jones and C.Woodward, *A Guide to the Architecture of London*, Weidenfeld and Nicolson, p 84.
28. B.Weinreb and C.Hibbert, *The London Encyclopaedia*, Macmillan, 1995, p 19.
29. E,Jones and C.Woodward, *A Guide to the Architecture of London*, Weidenfeld and Nicolson , p 84.
30. Ibid, p 392
31 Ibid, p.347.
32 R.Tames, *A Travellers History of London*, Cassel & Co, 2002, p 148.

Index

510

CPSIA information can be obtained at www.ICGtesting.com
Printed in the USA
LVOW02s1147290914

3717LVUK00007B/18/P